A. G. LAFLEY is the chairman and C  is consistently recognized as one of th the world and a great developer of bu CEO of the year in 2006 by *Chief Executive* magazine and serves on the boards of GE and Dell. His first opportunity to manage a business came when he was in the Navy and in charge of retail and services businesses for ten thousand Navy and Marine Corps people and their families. After the Navy he went to Harvard Business School, and then joined P&G following graduation. He started as a brand assistant for Joy in 1977 and was appointed CEO in June 2000.

RAM CHARAN is co-author of the bestseller *Execution* and the author of many other books. Dr Charan grew up in India, where he first learned the art and science of business in his family's shoe shop. After earning his MBA and DBA from Harvard Business School, he taught for a number of years at Harvard and Northwestern. He now advises the leaders and boards of companies around the world, including GE, DuPont, Nokia, Verizon and The Thomson Corporation. He is admired around the world for his practicality and for the value he provides in helping to solve business problems. For more information on Ram Charan and his work, visit www.ram-charan.com.

Also by Ram Charan: *Leaders at All Levels, What the Customer Wants You to Know, Know-How, Profitable Growth Is Everyone's Business, What the CEO Wants You to Know, Boards at Work, Boards that Deliver.*

Co-authored by Ram Charan: *Execution, Confronting Reality, Every Business Is a Growth Business, The Leadership Pipeline, E-Board Strategies, Strategic Management: A Casebook in Policy and Planning.*

THE GAME-CHANGER

How Every Leader Can Drive Everyday Innovation

A. G. LAFLEY & RAM CHARAN

P

PROFILE BOOKS

First published in Great Britain in 2008 by
PROFILE BOOKS LTD
3A Exmouth House
Pine Street
London EC1R 0JH
www.profilebooks.com

Published in the United States by Crown Business, an imprint of the
Crown Publishing Group, a division of Random House, Inc., New York

1 3 5 7 9 10 8 6 4 2

Printed and bound in Great Britain by
Clays, Bungay, Suffolk

A CIP catalogue record for this book is available from the British Library.

ISBN 978 1 84668 162 2

FSC
Mixed Sources
Product group from well-managed
forests and other controlled sources
Cert no. SGS-COC-2061
www.fsc.org
© 1996 Forest Stewardship Council

The paper this book is printed on is certified by the © 1996 Forest Stewardship
Council A.C. (FSC). It is ancient-forest friendly. The printer holds FSC chain of
custody SGS-COC-2061

Dedicated to the hearts and souls of the joint family of twelve siblings and cousins living under one roof for fifty years whose personal sacrifices made my formal education possible.

—Ram Charan

Dedicated to Gil Cloyd—my innovation partner at Procter & Gamble.

In the early days of 2000, we stood alone. We knew we needed to change—both the business and the R&D leadership approach, and the culture of the Company and R&D—but we didn't know exactly how, or even at first where to begin.

We knew we had to open the Company up to make the Company a lot more externally focused and to encourage a lot more collaboration and cooperation internally across business units, geographic regions, and functions.

It was *very* lonely, but we stood together.

Gil has been a real change agent and a consummate innovation leader. He preserved the essential part of P&G R&D—world-class technologists who are masters of core technologies critical to P&G's household and personal-care businesses—but was willing to change virtually everything else.

Gil is my innovation partner and, together with fellow innovation leaders in the businesses and functions across P&G, we are trying to unleash the power of the consumer and a host of external innovation partners to create brands and products that touch more consumers' lives and improve each day of their lives.

It hasn't been easy, and we still have a lot to do. But, every step of the way, it has been a privilege and a pleasure to work with Gil.

—A. G. Lafley

GAME-CHANGER

A Definition

GAME-CHANGER (gām chang'er) **1.** a visionary strategist who alters the game his business plays or conceives an entirely new game. **2.** a creator who uses innovation as the basis for sustaining profitable organic growth and consistently improving margins. **3.** a leader who understands that the consumer or customer—not the CEO—is boss. **4.** a catalyst who uses innovation to drive every element of a business from strategy to organization, and from budgeting and resource allocation to selecting, rewarding, and promoting people. **5.** an integrator who sees innovation as an integrated end-to-end process, not a series of discrete steps. **6.** a breaker of the chains of commoditization who creates differentiated and value-added brands and businesses through innovation. **7.** a hardheaded humanist who sees innovation as a social process and understands that human interaction—how people talk and work together—is the key to innovation, not just technology.

CONTENTS

Contents

PART TWO: MAKING INNOVATION HAPPEN

PART THREE: THE CULTURE OF INNOVATION

OUR GOAL

Winning is pretty much the same in today's business world as it has been for decades: Create new customers, new products, and new services that drive revenue growth and profits. What's different is *how to do it*.

The acceleration of change today is unprecedented. It creates opportunities as well as the threat of obsolescence.

The best way to win in this world is through innovation. But innovation has often been left to technical experts or perceived as serendipity or luck. Lone geniuses working on their own have, indeed, created new industries or revolutionized existing ones. But there is a problem. You can't wait for the lightbulb to go off in someone's head. The fruits of innovation—sustained and ever-improving organic revenue growth and profits—have to become integral to the way you run your business. That means making innovation central to the goals, strategy, structure, systems, culture, leadership, and motivating purpose and values of your business.

Our goal is to provide you with a new way to think about and manage your business—with a new management process for making innovation central to every driver of your business. It is a process that has been extracted from our practice and research. It is based on what works in the real world and provides a new way to manage a business of any size or at any level within an organization.

This new management process is practitioner-oriented and is presented in what we believe are concrete and actionable terms. You can, in fact, start using it on Monday morning.

The Game-Changer is the result of A. G. Lafley's experience with setting Procter & Gamble on a new path for increasing organic growth and Ram Charan's wrestling for more than a decade with why making innovation happen routinely was such a dilemma, much talked about but elusive in terms of getting much done.

In early 2001, Ram began working with one company on a framework to operationalize the way an idea moves from the person who has it to a product that is successful in the marketplace. While the company was successful in bringing innovations to market, its success was episodic. The reason, Ram observed, was that the process of innovation was fragmented. It was done "mechanically" and missing key social interactions. For example, as is common, the people in technology created something and then "threw it over the wall" to marketing with no productive interaction along the way. There was no disciplined, repeatable, and scalable process of innovation connecting various social interactions among the silos.

The problem accelerated Ram's interest and research. And, in the fall of 2005, he had the opportunity to meet A. G. Lafley, after following the progress that P&G made since A. G. became CEO in June of 2000. A. G., Ram observed, seemed to have made a breakthrough. Innovation at P&G was granular. It was part of what business unit managers did day in and day out. It was more than just brainstorming ideas, but at the heart of the management process and the reason for P&G's turnaround.

The goal, they both agreed, was to distill their experience and research and extract the lessons that could be used by others.

THE
GAME-CHANGER

CHAPTER ONE

HOW AND WHY INNOVATION AT PROCTER & GAMBLE CHANGED ITS GAME

My* job at Procter & Gamble is focused on integrating innovation into *everything* we do.

Every business has some central organizing principle that people use as the basis for making decisions, meeting challenges, and creating opportunities. For P&G, it is innovation.

Innovation must be the central driving force for any business that wants to grow and succeed in both the short and long terms. We live in a time when the rate of change is such that today's unique product or service becomes tomorrow's commodity. Winning—playing the game better than your competitors and changing the game when necessary—requires finding a new way to sustain organic revenue and profit growth and consistently improve margins.

This means seeing innovation not as something left to the R&D department, but as the central foundation in the way you run your business, driving key decisions, be they choice of goals, strategy, organization structure, resource allocation, commitment to budgets, or development of leadership.

All too often, managers decide on a business strategy—what markets to pursue and what products to make—then turn to innovation

---

* This chapter is in the voice of coauthor A. G. Lafley.

1

to support it. *This is the wrong way around.* Innovation needs to be put at the center of the business in order to choose the right goals and business strategy and make how-to-win choices. It is central to the job of every leader—business unit managers, functional leaders, and the CEO. The CEO, in fact, must also be the CIO—the chief innovation officer.

While we will both hone our definition of innovation and fully develop the practical tools for becoming an innovation-centered business, let's simply say that innovation is the foundation for controlling your destiny. It was for P&G (in my experience) the real "game-changer"—the real source of sustainable competitive advantage and the most reliable engine of sustainable growth. Innovation is the answer. That's what I learned in the weeks and years after I received an unexpected phone call.

ARE YOU READY?

It came on June 6, 2000, a few minutes before a business meeting in California. On the line was John Pepper, former chairman and CEO of P&G.

John got right to the point: "Are you prepared to accept the CEO job at P&G?" I was stunned. Just the afternoon before, I had been speaking with chairman and CEO Durk Jager about our plans for the final month of the fiscal year.

"What's happened to Durk?" I asked.

"He resigned."

"Why? What happened?"

"I don't have time to go into that now. I just need to know whether you're prepared to do the CEO job for P&G."

"Of course I am."

"Then get on a plane as soon as you can and come directly to my office when you arrive back in Cincinnati."

"OK."

I turned to my colleagues and told them something had come up. I had to leave. On the plane, I considered this sudden and totally surprising turn of events.

I tried to put first things first: What would I need to do in the next twenty-four, forty-eight, seventy-two hours? And what would I need to do in the first week, first month?

No question. P&G was struggling. We'd issued a big earnings profit warning in March, and the business was still coming in below expectations. While one of my areas of responsibility, North America, was delivering, my other business, Global Beauty Care, was not going to make its numbers. Other businesses were in even worse shape.

Stepping back, I reflected on P&G's recent history. We'd moved to a new global-business-unit-led strategy. We'd totally changed the organization structure—moving from local country to global category profit centers. We were adjusting to more global competition, a faster-changing industry landscape, and the challenges of the Internet and the so-called new economy. Most of our managers were in new roles. I'd worked in P&G's beauty business for exactly eleven months. In the midst of all this, we'd raised the company's goals to unprecedented levels—7 percent to 8 percent growth in net sales and 13 percent to 14 percent earnings growth.

Stretch, innovation, and speed were the orders of the day. Stretch for higher goals. Innovate in all we do. Go fast. Take more risk. All of these are good things in and of themselves. In hindsight, though, we were trying to change too much too fast. Many of our businesses were in no shape to stretch. Too many new products, businesses, and organization initiatives were being pushed into the market before they were ready. Execution suffered, as we too often fired before aiming. We had to come to grips with reality, to see things as they were, not as we wanted them to be.

Job one was to determine the state of P&G's business. At 6 a.m. on June 7, I began digging into the numbers—business by business, region by region, customer by customer. Unfortunately, we were in worse shape than I suspected. We were twenty-three days from year-end and there was no way we were going to make the month, the April–June quarter, or the 1999–2000 fiscal year. After briefing the board on Thursday, June 8, we issued another profit warning. P&G's stock opened more than $3.00 lower on the morning I was announced as CEO. By the end of the week, P&G's stock price was down more than $7.00 from Monday's close. It was not exactly an early confidence booster for me. (All told, our stock had dropped more than 50 percent over six months since January, a loss of more than $50 billion in market capitalization.)

I knew it would take another three to six months to know whether the business bottomed out. In the meantime, I had to retain the people at P&G who would be critical for future success. I talked one-on-one with each leader, as clearly and directly as I could about my expectations. We needed to come to a clear and common understanding of the business challenges and opportunities, and to get the fundamentals back in place quickly to get P&G growing consistently again. I shared with the leaders what was expected of them and what we needed to do together. I encouraged them to compete like hell externally but to collaborate like family internally. Just about everyone signed on to this vision.

What follows in the rest of this chapter is a disciplined crystallization of what was accomplished and how we did it. *While I had the fundamentals, cultivated over a long period of time, in my mind, the reality is their sequencing and actual execution evolved by "muddling through."* While I now have more clarity, I certainly did not have all the answers when I started.

WHAT WE HAD TO DO

Proud P&Gers, we were embarrassed by recent results. We wanted to turn this ship around. To do so, we focused on a few simple but powerful things.

We put the consumer at the center of everything we do. Three billion times a day, P&G brands touch the lives of people around the world. In our company, the consumer—not the CEO—is boss. Regardless of the original source of innovation—an idea, a technology, a social trend—the consumer must be at the center of the innovation process from beginning to end. In ways large and small, P&G was not living up to the "consumer-is-boss" standard; that is why we were losing market share in core categories like disposable diapers and toothpaste. Now we spend much more time with consumers, in stores and in their homes and in consumer-testing centers of all kind—to watch them use our products, to listen to them, and to learn from them what they want from us.

Our goal at P&G is to delight our consumers at two "moments of truth": first, when they buy a product, and second, when they use it. To achieve that, we live with our consumers and see the world and opportunities for new-product initiatives through their eyes. We do this because we win when more consumers purchase and use our brands— and do so repeatedly. We win when consumers use our brands more loyally. We win when consumers trade up to higher-priced, higher-margin brands. Consumers are now at the center of every key decision we make in a routine and disciplined, not episodic way.

We opened up. Long known for a preference to do everything in-house, we began to seek out innovation from any and all sources, inside and outside the company. Innovation is all about connections, so we get everyone we can involved: P&Gers past and present; consumers and customers; suppliers; a wide range of "connect-and-develop" partners; even competitors. The more connections, the more ideas; the more ideas, the more solutions. And because what gets measured gets managed, I established a goal that half of new product and technology innovations come from outside P&G. We are already beyond that figure, compared to 15 percent in 2000.

We made sustainable organic growth the priority. Innovation enables expansion into new categories, allows us to reframe businesses considered mature and transform them into platforms for profitable growth, and creates bridges into adjacent segments. So we changed our emphasis to organic growth, which is less risky than acquired growth and more highly valued by investors. In the second half of the 1990s, top-line growth had slowed, and some of P&G's most venerable brands were weakening—a vulnerability that competitors were quick to attack. I felt P&G could do—had to do—better. That, of course, is easier said than done. P&G is now an $80+ billion company; increasing revenues 5 percent a year means adding the equivalent of a brand like Tide or a market like China—year in, year out—against world-class competitors like

Colgate-Palmolive, Henkel, Johnson & Johnson, Kao, Kimberly-Clark, Unilever, and L'Oréal, as well as retailer private labels and popular low-cost local brands in developing markets like Brazil, China, and India.

Innovation now drives virtually all of P&G's per annum organic sales growth. We now only count on 1 percent of our 5 percent to 7 percent sales growth to come from acquisition activity; the balance must be innovation-driven organic growth. From fiscal 2001 through 2007, even against a background of rising energy and commodity costs, we have improved operating margins by more than 4 percentage points (i.e., 400 basis points). Profits have more than tripled to $10+ billion while free cash flow has totaled $50 billion over the same period. Innovation-driven value creation and incremental sales growth from innovation have nearly doubled since 2001. That has helped us average 12 percent earnings per share growth and increase our market cap by $100 billion, making us one of the ten most valuable companies in the United States. Since fiscal 2000 through November 2007, P&G's share price has increased nearly threefold, reaching a record high on December 12, 2007.

We organized around innovation to drive sustained organic growth. To get organic growth, we needed to innovate. We had to become a more consistent operator, and a much more consistent and reliable innovator. I consciously set out to restore innovation to the heart of P&G. My goal was and is to create an organization of sustainable innovation, which, in turn, drives sustainable organic growth through:

- Thinking about innovation as a strategy—a capability we wanted to build and to strengthen and to turn eventually into sustainable competitive advantage

- Regular business strategy and brand equity reviews that focus on innovation as the competitive advantage and game-changer

- Regular innovation reviews for every global business unit that focus on growth goals, innovation strategies, plans, and major initiatives

- The careful selection and use of the right metrics, recognition, and rewards to encourage innovation

- The process of evaluating, developing, and promoting outstanding business leaders who are also outstanding innovation leaders

- The allocation of resources—financial and human—to drive the successful commercialization of outstanding innovation

By running a disciplined development, qualification, and commercialization process, we have proved we can manage a large portfolio of innovations in various stages of development. Innovation is now P&G's lifeblood and is at the core of our business model. Every day, more P&Gers are involved in innovation. Consumers expect P&G brands to improve their lives with new innovations. Retail customers count on P&G innovation to grow their business and create value. P&G investors and shareowners look to innovation as an indicator of overall future financial performance.

We began thinking about innovation in new ways. We started from the premise that it is possible to run an innovation program in much the same way we run a factory. There are inputs; these go through a series of transformative processes, creating outputs. It is possible to measure the yield of each process, including the quality, the end product, and the financial and market results. The necessary dynamics to talk about innovation this way—opening the innovation process, focusing more on the consumer, and building teamwork and processes—cannot be done in isolation. To work at all, they have to work together and be integrated into the main decision making of the business.

Second, we broadened the way we thought about innovation to include not just products, technologies, and services, but also business models, supply chains, and conceptual and cost innovations. We also saw innovation not just as disruptive—the proverbial home run—but also incremental, the less glamorous but highly lucrative and profitable "singles and doubles."

And, third, while everyone knows that innovation is risky, we have learned how to pinpoint the sources of those risks and have developed the tools and know-how for managing them. We've made learning from failure a regular practice to improve our ability to manage risk.

HOW WE DID IT . . . FIRST THINGS FIRST

That is what we did. What you want to know is how we did it.

The first step was to improve our execution so we could then focus more resources on innovation. In June 2000, it was crystal clear that we were not executing very well—and in the fast-moving consumer goods industry, execution is often decisive. As a result, we were not delivering on business and financial commitments to our shareholders, customers, suppliers, and employees. The obvious question was "Why?" The answer: We were trying to do too much, too fast, and nothing was being done well. P&G needed clarity and focus. What were the critical choices to make? What would be the key priorities? What was the right *balance?*

Our first choice was growing the core—categories like fabric care, feminine care, and hair care. We had been harvesting or milking these businesses to invest in new brands and products, and/or in new geographic expansion. We would obviously like to do both to maximize short-, medium-, and long-term growth, but we had swung the pendulum too far. We had to get these core businesses and leading brands growing more consistently and more profitably as soon as possible.

In doing so, we placed a laser-sharp focus on current consumers, who at least occasionally bought and used our brands and products, and current retailers, wholesalers, and distributors we worked with. We also needed to improve the discipline with which we managed the operating fundamentals of P&G businesses. For example, in June 2000, we were able to ship only about 97 percent of the cases ordered by customers. That meant we were leaving up to 3 percent in potential sales "on the table." Every Monday morning, my leadership team was asked to report on missed cases and what actions were taken to fill orders. We continued the practice until missed cases were in much better control. Today, missed cases run less than 0.4 percent, and they are no longer a major cause of lost sales and profits.

Pricing was another area of focus. On too many brands and product lines, in too many countries, P&G prices were too high. We needed to find the pricing "sweet spot" that represented a better value for consumers, gave retailers a fair profit, and would drive P&G to improved market share, net sales, and margin performance. This was incredibly important because P&G's business model is driven by well-differentiated brands and superior-performing products that can command modest price premiums and more loyal-consumer purchase and usage. We worked the issue hard and took about two points per year out of net pricing between 2000 and 2002 to ensure better consumer value for P&G brands.

While missed cases and winning the consumer value equation were important areas to work on, we knew that innovation would be the key to winning over the medium and long term. Why? Fundamentally, P&G had been built on a strategy of differentiation—of differentiated, branded consumer household and personal-care products. Brands are promises of something different and better in terms of performance, quality, and value. Brands are guarantees of consistent quality, performance, and value.

But the critical questions were, *how* could we put innovation at the center of everything we do? *How* could we turn innovation into more consistent, more decisive, and more sustainable competitive advantage? And, *how* could we manage the risks associated with our all-in and full-on commitment to innovation? Could we identify and take advantage of the opportunities innovation might offer us? With this in mind, we looked at what we believed would be the key enablers or drivers of an innovation strategy; the drivers that would create an innovation-led operation and build an innovation culture; the drivers that would result in game-changing innovation that would touch more consumers and improve more lives.

INNOVATION IS AN INTEGRATED MANAGEMENT PROCESS

For innovation to have a payoff—for it to generate sustainable organic sales and profit growth—it must be integrated into how you run your business: its overall purpose, goals and strategies, structure and systems, leadership and culture. As illustrated in the diagram on the next page, there are in fact eight elements of any business that ultimately must be organized and led to drive innovation. These eight drivers work together; that is, they are integrated with one another and with the everyday operation of the business. It's important to keep in mind that this is a model, not a lockstep process that must be rigidly followed. It is intended as a guide for breaking down into manageable pieces the seemingly overwhelming challenge of making an organization more innovative. Adapting it as conditions change and idiosyncratic challenges arise is crucial to its usefulness. While we describe the model in a linear, sequential way in order to make it understandable, the reality is that the model doesn't have to be implemented in any particular sequence. You can begin to integrate innovation into your organization through any of these drivers and through more than one at a time. Being adaptable, commonsensical, practical, and "muddling through" to see what works best for your company given the situation at the time are important to making the model work and for innovation to take root.

The overarching or guiding principle for game-changing innovation that delivers sustained organic growth and profits, no matter whether your business is consumer products, services, or business-to-business industrial products, is placing the consumer or customer at the center of this framework. While many say they are "customer-centric," few actually put the customer as boss in the center of the innovation process. The goals of sustaining organic growth and differentiation from the competition are best fulfilled when all eight drivers are fully working together.

1. Motivating purpose and values   Companies centered on innovation are inspiring places to work, and the people who work there are

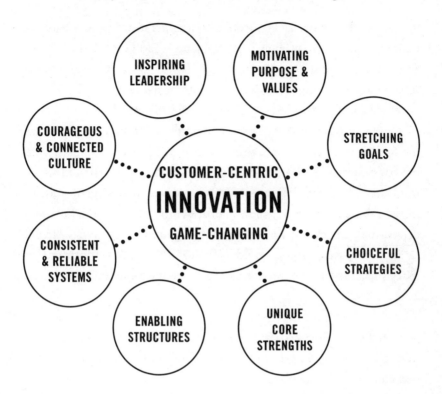

turned on by a higher purpose. Having a sense of purpose larger than delivering numbers that keep Wall Street happy gives meaning to one's work and unifies an organization.

P&G is purpose-led and values-driven. Billions of people around the world are striving to improve their lives through accessible and affordable products and services. Our purpose is to improve their everyday lives in small but meaningful ways with brands and products that continually deliver superior performance, quality, and value better than the best competition.

Our values—integrity, trust, leadership, ownership, and a passion for serving and winning with consumers—translate purpose into action and show up in everyday behaviors, beginning with how we treat the consumer and each other.

Our purpose and values are not unique, but they *are* powerful because our employees have been embracing and practicing them for generations. The key is translating them so they are relevant to winning in today's marketplace. For example, a generation or two ago, we mainly focused on serving middle-income mothers in the United States, Canada, and Western Europe. Today, we aspire to serve a much broader array of people of different income levels and lifestyles in both developed and developing countries around the world.

Our purpose inspires us. Our values unite us. Emphasizing them was the first critical step in the transformation of P&G as a company with the consumer as the boss and innovation at its center. The linkage of purpose and values with innovation energized management and inspired P&G employees in ninety countries around the world. Purpose-driven innovation, everyday-life–improving innovation, was a higher calling—a cause everyone could embrace, a very real opportunity to make small but meaningful improvements in the human condition.

2. Stretching goals   Goals influence every other critical choice. Identifying a few critical goals creates clarity in focusing on strategies that win and align everyone's energy.

In creating game-changing innovation, therefore, it is important to get the growth goals right—goals that are stretching but achievable, yet cannot be reached without a sustained process of innovation, driven by leaders who see it as *the* way to change the game.

The problem in 2000 was that we had committed to stretching goals that we had less than a fifty-fifty chance of delivering. One of the first things we did was to reset our three external growth goals so that they were still stretching but achievable, for example, 4 percent to 6 percent sales growth in categories typically growing 2 percent to 3 percent a year. These goals would elicit bolder, more innovative business unit strategies and more ambitious operating plans.

3. Choiceful strategies   Once goals are set, you have to figure out how to achieve them. Strategies are the few critical choices required by clear goals—choices that result in winning *with* consumers and customers and *against* competition. Putting innovation at the center of our thinking enabled us to see strategic choices in a different light. Businesses and brands previously considered "mature" could then be looked upon as growth opportunities. Innovation thus energized our leaders to grow our four core businesses (fabric care, hair care, baby care, and feminine care) and ten leading brands that each generated a billion dollars or more in sales. Innovation also enabled us to make decisions about where *not* to play. For example, we decided to exit most food and beverage businesses. While profitable and earning cost of capital, they neither had the potential for growth through innovation nor for long-term competitive advantage. Resources, then, were freed up and deployed toward faster-growing, higher-margin, more asset-efficient beauty, health, and personal-care businesses. Innovation also opened up an entirely new opportunity to capture more than a billion new lower-income consumers, particularly in the fastest-growing developing markets.

4. Unique core strengths   Once we made our choices about *where to play*, we then focused on *how to win* by building on, enhancing, and deploying our unique core strengths. Core strengths enable you to play successfully in your industry and are consistent with what your company does or could do best. They create and sustain competitive advantage; they can be integrated in different ways to meet new and unforseen needs. P&G's core strengths include a deep understanding of consumers and placing them at the center of all decision making; creating and building brands that endure; the ability to create value with customers and suppliers; and effectively leveraging global learning and scale into competitive advantage.

We invested serious money, resources, time, and management intensity to make our core strengths stronger. For example, we've reinvented our highly valued market research organization and focused it on deep consumer understanding. Our research has moved away from traditional focus group research and invested heavily, to the tune of a billion dollars (double the industry average), in consumer and shopping research, with particular focus on *immersive* research.

We're spending far more time in context with consumers—living with them in their homes, shopping with them in stores, and being part of their *lives*. These real-world connections lead to richer consumer insights, faster speed to market, and lower risk. It alters the mind-set of P&G leaders and changes their decision making. Total immersion gives real meaning to the power of "consumer is boss" in practice.

The effect has been not only to improve our performance in each unique core strength, but also to create real competitive advantage from their combination. When we put it all together through our deep local knowledge and close retail partnerships, we see and create more innovation opportunities. We use P&G's leading global brands as platforms for innovation. And we commercialize innovation more consistently—all of which leads to more *sustainable* growth and to *superior* shareholder returns.

5. Enabling structures The execution of a chosen strategy and the deployment of unique core strengths require the design of an organization structure that supports innovation at the center of the business. While there is *no* one best way to structure an innovation-centered company, it is clear that the sun is setting on the internally focused, vertically integrated organization. We are in the era of the open corporation. The behavior and psychology of managers has to be in tune with this phenomenon; they need to be comfortable designing structures and processes that bring in and commercialize outside ideas. At P&G, we call it "Connect and Develop." It is the structure and process that brings in more than 50 percent of our innovations and produces billions of dollars in revenue. Structure—which *could* be a liability, particularly in a large, global, diversified company—instead becomes a powerful, sustainable source of competitive advantage.

6. Consistent and reliable systems Innovation is creative but not chaotic. It is a systemic way of moving from concept to commercialization. The process of innovation has well-defined success criteria, milestones, and measures. It is integrated with the mainstream of managerial decision making, particularly the choices of where to play, specific time-based goals, and key performance indicators. Innovation is also linked with budgetary revenue growth and cost targets, resource allocation and reallocation, people development and promotions, and performance appraisals and rewards.

7. Courageous and connected culture   A culture is what people do day in and day out without being told. In an innovation-centered company, managers and employees have no fear of innovation since they have developed the know-how to manage its attendant risk; innovation builds their mental muscles, leading them to new core competencies. They know that the culture of innovation will continue to help the organization be agile and not only adapt to change, but also cause change. A forward-looking culture of innovation continuously transforms a company at the speed of external change.

At P&G, there is a broader, stronger, more-consistent innovation culture today than at any time in our history. It is not perfect, nor where we ultimately want it to be. But we're getting there. P&G leaders, management, and employees are more connected to consumers whose lives they are committed to improving, more connected to customers and suppliers—who are important innovation partners, and more connected to each other as we move from a "not-invented-here" culture to an open-learning culture that "applies and reapplies with pride." They are more courageous and more curious and open to any and all new ideas. They are willing to take more risks because they understand that failure is how we learn.

8. Inspiring leadership   No organization can work without leadership. In the integrated process of innovation, it is the leaders who link all the drivers of innovation together, energize people, and inspire them to new heights. Leaders are instigators. They continually look over the horizon to gauge the changing landscape in their industry. They set the goals that are stretching but achievable and require innovation. They know innovation is a team sport and exercise both their IQ and EQ, enabling them to work with diverse people whose creativity needs to be converted into practical results. Innovation leaders are passionate about knowing the consumer, personally immersing themselves into finding insights about consumer needs. Over time, they learn and develop confidence about how to deal with the risk and failure inherent in innovation. They become confident in the art of balancing possibilities and practicalities. They are intellectually honest about diagnosing the causes of both failure and success. Above all, they know innovation is a highly integrated process that is systemic and replicable and produces results.

A WORK IN PROGRESS

Once our purpose was reaffirmed, clarified, and focused, I could turn to those drivers of game-changing innovation where I believed I could make the biggest impact as CEO. While all eight are important innovation drivers, and each can be addressed in a different sequence, I chose to focus on those I "owned" as CEO and where I could make the biggest impact—goals and strategies, and leadership and culture. What you choose to focus on will vary with your specific responsibilities, your current business situation, and which innovation drivers are either working or need improvement.

I think you'll find, as I have, that you can evaluate any program against these innovation drivers and see where the problems and opportunities are. They are both a description of what we want to achieve and a diagnostic tool.

The most important part of the system is the one in the middle: the consumer. Everything begins and ends with the consumer. We have figured out how to keep the consumer at the center of all our decisions, actions, and behaviors. As a result, we don't go far wrong.

In fact, P&G is getting it right more often. Now we can say that P&G's strategy and structures empower innovation. Our systems enable innovation. Our culture is more an innovation culture. The numbers tell the story. Sales growth and net present value of the total innovation portfolio have more than doubled. Shareholders who stuck with us have been rewarded. R&D productivity is up 85 percent, even though R&D dollars are modestly up versus 2000. Capital spending, which was 8 percent of sales in 2000, is only 4 percent now—and we have not foregone investment in a single unit of capacity to support a growing business or a single innovation initiative to sustain growth.

We have created new products that serve our consumers in new ways, such as Swiffer, Crest Whitestrips, and Tide Coldwater detergent and its international counterpart, Ariel Cool Clean. Consumers tell us they are delighted. Pick a measure, any measure, and P&G is a healthier, more-prosperous, and more-dynamic company today than it was at the turn of the millennium.

The Game-Changer is about what I have learned over the course of a lifetime in business, but particularly since I became CEO of P&G, one of the world's most admired companies. Through many trials and too many errors, I have learned that innovation is an integrated process and that innovation is a game-changing and winning strategy that can transform the everyday work and behaviors of managers and employees. We have not perfected the process of innovation—not by a long shot. But I have no doubt that the right building blocks are in place because we have thought innovation through, step by step.

CHAPTER TWO

WHAT P&G'S INNOVATION TRANSFORMATION MEANS FOR YOU

P&G is one of the few companies that has been able to break the chains of commoditization and create organic growth on a sustainable basis through implementing and managing the integrated process of innovation.* Most companies have pieces of this process—for example, the launch process for bringing a new product to market. All too often, though, each piece of the innovation process is discrete. They are neither connected to each other nor integrated into normal business management and main decision routines, such as budgeting and resource allocation. *P&G's managerial breakthrough was to conceive of and implement innovation as an integrated process based on the idea of customer is boss.* Many think of innovation as serendipitous, risky, and not as manageable as other business processes. The P&G experience clearly demonstrates that innovation can be part of a leader's day-to-day routine. This is a huge step forward in the practice of leadership, especially the ability to drive organic growth day in and day out.

As a key goal, the leaders of P&G chose to exceed industry and GDP growth rates by an order of magnitude of 50 to 100 percent or more.

Announcing and meeting such an ambitious goal required courage based on the confidence that the innovation process would be executed.

---

* This chapter is in the voice of coauthor Ram Charan.

It would not have been possible through cost cutting, productivity improvement, and restructuring the business portfolio alone.

It's important to understand not only what P&G did to execute its turnaround, but also what it didn't do. Usually, when a large company gets in trouble, the knee-jerk reaction is to restructure, resize, and realign. To get back on track, the financial folks get behind the steering wheel; their outlook focuses on reducing costs and narrowing the scope of the business. While P&G had to be refocused and restructured, A.G. and his team took a longer view.

Simply taking cost out would have helped meet short-term goals but would not have put P&G on the path of sustainable organic growth. What the "tried-and-true" approach leaves out is how a continual innovation process can change the landscape of the business. Innovation can redefine what may seem like a low-growth market into a higher-growth opportunity or show how a less-than-attractive industry could be dissected into some very attractive segments, thus paving the way for sustainable growth.

The P&G leadership also made a seminal change in the psyche and working of the organization. P&G changed from a technology-push innovation model to a customer-pull one. This is a radical change in the way a company works and is based on making operational the new approach of customer is boss. By demonstrating that innovation investments could bring tangible returns, P&G's leadership built credibility and created the momentum to do more. Innovation is now firmly yoked to P&G's choice of goals and strategy, resource allocation, review systems, and the selection, promotion, and reward of key people. Only a handful of corporations come close to matching P&G's thorough and systematic integration of innovation into every aspect of its operations. In the best sense of the word, innovation is routine at P&G.

A similar confidence in innovation as a game-changer took place when Jeffrey Immelt became the CEO of General Electric. With $130 billion in revenue in 2001, skeptics abounded about Immelt's ability to meet his goal of increasing organic top-line growth at two to three times the rate of world GDP growth, while maintaining the desired return on investment and operating margins. Confidence in executing his "imagination breakthrough" process gave him and his team the courage to take GE to the next level. For the last four years, GE, just like P&G, has delivered these goals.

Nokia is another example. It is changing the game in the global telecommunications industry, particularly in the handset devices segment. Despite holding the world's highest market share, with a wide gap separating it from the player in second place, Nokia went on the offensive to break the chains of rapid commoditization and capitalize on emerging fast-growth information consumption by the billions of customers coming into the market, particularly in low-income countries. Confidence in its ability to execute the integrated process of innovation gave CEO Olli-Pekka Kallasvuo and his team the courage to announce in July 2006 the goal of becoming more of an Internet company.

Part of future organic growth for Nokia lies in the usage revenue that will come from customers using its mobile handsets for content, information, and entertainment, even if mobile devices remain the major source for Nokia's revenues. However, while the number of handsets sold will substantially increase, revenues from devices will not grow at the same rate because of fast declining price points. (Nokia has, though, been able to maintain its margins and has just raised its one- to two-year margin targets for devices.) Nokia is now using its core strengths—brand, scale and technology, its innovation process, and its unmatched connection with the customer—to rapidly fulfill its promise to be an Internet company. Nokia is thereby starting to change the game not only for other handset players, such as Motorola, but also for carriers like Vodaphone, Internet companies such as Google, and entertainment companies such as Warner Music.

Still another example of game-changing innovation comes from the hand-to-hand combat between Dell and HP. Dell's innovative direct-to-customer and made-to-order business model is legendary. In 2005, when Todd Bradley became head of HP's personal computer unit, it was a money loser and seen as the also-ran number two market shareholder. While Bradley first got his house in order through cost control and focusing the business, he realized that the future depended on developing and implementing an integrated process of innovation. His unit's new organizational structure is based on the need to move fast in the ever-changing rapidly commoditizing PC industry. Bradley and his team created new products in less than two years, won market share consistently, and improved profits and cash flow. As of this writing, HP is number one in market share. The new game in the PC business will not be won on the basis of the supply chain but on differentiation and effectiveness of the processes of innovation. An added benefit for HP is that the innovation process pioneered by Bradley will be implemented in the other divisions of the company. However, the battle won't be easy. Dell is fighting back with several new innovations that have won new product and design awards.

WHAT IS REAL INNOVATION?

To understand innovation, you first have to see the differences between an invention and an innovation. An invention is a new idea that is often turned into a tangible outcome, such as a product or a system. *An innovation is the conversion of a new idea into revenues and profits.* An idea that looks great in the lab and fails in the market is not an innovation; it is, at best, a curiosity. As Jeff Immelt once put it, "Innovation without a customer is nonsense; it's not even innovation."

Invention is needed for innovation to take place. But invention is not innovation. In many companies, inventions that result in patents are considered innovations. These companies are often touted as "innovative." In fact there is no correlation between the number of corporate patents earned and financial success. Until people are willing to buy your product, pay for it, and then buy it again, there is no innovation. A gee-whiz product that does not deliver value to the customer and provide financial benefit to the company is not an innovation. Innovation is not complete until it shows up in the financial results.

Real innovation can change the context—the market space, the customer space, the competitive space, the societal space—in which a business operates. Changing the game, then, means not being hamstrung by the deep-rooted conventional wisdom of your business and industry, but rather seizing the initiative to imagine a new game or a new space and, thus, shaping and controling your destiny. Game-changing leaders search for and execute ideas that put the company on a long-term path to prosperity. For example, P&G created a new market space by introducing the disposable diaper; with the iPod, Apple likewise created an entirely new market space and changed the game for those who were not its usual competitors, such as music, media, and consumer electronics companies. Both P&G and Apple refused to be hemmed in by current conditions; instead, they redefined them. In the process, they forced the competition to play their game. It did not end there. The iPod, with its sleek design, built new capabilities within Apple and was a harbinger of the iPhone, which is changing the game for the cell phone companies.

There is an increasing advantage to being a game-changer—and higher risk for trying to survive on the defensive. Innovation enables you to be on the offensive. The speed of change is such that compared even to two decades ago, "innovate or die" is truly the name of the game. P&G's core products are increasingly challenged by private labels and without continuous innovation would be threatened by commoditization. Commoditization drives down prices; the differentiation that comes from innovation carries an economic premium. Moreover, the competition is tougher than ever—and only getting more so. Thanks to the Internet, there is more transparency than ever on prices, which reduces margins. A more-open trading system and more-efficient shipping have shrunk the economic globe; better communications and the Internet have tolled the death of distance. The development of venture capital and the rise of bold capitalists in places like China and Brazil have led to a host of new competitors. The only way to stay ahead is to keep innovating.

WHY INNOVATION MATTERS

Innovation is the key idea that is shaping corporate life, helping leaders conceive previously unimagined strategic options. Take acquisitions, as an example. Most are justified on the basis of cost and capital reduction: for example, the merger of two pharmaceutical companies and the global rationalization of overhead and operations and the savings from combining two sales forces and R&D labs. You can, however, buy earnings through acquisitions for only so long; cost-control, however necessary, is a defensive strategy.

Innovation enables you to see potential acquisitions through a different lens, looking at them not just from a cost perspective, but also as a means of accelerating profitable top-line revenue growth and enhancing capabilities. For example, the innovation capabilities of P&G were enhanced by its acquisition of Gillette. Its market-leading brands (such as Gillette, Venus, Oral B, and Duracell) are platforms for future innovations; and core technologies in blades and razors, electronics, electromechanics, and power storage strengthen the technology portfolio from which P&G can innovate in the future.

Innovation also provides an edge in being able to enter new markets faster and deeper. In large part, it is P&G's revived innovation capacity that is allowing it to make inroads into developing markets, where growth is double that in rich countries.

Innovation puts companies on the offensive. Consider how Colgate and P&G, effective serial innovators, have innovated Unilever out of the U.S. oral-care market. The company that builds a culture of innovation is on the path to growth. The company that fails to innovate is on the road to obsolescence. The U.S. domestic automakers and major companies such as Firestone, Sony, and Kodak all used to be industry leaders, even dominators. But they all fell behind as their challengers innovated them into second place (or worse).

Peter Drucker once said that the purpose of a business enterprise is "to create a customer." Nokia became number one in India by using innovation to create 200 million customers. Through observing the unique needs of Indian customers, particularly in rural villages where most of the population resides, it segmented them in new ways and put new features on handsets relevant to their unique needs. In the process, it created an entirely new value chain at price points that give the company its desired gross margin. Innovation, thus, creates customers by attracting new users and building stronger loyalty among current ones. That's a lot in itself, but the value of innovation goes well beyond that. By putting innovation at the center of the business, from top to bottom, you can improve the numbers; at the same time, you will discover a much-better way of doing things—more productive, more responsive, more inclusive, even more fun. People want to be part of growth, not endless cost cutting.

A culture of innovation is fundamentally different from one that emphasizes mergers and acquisitions or cost cutting, both in theory and practice. For one thing, innovation leaders have an entirely different set of skills, temperament, and psychology. The M&A leader is a deal maker and transactionally oriented. Once one deal is done, he moves to the next. The innovation leader, while perhaps not a creative genius, is effective at evoking the skills of others needed to build an innovation culture. Collaboration is essential; failure is a regular visitor. Innovation leaders are comfortable with uncertainty and have an open mind; they are receptive to ideas from very different disciplines. They have organized innovation into a disciplined process that is replicable. And, they have the tools and skills to pinpoint and manage the risks inherent in innovation. Not everyone has these attributes. But companies cannot build a culture of innovation without cultivating people who do.

MYTHS OF INNOVATION

The idea of innovation has become encrusted by myth. One myth is that it is all about new products. That is not necessarily so. New products are, of course, important but not the entire picture. When innovation is at the center of a company's way of doing things, it finds ways to innovate not just in products, but also in functions, logistics, business models, and processes. A process like Dell's supply chain management, a tool like the monetization of eyeballs at Google, a method like Toyota's Global Production System, a practice like Wal-Mart's inventory management, the use of mathematics by Google to change the game of the media and communications industries, or even a concept like Starbucks's reimagining of the coffee shop—these are all game-changing innovations. So was Alfred Sloan's corporate structure that made GM the world's leading car company for decades, as was P&G's brand management model.

Another myth is that innovation is for geniuses like Chester Floyd Carlson (the inventor of photocopying) or Leonardo da Vinci: Throw some money at the oddballs in the R&D labs and hope something comes out. This is wrong. The notion that innovation occurs only when a lone genius or small team beaver away in the metaphorical (or actual) garage leads to a destructive sense of resignation; it is fatal to the creation of an innovative enterprise.

Of course, geniuses exist and, of course, they can contribute bottom-line-bending inventions (see Jobs, Steven). But companies that wait for "Eureka!" moments may well die waiting. And remember, while da Vinci designed a flying machine, it could not be built with the technology available at the time. True innovation matters for the present, not for centuries hence. Another genius, Thomas Edison, had the right idea: "Anything that won't sell, I don't want to invent. Its sale is proof of utility and utility is success," he told his associates in perhaps his most important invention—the commercial laboratory. "We can't be like those German professors who spend their whole lives studying the fuzz on a bee," he said. Generating ideas is important, but it's pointless unless there is a repeatable process in place to turn inspiration into financial performance.

INNOVATION IS A SOCIAL PROCESS

To succeed, companies need to see innovation not as something special that only special people can do, but as something that can become routine and methodical, taking advantage of the capabilities of ordinary people, especially those deemed by Peter Drucker as knowledge workers. It is easy to put it off because you are rewarded for today's results, because the organization doesn't seem to support or value innovation, because you don't know where to find ideas, because innovation is risky, or because it is not easily measured. But these are excuses, not reasons. We have both observed and practiced innovation as a process that all leaders can use and continue to improve. It is broader, involves more people, can happen more often, and is more manageable and predictable than most people think.

But making innovation routine involves people. In real life, ideas great or good do not seamlessly work their way from silo to silo. No, from the instant someone devises a solution or a product, its journey to the market (or oblivion) is a matter of making connections, again and again. Managing these interactions is the crux of building an innovation organization. In a phrase that will recur throughout this book, innovation is a social process. And this process can only happen when people do that simple, profound thing—connect to share problems, opportunities, and learning. To put it another way, anyone can innovate, but practically no one can innovate alone.

When you as a leader understand this, you can map, systematize, manage, measure, and improve this social process to produce a steady stream of innovations—and the occasional blockbuster. Innovation is not a mystical act; it is a journey that can be plotted, and done over and over again. It takes time and steady leadership, and can require changing everything from budget and strategy to capital allocation and promotions. It definitely requires putting the customer front and center, and opening up the R&D process to outside sources, including competitors. But it can be done.

And no, belying another myth: Size doesn't matter. Innovation can happen in companies as large as P&G, Best Buy, GE, Honeywell, DuPont, and HP and as small as my father's shoe store in India. I remember vividly how we used to sit up on the roof to get a whiff of relief from the evening heat, talking about what to do better and how. When I was nine years old in 1948, we changed the game of the shoe business in Hapur, the town where we lived and our business was located. Even though we had no sophisticated understanding of branding—in fact we never used the word *brand*—we named a line of shoes "Mahaveer" (after my cousin) and targeted it at the "rich people" largely associated with the local grain trading exchange, the second largest in India. We persuaded manufacturers to produce a special line of shoes for this target audience and became number one in town in less than two years. The profits from this innovation funded my formal education in India.

GETTING A HANDLE ON INNOVATION

For all the talk about innovation—and there is a veritable Niagara of talk—and how important it is for future growth, many middle managers I speak to are unmoved. They see their careers progressing because of other day-to-day operating priorities, such as making the numbers or cutting costs, and see betting their futures on innovation as risky and daunting. "What's the use of trying to come up with something new? Nobody here will give me the resources to pursue it," one complained to me. "Before I could finish my sentence, people poked holes in my ideas," said another.

Those comments have a ring of truth, but they are irrelevant in terms of building your capability for succeeding in the future. Every leader in charge of a P&L has to make innovation happen, even if the company lacks a culture of innovation. I'll go further, and ask of middle managers reading this: Are you actively participating in one or more innovation-centered growth projects? If not, you should be worried, because you will be left behind or risk obsolescence in the skills that will be required in the future. Without this experience, you are neither building your capabilities nor learning how to deal with uncertainty and managing risk. Figuring out how to make decisions across silos—bringing together all the skills from people across the company to make innovation happen—can help to make you CEO material. No matter what your job is as middle manager, you must practice and master the art of observing customers and detecting insights for innovation.

As I see it, innovation failure is less the ability to find new ideas and more often the failure to make the right connections and have the right conversations. Managers have to do the hard work of putting innovation at the center of their thinking and decision making, and creating the organizational mechanisms that convert ideas into profits.

Consider: Every company has a budgeting process that is repetitive, refined, and ingrained into the company's DNA, with every manager participating in the process to some degree. But few corporations can say the same when it comes to innovation. We will describe such a process, drawn from deep observation of practice at P&G, and other leading companies, such as LEGO, Honeywell, DuPont, GE, and Nokia.

To prosper, companies need to do four things well: develop leaders of the future, improve productivity, execute strategy, and create innovation. Innovation is the glue that binds everything together. Without sustaining the practice of innovation, no company can excel—or survive.

As A.G. has demonstrated, creating an innovation culture is doable. It is, however, one that is never finished. And that's OK. Relax. Humans are wired for creativity; we long to express it. By emphasizing innovation, you will be tapping into your staff's deepest intellectual and professional desires. There is no question that P&G is a happier place than in 2000—and this is not strictly because people have seen their business grow steadily and their company stock rise in value (although this certainly helps). It is also because more people are more charged up when they come to work. They are more engaged because they are drawing on more of their capabilities, in ways they never anticipated.

And finally, there is no choice. The company that fails to innovate consistently, and elegantly, will fail. Every leader, therefore, must make innovation a driver of her unit's strategy. That means building an organization that supports innovation as a goal and a social process that delivers it. Done consistently over time, the company with these characteristics delivers better results than otherwise by being comfortable with managing risk as a routine. Like the power of compound interest, the innovations that ensue—both small and large—accumulate year in, year out, to create ever-increasing distance against the competition.

Game-changing innovation is not only the primary engine of sustainable growth and superior value creation, but also the catalyst for transforming a company's strategy, organization capability, culture, and leadership. We address the fear that the task is too big, broad, or complicated to achieve success. It's simply not the case. The required tool kit is actually fairly small. To create an innovation culture, you need a strategy; ideas; a process that moves these ideas to market; and an organizational structure that supports innovation (and protects and rewards innovators) up and down the line. Properly adapted, we are confident the framework we present is replicable across companies with widely varying cultures at the corporate, business unit, and functional levels because it comes from actual practice.

PART ONE

DRAWING THE BIG PICTURE

In mid-2000, it was obvious that P&G would have to change its game. Most simply put, it was not winning in the marketplace, missing financial commitments to investors, and losing market share to key competitors. It was neither its customers' best supplier nor its suppliers' best customer. It was definitely not delighting customers and improving their lives with brands and products of consistently superior performance quality and value.

The core issue was customers. Not enough new ones were being attracted to P&G brand and product lines, and not enough were delighted when they used P&G products and thereby converted to loyal usage. P&G's fundamental business model relies on higher brand and product trial rates and higher customer and household conversion or loyalty rates. If more customers try its brands and more like its products, then more will use them on a more regular or loyal basis. This is what drives category and industry leading market shares for P&G brands. This is what results in higher margins and profitability.

P&G was not winning with the customer at the first moment of truth (when she decides what to buy or try) or at the second moment of truth (when she puts the product she bought and tried to the usage test). P&G, as you will learn in chapter 3, had to make the customer the boss.

Putting innovation at the center of your business helps make breakthroughs. It provides the foundation to choose goals that are more ambitious but are still realistic. These ambitious goals become inspirational when employees gain confidence that with the capability to innovate, the goals can be achieved.

Determining the right, ambitious goals requires that you be resourceful and creative in defining new market spaces or reconfiguring existing ones and casting for new ways to compete in those spaces. In short, you must determine where to play and how to win.

Innovation revitalizes the core strengths of a business. It enables you to combine them in unique ways to create new core strengths that better capitalize on opportunities for where to play and how to play.

By constantly searching for a new game and executing it well, you serve notice to competitors that you have changed the rules of the game or the game itself, and that they will have to play a different game entirely. That is the essence of what being a game-changer is all about.

In the section to follow, we illustrate the power of putting the customer first and choosing the goals and new strategy plays that cannot be accomplished without innovation. As well, we look at how the *dynamic combination* of core strengths enables you to win in areas that conventional wisdom would see as "off-limits" to your business.

CHAPTER THREE

THE CUSTOMER IS BOSS

The Foundation of Successful Innovation

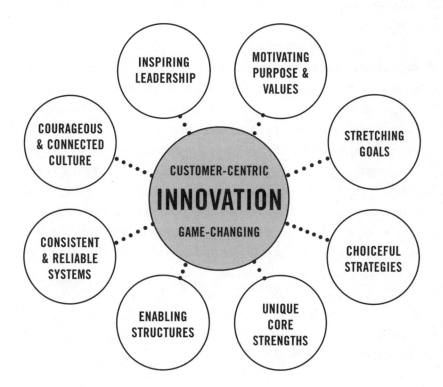

Every culture has a language; and the corporate culture at P&G is rich in words and phrases that convey what it is trying to do. Of these, the most important is a phrase that sums up all its priorities: The consumer is boss. The people who actually buy and use P&G products are a rich source of innovation—if only you listen to them, observe them in their daily lives, and even live with them. For P&G, the end user is the consumer, what other businesses may refer to as their "customer." At P&G, the consumer is often referred to as "she" or "her" because the majority of purchasers and users of P&G brands and products are women.

Consumer is boss is far more than a slogan. It is clear, simple, and inclusive—not just internally for employees, but also for external stakeholders, like suppliers and retail partners.

"Our business is pretty simple," I told employees in one town hall meeting after another during my first months as CEO. "The consumer is our boss, and we have to win with her at two moments of truth day in and day out. We face the first moment of truth at the store shelf, when she decides whether to buy a P&G brand or a competitor's. If we win at the first moment of truth, we get a chance to win at the second, which occurs at home when she and her family use our products and decide whether we've kept our brand promise. Only by winning at both moments of truth—consistently, every day—do we earn consumers' loyalty and sustain the company's growth over the short and the long term. And, we have to win *both* moments of truth *millions* of times a day in more than 180 countries worldwide."

P&G puts the consumer at the center of the innovation process—from the beginning during the ideation stage through the end, when she ultimately buys the product. As the saying at P&G goes, "The consumer is at the heart of all we do."

KNOW/APPRECIATE/RESPECT THY WHO

The most essential component to game-changing innovation is deeply understanding your consumer at both the rational and the emotional levels. This goes well beyond basic demographics and psychographics. It requires deep understanding of what drives their *emotions*. It requires understanding not only their needs, but also their *aspirations*. You must get an appreciation for who they are, how they live, and—yes, of course—how your product can best improve their lives.

Making the consumer the boss is a promise to identify with her, to respect and serve her, and to take her needs and wants seriously.

As Peter Drucker put it, "The customer has to be assumed to be rational. His or her reality, however, is usually quite different from that of the manufacturer." Understanding the boss's reality helps identify meaningful insights. Consumer insights lead to innovation opportunities. Once you know where the opportunities are, you can bring tremendous innovation resources to the task. P&G needed to see things as they really are—through the eyes of the boss.

I consistently encourage P&G employees to stay externally focused on the men, women, children, babies, and pets we serve. Get out of the office and into homes and stores, no matter what their work is. Understand consumers' reality—for sure!—but, also understand their dreams. It is *always eye opening* to spend time with consumers to understand why they buy or do not buy P&G products. And it is always *inspiring* to understand their lives and how we can help make their everyday household and personal-care experiences more satisfying. I personally make time to visit with shoppers and consumers at least once a month, and I never fail to learn something I can apply to the business.

At P&G we often ask, "Who is your WHO?" How a product innovation team applies their consumer understanding can show up in many different ways. For example, the team preparing for the launch in the United States of the heartburn medication Prilosec as an over-the-counter product created a life-sized cardboard cutout of a consumer they named Joanne. She represented their most important WHO, or consumer. In order to keep Joanne front and center, the team put the cutout of Joanne in a chair in their conference room. Often during meetings, to cut through the debates and focus only on those innovations that would meaningfully impact her life, they turn to her and ask, "What would Joanne think?"

UNDERSTANDING THE WHOLE PERSON

"The human condition," says Jeneanne Rae of Peer Insight, a consultancy that specializes in service innovation, "is a much more fruitful starting point given the level of competition today."

You might think that P&G, of all places, would know this. After all, the company created the first market research department and has long been acknowledged for the almost relentless way it seeks knowledge of consumers. What it was not doing well enough, often enough, was seeing consumers as active participants in innovation. Their role was essentially passive: responding to stimuli in experiment after experiment to provide "quantitative research data"—numbers that could be crunched—instead of being sources of innovation and inspirational partners in innovation.

P&G needed to look at consumers more broadly. It tended to narrow in on only one aspect of the consumer—for example, their mouth for oral-care products, their hair for shampoo, their loads of dirty clothes and their washing machines for laundry detergents. P&G had essentially extracted the consumer out of her own life (and, at times a particular body part as well!) and myopically focused on what was most important to the company—the product or the technology. P&G has since learned to understand and appreciate her and her life—how busy she is; her job responsibilities; the role she plays for her children, husband, and other family members; and her personal and family aspirations and dreams. This has enabled the identification of innovation opportunities that truly provide meaningful solutions to her household and personal-care needs and wants that otherwise wouldn't have been discovered through more-traditional, more-narrow, and often more-superficial methods.

Understanding how a family's income influences the daily decisions they make about the brands and the products they choose to buy and use is another important aspect of consumer understanding. The consumer-is-boss orientation—the understanding and appreciation of the WHO as a whole person—is illustrated in the following story of Carlos and Marta.

THE STORY OF CARLOS AND MARTA

Through a gate on a backstreet in Mexico City, into a courtyard, and up two flights of stairs is the modest two-bedroom apartment of Marta and Carlos. Marta, thirty-two, is a stay-at-home mother of two basketball-crazy girls; Carlos is an accountant at a car repair shop. Their home is no larger than a good-sized hotel room, with a tiny kitchen and a dining room just big enough to hold a table and four chairs. There are no closets, so the couple has put up wooden shelving for their clothing. The walls are scattered with family pictures; on the door is a printed prayer and two crosses. This home is truly their castle. They saved for twelve years, living with Marta's parents, to buy it. Marta takes meticulous care of every inch; even the family toothbrushes are kept in order, snapped to attention by a device that hangs on the wall above the sink. Marta is P&G's kind of consumer. And, in fact, she is a P&G consumer—Ariel laundry detergent, Downy fabric softener, and Naturella feminine protection.

Carlos makes the equivalent of about $600 a month, almost exactly the country's average. In P&G terms, the family is part of the Mexico lower-income consumer market, which is defined as households with income between $215 and $970 a month. These families account for about 60 percent of the country's 106 million people.

The poorest 25 percent of Mexico's people do not have the disposable income to be much interested in what P&G has to offer; as far as the top 15 percent, since P&G entered the country in 1948, it has done pretty well. But for a time it was not as successful with the middle 60 percent, which also happens to be where the most population growth is. "We have to win in this segment today, since the proportion of the low-income segment will not decrease in coming years," the P&G Mexico office concluded in an internal study. It went on to ask, "What are the business opportunities we have with them and why?"

Those are the right questions, and the failure to think them through was costly to us. In one case, innovation did deliver a better product— but it still failed because of faulty understanding of the WHO's beliefs and habits. In the late 1980s, Ariel Ultra laundry detergent was launched. It delivered better cleaning performance while using only half as much. P&G saw this as a significant benefit because most lower-income households have limited storage space—a single shelf, like in the kitchen of Marta and Carlos. Ultra also had enzymes that delivered better cleaning. So convinced was P&G that it had a big winner that most of production was switched over to Ultra and a huge campaign was initiated. Mexican women told P&G otherwise. For one thing, they didn't believe that they could really get their laundry clean by using so little. For another, Ariel Ultra didn't foam. Many members of lower-income households do manual labor and are acutely conscious of odor; they considered foam a signal that their perspiration was being rubbed out. "We totally missed how important aesthetics and visual signals of performance were to the low-income consumer," says P&G's Herrera Moro. In a matter of months, Ariel Ultra was discontinued from the market. He put it bluntly: "We could have understood. We should have understood. We didn't so we failed." And this was not the only time P&G missed the mark with the lower-income consumer.

Starting in about 2001, P&G changed tack. To reach the middle 60 percent, it had to know them better. All it really knew was there was a gap between what it was offering and what the majority of Mexicans wanted.

The "consumer closeness program" developed ways to get people literally closer to the consumer. *Living It* is a program in which P&G employees live for several days with lower-income families (see pages 48–49 for more program details).

Downy Single Rinse is one highly successful example of how to convert insights from such experiences into profitable products. In the early 2000s, the Mexican market share for Downy fabric softener was low and stagnant. P&G wasn't sure what could be done about this since the assumption was that people who didn't have washing machines didn't use softener. Not wanting to compromise the Downy brand by dropping the price too much, the decision was made to see if something specific to the needs of the lower-income consumer could be designed.

One of the things P&G people noticed—often to their shock—by Living It and similar experiences was the problem of water. Before the Europeans arrived in the sixteenth century, Mexico City was surrounded by a lake; now it is parched. Suspicion of drinking water is high; Carlos and Marta buy bottled water, as do a large proportion of families who make much less than they do. Millions of rural women still lug buckets back from wells or communal pumps; in the cities, many have running water for only a few hours a day. Most homes do not have fully automatic washing machines; even fewer have dryers. All this makes doing the laundry a seriously draining chore.

At the same time, lower-income Mexican women take laundry very, very seriously. They cannot afford to buy many new clothes very often, but they take great pride in ensuring that their family is turned out well. Sending your children to school in clean, ironed, bright clothing is a visible sign of being a good mother. On Marta's wooden shelves and hangers, every single item, from jeans and T-shirts to Carlos's suits, is tautly ironed—and she is the rule, not the exception. P&G found that Mexican women spend more time on laundry than on the rest of their housework combined. More than 90 percent use some kind of softener, even women who do some or all of their laundry by hand.

"By spending time with women, we learned that the softening process is really demanding; it required a lot of energy and time," recalls Antonio Hidalgo, P&G brand manager for Downy Single Rinse at the time of its debut in March 2004. A typical load of laundry went through the following six-step process: wash, rinse, rinse, add softener, rinse, rinse. No problem if all this is just a matter of pressing a button every once in a while. But it's no joke if you have to walk half a mile or more to get water. Even semiautomatic machines require that water be added and extracted manually. And if you get the timing wrong, the water supply might run out in the middle. "The big 'aha!' " says Carlos Paz Soldán, vice president of P&G Mexico and Central America, was discovering how valuable water is to lower-income Mexicans. "And we only got that by experiencing how they live their life."

Putting it together, here is what was known. Lower-income Mexican women liked to use softener; they had high standards for performance; and doing the laundry was arduous, time consuming, and required plenty of water for multiple cleaning and rinsing steps. These ideas were put through the wringer, doing the kind of large-scale quantitative research that P&G is known for. They stood up to the scrutiny.

Having identified a problem to solve (making laundry easier and less water intensive) and a consumer benefit, all that was left was to figure out was what product to offer. Specs for performance and target costs were sent to the labs, and they came up with an answer: Downy Single Rinse. Instead of a six-step process, DSR reduced it to three—wash, add softener, rinse. Cutting down on the number of rinses saves enormous time, effort, and water. DSR was launched with the endorsement of the Mexican water and environment agency. There were lots of in-store demonstrations so women could see it work.

DSR was a hit from the start. Hidalgo recalls when he told one mother that he had worked on DSR, her face lit up. "She thanked me," he says, with satisfaction, "and asked me to please bring more of these kinds of products to her life." Hidalgo is, of course, trying to do just that.

Particularly when innovating for lower-income markets, it is important to think about affordability, not price. Lower-income consumers are price sensitive, of course, but the better way to think of it is that they are value sensitive.

By listening to women like Marta, a trusted brand and a profitable product was created. Marta positively purrs when her nieces tell her, "Your clothes smell so good."

BREAKING INTO A NEW MARKET
BY UNDERSTANDING THE WHO

Another example of deeply understanding the WHO comes from Nokia, which adapted its business to conditions within India. In the process, it has come to dominate the Indian market for cell phones.

All too many companies trying to tap into the booming markets outside the Western world—China, India, Brazil, and Russia, for example—tweak product offerings and then "push" what worked in their traditional markets. Nokia's success in India is based on its being attitudinally willing to accept that "what worked here is not likely to work there." They were psychologically open to the possibility that their existing conceptions and capabilities—indeed, their entire business model—might not apply.

Understanding and catering to the needs of a new market is not just about marketing, it is also a fundamental business challenge. Being open-minded and willing to listen and probe for insights about not just the product, brand, or advertising, but also the distribution system, the supply chain, and other aspects of the new market, are crucial. This information is the raw material for innovation. Building an organization that can unearth and act on these insights provides the strategic and organizational agility to stay ahead in different markets.

Learning, curiosity, and probing for the precise need gives you that edge. That is what led Nokia to discover that building the market for mobile phones in India would take more than a few tweaks to its existing product. What India required was a new business model, and Nokia created it.

Nokia's senior leadership knew the market for mobile phones in India could be huge. When Nokia first set its sights on India in 1996, only one out of a hundred Indians had a landline phone. The Nokia team imagined how significant mobile communications could be to people who otherwise delivered messages by riding a bicycle from one town to another, or who lost touch with family members—even spouses—for months at a time. But while the people at Nokia imagined the possibilities, they didn't assume they knew exactly how to meet India's mobile phone needs. They first assigned a carefully chosen team with a broad mandate to understand the Indian market from the ground up. While the team included Nokia employees from California and Finland, it was slanted toward native Indians, for the obvious reason that they would have a better ear for listening to and a keener eye for observing local tastes, values, habits, and culture.

As Nokia was making the effort to understand the Indian market, it looked at the other side of the coin as well and ensured that the new Indian employees understood Nokia. They were brought to headquarters in Finland for several weeks of intensive training. Explains Tero Ojanperä, Nokia's chief technology officer: "We relocate people to headquarters for a while so that they get to know people in the company, and understand the company culture. This is especially important if they were recruited from outside. Then when they return to the country where they are going to work, they not only have a deep connection with the local culture, but they also have Nokia culture in their veins. They get a viewpoint that is both global and local." Frequent visits from Nokia senior managers and product development people also reinforce Nokia culture.

Early on, Nokia recognized that getting mobile phones into the hands of India's vast population would be a major challenge. The big retail outlets selling durable consumer electronics wanted nothing to do with the nascent mobile phone market, because margins per handset in absolute terms were too slim and volume too low. Ojanperä explains, "We realized just how different this market is. To reach this vast market, we needed to redesign the whole business model from scratch: the price points, the value propositions, the product design, and also how we market and distribute."

Nokia turned to HCL, a personal computer manufacturer and distributor, to help it crack the distribution nut. HCL shared Nokia's vision of affordability and distribution far beyond traditional electronics stores that carry products with much-higher price points. HCL also shared many of Nokia's values and became a true partner. Many companies change distributors every two or three years, but the Nokia-HCL partnership has endured since the outset, even as Nokia has, at the same time, expanded its distribution and partner network.

The India business development team talked with a huge number of Indian consumers and soon realized that the mobile phone would have to meet many different needs and be used under a variety of conditions. The team landed on what Shiv Shivakumar, Nokia's vice president of sales in India, refers to as "a digital convergence at the bottom of the market"—that is, the idea that a mobile phone could also function as an alarm clock, a radio, and a flashlight, products that cost 700 to 900 rupees ($14 to $18) apiece, at that time. (As of this writing, it would be $17.50 to $22.50.) People would need to use the phone in arid conditions with a lot of dust, in bright sun that created a lot of glare, and in hot, humid places where hands got sweaty and slippery. Moreover, the vast population of people living in Indian villages have neither plumbing nor electricity and are extremely poor. Their ability to afford a phone increases when multiple families use the same set. With electricity scarce in many places, lighting was a problem.

These keen observations pointed to desirable product features: a better grip, a dustproof phone, a built-in flashlight, a polarized screen. Nokia India, Nokia Global, and HCL discussed the issues with the aim of identifying a product that could be built off Nokia's technology platform and in keeping with the Nokia brand at the right price.

The "right" price wasn't necessarily rock bottom. Indian users couldn't afford the price of a mobile phone in the Western world, but they were willing to pay for value. Initially, the price was about $50, down to about $20 as of late 2007. Those pricing levels enabled Nokia to provide what Indian consumers wanted and still have desirable margins. As president and CEO Olli-Pekka Kallasvuo explains, "Some people try to optimize for cost in developing markets, but you may need to spend a little more to design and produce a better product." Nokia finds, for instance, that some 63 percent of Indians look for style when they buy a phone—which for some means it has great technological features; for others, appearance is what counts; and still others, the sensory aspects, like the screen and keypad, are appealing.

Nokia's biggest insight, however, had nothing to do with the product itself. It recognized that because the big retailers were unwilling to sell mobile phones, Nokia would have to create its own distribution system. Here again, by being close to the market and taking time to understand the particulars of the country without being tainted by previous success, the Nokia team found a solution that worked for the

Indian market. They developed a network of people willing to sell Nokia phones from small stands, about the size many vendors use to sell fruit and vegetables all across India, from the bustling cities of Mumbai and Delhi to the tiniest villages in the hinterland. Nokia, in partnership with HCL, found people who were interested in the opportunity and trained them. There were plenty of entrepreneurial people eager for the chance to make a decent living. The right product at the right price point sold through tiny outlets that could be located just about anywhere gave Nokia tremendous reach and acceleration.

Nokia and HCL's insights extended to the motivations and needs of the individual vendors, discovering that they expected to make their money by turning over the merchandise quickly, not from high margins. The main concern was velocity—how quickly the vendors could sell their items. The vendors did not want to have their money tied up in inventory, even overnight. Fruit vendors typically emptied their cart by the end of the day. Vendors selling mobile phones expected to do the same. In fact, if the products were priced with a 10 percent margin, the vendor would undoubtedly sell it at a lower price, whittling the margin closer to 2 percent, to move the merchandise. What mattered was a steady supply of product and avoiding financial risk. Recently, existing retailers such as pharmacies and supermarkets have begun to sell Nokia mobile phones. As Shivakumar explains, "Now people realize that mobile phones actually increase foot traffic, so every organized trader or big retailer wants to sell mobile phones." In fall 2007, there were one hundred thousand retail outlets selling Nokia products.

Nokia now dominates the Indian market for mobile phones by a wide margin. It has established manufacturing and R&D facilities in India, allowing the product innovation cycle to move even faster. Getting deeper into the Indian market also provides the fuel for continual innovation. For instance, Nokia has identified seven distinct market segments, each with its own priorities. Ojanperä says, "Results are now showing that we seem to have done something right. We have been able to sustain reasonable margins at those very low price points, which none of our competitors seem to be able to match at this point of time."

Product features designed for the Indian market are now part of the portfolio other country teams can draw on as they expand to places like Indonesia and sub-Saharan Africa. But even if members of the Nokia India team are involved, you can be sure they will work hard to define the needs of the new local market. As Ojanperä says, "It is about being close to the market and realizing the diversity of the market and then innovating very close to the market. There is no way our people in corporate headquarters can realize what is going on in India, or what is going on in Africa. Every location is different, and requires an open mind and fresh thinking about the product and every element of the business."

ARTICULATED VS. UNARTICULATED NEEDS

Great innovations come from understanding the customer's unmet needs and desires, both articulated and unarticulated—that is, not only what they say, but, more important, what they cannot articulate or do not want to say. Unarticulated needs help uncover the boss's "real reality." It may include getting a real-world appreciation of their lifestyle and what's most important to them; understanding how they use a product and their real motivations for doing so; beginning to understand their emotions and feelings. Unarticulated needs may also be uncovered by looking at the contradiction between what people say they do and what they actually do. Done well, you uncover *unarticulated* reasons why a customer chooses one brand over another. For example, a woman may say she buys a certain fine fragrance "because it reminds me of my first boyfriend." With insights like this, you can determine which groups of customers have the highest potential to be attracted to your offerings and develop innovations precisely targeted to them.

A good example comes from L'Oréal. The French beauty company designed a mascara for Japanese women, whose short, straight lashes meant they traditionally did not use the product. Therefore, there was no demand for it. If L'Oréal had listened to the market, it would have shrugged and gone on to something more promising. Instead, it came up with the idea of a special mascara that could lengthen and curl lashes. It was a hit. As CEO Jean-Paul Agon told the *Financial Times*, "We never would have seen [the potential] in a focus group." L'Oréal's mission, Agon noted, is to introduce or invent products that customers come to love; that requires anticipating their needs, not just giving them what they ask for.

Just about every P&G billion-dollar brand was launched with a product innovation discontinuity—that directly addressed unmet customer needs—and, as a result, stimulated new consumption. Pampers was the first mass disposable diaper, giving mothers a more-effective, more-convenient alternative to cloth. Head & Shoulders was the first shampoo to provide no trade-off between antidandruff protection, scalp care, and beautiful, clean hair.

In the end, customers cannot always tell you what they truly want. It is up to you to listen, to observe, to make connections, and to identify the insights that lead to innovation opportunities.

Industrial companies also have to know the end user, despite the fact that their offerings often become part of another company's product. Making that connection with customers is the only surefire way to stay relevant. That's how 3M's Optical Systems Division has generated hundreds of millions of dollars in revenues a year and makes a major contribution to 3M's bottom line, despite the fast product introduction-obsolescence cycles and rapid price erosion that characterize the consumer electronics industry it serves. When you use a laptop computer, PDA, or LCD TV, chances are it's using a product from 3M's Optical Systems business. The displays of many consumer electronic products sold by companies such as Sony, Nokia, Sharp, HP, and SAMSUNG use 3M films that "manage" light, making the display more energy efficient and easier to read or even directing the light toward you and not the person in the plane seat next to you.

3M has great technology platforms to draw on, which the Optical Systems team has to be intimately familiar with to build new products. Combining and applying those technologies in innovative ways works only after the team has figured out what the consumer really needs. As

Jeff Melby, optical systems business director and former technical director, explains, "Before you can identify how to put together the 3M technologies, you have to be able to identify what type of product would absolutely delight the consumer while providing real value to the display manufacturer that is your customer. You have to ask a lot of questions and get information from a lot of external sources.

"If you ask a big manufacturer what's important, they'll tell you cost, cost, cost. But that's only one part of what consumers care about. Did you ever look at your laptop computer and say, 'Gee, I wish the backlight were three times brighter'? Probably not. Those are the unarticulated needs. They're harder to discover, but when you find them and meet them, the opportunity is large. Getting at them is the work you have to do."

HOW TO GET ACQUAINTED WITH YOUR WHO

Several years ago, P&G realized that though it talked to a lot of people, it wasn't really hearing them. It has overcome this barrier by taking one of industry's more traditional market research organizations and turning it into a consumer-understanding powerhouse and consumer-insight generator. By investing more than a billion dollars in consumer-understanding research between 2002 and 2007 and conducting research with more than 4 million consumers a year, P&G has moved away from traditional, behind-the-mirror focus groups to more immersive research techniques. In fact, spending on immersive in-store and in-home research is up fivefold since the beginning of the decade.

This is an important shift. Investing these dollars in smarter ways has paid bigger knowledge dividends, unlocked deeper insights, and led to bigger innovation opportunities.

P&G spends far more time *living* with consumers in their homes, *shopping* with them in stores, and being part of their *lives*. This total immersion leads to richer consumer insights, which helps identify innovation opportunities that are often missed by traditional research.

LIVING IT, WORKING IT

One example comes from Latin America. The P&G management in the region, as noted earlier, knew there was a gap between what its brands were offering and what lower-income consumers wanted. "We tend to hire from relatively high (Level 'A') socioeconomic classes," notes Carlos Paz Soldán. But our primary consumer—where most of the consumption and growth is—comes from what we call "C" and "D" household incomes. Continues Paz Soldán, "We were pretty ignorant about them in a deep way. So we couldn't just have our employees do a focus group or conduct some quantitative research of one design or the other. We had to get out of our offices and become immersed in the real-world and daily routines of lower-income consumers and in the stores of the retailers we partner with."

In 2002, P&G created specific consumer immersion programs. *Living It* enables employees to live with consumers for several days in their homes, eat meals with the family, and go along on the shopping trips. Employees experience firsthand these consumers' demands for their time and their money, the way they interact with their social networks, what's most important to them, and which products they buy, how they use the products, and how the brands and products fit into their lives. Another program, *Working It*, provides employees with the opportunity to work behind the counter of a small shop. This gives them insights about why shoppers buy or do not buy a product in a store. They also gain an appreciation of how the innovations they bring to market may make shopping for a product easier or cause confusion at the store shelf—for the person stocking the shelf and for the shopper. Why do these immersion programs work?

• Top managers set the tone in two ways. First, they participate (about 70 percent of P&G executives at all levels and functions have completed at least one of these experiences). Second, they set the expectation that employees participate in these programs as part of their daily work. In fact, participation in the consumer closeness program is mandatory for all new employees to educate the future P&G leaders on the importance of external focus and the consumer is boss from day one.

• Employees have increased job satisfaction when they get out of the office and into the real world. It enables them to connect with the consumers they serve on a human level—gaining an appreciation of their complete lives, which are so different from their own.

• Richer, more actionable insights are identified from what is learned in the context of the real world. These insights and learnings inspire consumer-meaningful innovation ideas that otherwise would not have been discovered.

• Recognition systems are in place to reward innovation insights that were discovered during a consumer closeness session and subsequently commercialized with positive marketplace results.

Living It, Working It, home visits, and shop-alongs are how P&G bridges the gap in consumer understanding; innovation is how they turn consumer understanding into profit.

THE POWER OF OBSERVATION

Close observation of the boss, and her active participation in the process of innovation, results in a more precise definition of the key needs, the price points, the route to reach her, the business model, and the cost structure. And it all starts by doing something simple—keenly watching consumers, face-to-face, knee-to-knee, and listening, with ears, eyes, heart, brain, and your intuitive sixth sense.

Imaginatively connecting and distilling what you see and hear is how observation becomes insight. Marico, a company that makes some of India's best-known consumer products, has mastered this translation with its "Insighting" process. Dialogue with consumers is at the heart of Insighting. People who are Insight team members have to be able to think on their feet, spontaneously shaping the dialogue as it unfolds. They learn techniques to connect with consumers and draw out thoughts and feelings, developing their own style for doing it. The Insighting training also makes them aware of their own assumptions, so their minds are open to what people say. To be sure they absorb everything, the Insighting team members split into pairs or small groups to conduct the dialogues. That way, one person can take notes and observe while another asks questions. And they can cross-check the observations and any hypotheses that result.

The team then regroups to synthesize their findings. A lot of effort goes into sifting through the mass of information and distilling out the insights, and then choosing the ones that are most relevant to the business. While these sessions are typically a day long, they can get extremely intense. It's not uncommon for a team to be totally immersed and work into the wee hours of the morning trying to get to the bottom of the issue. Their passion and perseverance to keep diving deeper gets them to hit on the elusive insights that others miss. Throughout the process, the business that presented the problem stays away from the Insighting team so their biases don't inadvertently creep in.

Marico used Insighting to move sure-footedly and fast into men's hair cream with Parachute Advanced Aftershower. It achieved a dominant position, grabbing a 43 percent share of the market in less than a year. The Parachute brand had traditionally been targeted at women. While Indian men were increasingly interested in grooming, Marico wanted to find out whether marketing to men would dilute the brand. Many friends and industry experts warned that it would be a huge mistake.

An Insighting team explored with women, men, and barbers how they felt about hair care in general and the Parachute brand in particular. Men often ran their hands through their hair and cared about how it felt. The only time they really discussed hair care was at the barber. Consumers perceived that the core value of the Parachute brand was healthy hair, and a masculine marketing message did not seem to undermine it. These findings helped confirm that Parachute Advanced Aftershower would likely be well received, and also fed into the advertising and marketing programs. A new "barber influencing program," for example, has been giving them good results.

When Marico became interested in expanding its strong brand in edible oils—oils that were associated with a healthy heart—it used Insighting to explore the opportunity. Initial research showed that diabetes was a huge health problem, suggesting there was great potential to serve diabetic consumers. They first assembled a brand team to define the area of exploration, which zeroed in on the area of foods for diabetics. Then the project was assigned to an Insighting team to define the opportunity more specifically and test it. The Insighting team in this case comprised people from several different brands, technology, and HR; they were pulled from a range of organizational levels, from the chief technology officer to newly hired employees.

The brand team briefed the team on the opportunity as they envisioned it. Then the Insighting team got to work. The initial phase was to think through the task and clarify anything they were unsure about. The second phase was to gather and digest existing information, such as research reports. Third, they determined what questions and issues they wanted to probe. One team member suggested exploring post-therapeutic care for people who are serious diabetics, have undergone surgery, and are on an extremely regimented diet. Another suggested focusing on type 1 or type 2 diabetes. Along the way, the team raised the question: Can we make the current diet friendlier for diabetics? Then, a thought arose to look at snacks. The team explored all of those areas to see which was most promising, and then dug deeper.

As part of their "Insighting plan," the team weighed who would be the best sources of information. Diabetics and dieticians were obviously important sources. But the team believed family members of diabetics—spouses and even children—were also important, because they might know things the diabetics themselves wouldn't mention. From there, the team prepared its discussion guide, split into teams of two to conduct the interviews, and held their deep discussions to probe for insights.

As the team pooled their findings, they found that diabetics did want to have snacks. Family members confirmed that in fact they already consumed snacks, and they didn't like having to do so in a very controlled manner. The team learned from the medical community that doctors actually wanted their diabetic patients to have smaller, more frequent meals instead of heavy meals once in a while. These findings, combined with research showing that the number of diabetics was large and growing, pointed to an attractive opportunity for Marico to provide diabetic-friendly snacks. Further insights provided specific information to guide product development and launch.

Marico ultimately decided to start with a popular component of the Indian diet: roti, or Indian bread. In 2006, it test-marketed boxed mixes for preparing roti that would help manage cholesterol and diabetes, and in 2007, the product was scaled up across India. Early results have been strong.

SEGMENTING THE WHO TO MORE PRECISELY TARGET INNOVATION

As you work to better understand the WHO, you'll discover that people use your product for different reasons. They may have different occasions for when and how to use it; different attitudes about the benefits they want; differences about what they think is a good value, and what they're willing to pay. One size does not fit all.

Typically within a broader WHO target, there are subgroups of people who share common beliefs and/or habits. Identifying these clusters enables a team to more precisely understand, prioritize, and target the WHO for the innovations they create. Take, for example, the Charmin toilet paper business. Yes, consumers have different opinions and expectations, even for toilet paper. The Charmin innovation team conducted an intensive consumer segmentation analysis. Using a variety of qualitative and quantitative techniques, they identified several differentiated subgroups of consumers based on a combination of their various behavioral, attitudinal, psychographic, and demographic variables. For example, "Mindy" is a single mother who lives in a small apartment with one small bathroom. While she isn't willing to spend much on toilet tissue, she wants it to be soft enough for her children. Then, there's "Jacqueline," who sees her bathroom as her own private oasis—her time away from the husband and kids (albeit if for only a few minutes each day). Therefore, she is willing to spend on a little more luxury—including her toilet tissue. The team put together a road show to help bring the consumer segmentation model to life for others working on the business—for example, manufacturing-plant employees and retailer partners. The show included pictures of the different types of bathroom layouts, like Mindy's and Jacqueline's, and video clips from live consumers representative of each of the segment groups.

This segmentation is alive and actionable. Today, the Charmin organization has created its entire innovation pipeline tailored to its priority consumer segments—ensuring each innovation focuses on delighting its target consumer on what's most important to her. For example, in 2005, P&G introduced Charmin Basic—a toilet paper innovation that provides basic cleaning with minimal acceptable softness that is sold at a good price. This innovation was developed for Mindy and others like her. Importantly, the Charmin team's consumer understanding is not a onetime effort—it's ongoing. The team now gets data regularly for each consumer segment on every piece of key consumer research performed—including the product and TV commercial. This helps them further fine-tune and strengthen their understanding of the WHOs.

Another example of segmentation comes from Hugo Boss, one of P&G's fine-fragrance brands. The brand had sales of only $40 million at acquisition in 1992. At the time, P&G did not have much experience either in the fragrances category or in selling through department stores and perfumeries. "A lot of people didn't think we would be able to do beauty at all. They didn't believe consumer research or consumer understanding could give us any help," recalls Hartwig Langer, president of P&G's Global Prestige Products.

Early on, it was recognized that while the Hugo Boss brand starts with fashion, the job was to translate the brand's fashion equity into fragrance. (Langer does his part by typically dressing top-to-bottom in Hugo Boss.) So Langer and his team set out to understand what Hugo Boss meant to men. They found that different versions of Hugo Boss appealed to different men. One was named "Hugo"; the other, "Boss."

The "Boss" brand appealed to sophisticated, classic "winners"—successful alpha males who are accomplished and feel formidable. Younger men also go for the look as aspirational; they constitute a type called "the apprentice." Men who believe they have already made it, "the cool leader," also identify with Boss.

The "Hugo" brand, on the other hand, is for a man who sees himself as irreverent, who wants to succeed in his own cool way—but who definitely wants to succeed. (His rebellion does not stretch that far.) Hugo is more fashion forward, a little edgier. While Hugo has a bit of a bad-boy feel, this is a bad boy who also wants to be respected. It's a question of attitude, not age; fifty-year-olds can wear Hugo without feeling ridiculous.

The team came up with these personality profiles by spending a lot of time with men. There were conventional focus groups, of course, but it was found that the kinds of things they wanted to know about do not lend themselves to direct questioning. So they went out in the real world with the men: on shopping trips in department stores, attending fashion shows, and joining them in restaurants and nightclubs.

Once they knew who Hugo men and Boss men were, they could more precisely design fragrances, packaging, and marketing plans to suit each profile. They designed Boss with several different bottle shapes and colors (green, orange, black) for the different segments of its market. This segmentation allows the brand to focus on different emotional benefits, project slightly different images, and hit different price points, without cannibalizing the broad Boss consumer. Again, the fragrance followed the fashion. The original Boss fashion line is associated with the original Boss Bottled fragrance—a simple, classic fragrance in a simple glass bottle. Boss Orange corresponds to Boss in Motion, a metal, ball-shaped package—a little more style and surprise.

The packaging design is spherical to echo the dynamics of sport that the Boss Orange clothing line is designed for. Boss Black corresponds to the ambitious Boss man at the top of his game. He has arrived at the success level he strived for, but now wants to leave his mark. The corresponding fashion line is in exclusive fabrics with personalized details. The Boss fragrance bottle represents a fine-quality gentlemen's hip flask, and the selling line "Leave your mark" echoes the philosophy of the line. As for Hugo, it has a canteen-shaped bottle, with a canvas strap. The combination of a quasi-military look in a bottled fragrance is a perfectly rendered take on the slightly off-kilter take the Hugo man has on the world. While understanding the different segments of men and how Hugo Boss appeals to them may seem like a lot of effort, it has paid off. While the global fragrance market grows about 3 percent a year, Hugo Boss's compounded annual sales and profit growth rate have been in the steady double digits for the fifteen years P&G has owned the brand.

Another example of identifying groups of customers with similar buying behaviors comes from retailing. In 2002, when Brad Anderson became CEO of Best Buy, the giant retailer of consumer electronics, appliances, and PCs, he started searching for innovation that could reignite growth. He focused the business on groups of customers with common needs and expectations. Then, he combined this new focus with insights gained from employees' daily interactions with consumers to radically shift decision making and turn retailing on its head.

Retailers have long relied on merchandisers to make decisions about what the store will sell and, therefore, what and how much they (the merchandisers) will buy. Anderson wanted to make a profound shift in the flow of merchandising decision making, to let consumers—not merchandisers—drive these decisions. That meant getting to know consumers better, not just through the traditional means of focus groups but also by tapping insights from employees working on the sales floors of Best Buy stores.

Understanding groups of consumers was a starting point. Anderson and his team initially identified six distinct customer groups. They included "Barry," an affluent professional who wants the latest technology and best service; "Buzz," an active, young male who wants technology and entertainment; "Ray," a family man who wants technology that improves life for him and his family; "Jill," a busy suburban mom who wants to use technology and entertainment to enrich her family's lifestyle; and small business owners.

They then set out to define the needs of each of these customers more precisely by mining the gold mine of information at their fingertips: the one-on-one contact their sales assistants had with consumers all day long, every day of the week. Best Buy's employees' daily interaction with customers was a great opportunity to do what Anderson calls "belly-to-belly innovation." If sales assistants were trained and motivated to listen and observe customers and if that data got to the right places, decision making and business results would improve.

Best Buy sales assistants are now trained to better understand each individual customer, with an eye on the customer groups they may be a part of. They are encouraged to watch consumers for ideas and insights, and the company has created processes for capturing them. All employees are encouraged to test new ideas. One creative employee suggested they put together a package for real estate agents, who are part of the small business segment, based on his observation that Realtors often came in looking for one item, say, a digital camera, but often needed others as well, such as a GPS, a laptop computer, and software. He raised it with his general manager, who launched it as a test to see if the real estate package in fact generated more business.

If an idea works, area leadership can determine if it is unique to a particular store or applicable to a broader group of customers. For example, the manager of the Buzz customer group heard a recurring theme from the sales floor that Buzz was also interested in musical instruments. So they put a test project in a single store and watched the response. It was positive, so they expanded the test.

Better consumer insight is unearthing many opportunities for Best Buy to grow profitably and giving it the confidence to move decisively into new areas, whether it's adding more stores, expanding the range of services and capabilities in the stores, creating its own private label products, or tailoring advertising campaigns and physical displays. The consumer-insight work has led to the creation of Magnolia Home Theater stores, a small area within Best Buy stores that sells high-end audio/video and home-theater equipment, and the addition of the Geek Squad to service the PCs Best Buy sells. It even changed the company's view of the playing field. "We used to think we had room for one thousand stores in North America," Anderson explains, "but because of our customer-insight work, we now think there's room for at least eighteen hundred."

Best Buy also uses its firsthand consumer insight to help suppliers innovate, and sometimes to produce products of its own. One group of customers they were underserving was Jill, the busy female with kids. Early consumer-insight work revealed that Jill didn't like Best Buy very much, so the company worked hard to understand her better. Those observations led to the discovery that Jill needed a more durable portable DVD player for her young children. The screens on the existing players couldn't take the rough handling they often got. Best Buy decided to make a portable DVD player just for her, and it is now their best seller.

By digging deeper into consumer behavior, Best Buy came to realize that their appliance department was really serving two distinct groups of customers, younger families and empty nesters, as opposed to the thirty-something value-oriented females they thought they were selling to. That prompted a broader product range and the creation of Certified Appliance Specialists, who handpick people suited to sell to these customers and then train them extensively. The experts are compensated for their higher skill levels. Higher pay combined with work that is more meaningful and managers who actually want to hear their ideas lead to happier, more engaged sales associates. Retention of associates has risen, which means the average experience level is higher. With more experience come better insights, and with that, more innovation, and what follows next is greater customer satisfaction—thus the advantage steadily increases. Not incidentally, dollar profit per employee has increased despite the higher costs associated with raising employees' skill levels.

Other big retailers are adopting their own version of segmentation. Will they catch up? "It's the precision of your segmentation, your ability to organize around it, and then rigorously searching for the insights and acting on them that makes the difference," Anderson says, acknowledging that Best Buy is still learning. "Understanding those customers is the core of innovation. If we can tap that connection with the customer and act on it in a deep way—which we think we're on the cusp of doing—that is a game-changer."

As these examples show, WHO segmentation is a requirement for innovation but only valuable if it is actionable. An actionable segmentation enables a team to prioritize which consumer segments to focus on based on where there is the greatest business opportunity. Segmentation also helps focus the allocation and assignment of the precious and scarce resource of talent. The size of the opportunity needs to include an assessment of marketplace dynamics, consumer trends, and where your business can add the most value. Importantly, when doing consumer segmentation, it is essential that the different segments are large enough to provide sufficient business opportunity. Sometimes segmentation can get too fine and become too niche. Another consideration is to ensure that each group of consumers can be easily identified and reached with your product or service innovation and marketing efficiently and effectively. Developing an innovation without the ability to reach your WHO is time and money poorly spent.

COCREATING AND CODESIGNING WITH THE BOSS

There is one additional important element to the customer as boss: actually getting her involved in cocreation and codesign. At its foundation is clarifying, segmenting, and precisely targeting the WHO before engineering and formulating new-product innovations. That means involving her in the iterative, two-way creation and design of innovation, right from the start. For an example of how this works, consider the LEGO Group, the Danish toy company.

LEGO has three levels of consumer involvement: first, testing a product; second, cocreating a product; and third, designing custom versions. In important (and highly profitable) ways, the company has become a facilitator of consumer innovation.

LEGO is blessed with a loyal customer base. Not only children, but also some adults are fanatical about LEGO building systems. The company knew adults loved its products, because back in 1998 a student at Stanford University cracked the software code for LEGO MIND-STORMS, the kits that combine construction systems with robot technology, just four weeks after the first version was released. The student ended up creating a better version of the code. So in 2004, when LEGO was seeking ideas for the next generation of MINDSTORMS kits, they turned to the enthusiasts for help. Those who volunteered worked side by side with LEGO employees. By the time the product was released, more than a hundred users had been involved.

LEGO also found enthusiasts around some of their more-traditional product categories, such as LEGO Castle and LEGO City. People were buying old LEGO sets on eBay and exchanging information about their building projects online. Some of those fans knew more about how to create the perfect LEGO castle than LEGO's own designers. LEGO brought them into the fold to tap their ideas early in the development process and will soon be releasing some of the sets those users helped create. CEO Jørgen Vig Knudstorp says, "They are the best LEGO castles that have come out in many, many years." In effect, LEGO has expanded from about one hundred and twenty designers (the number who get their paycheck from the company) to something like a hundred thousand. There can be no more literal example of consumer cocreation.

While people at LEGO believe in "letting consumers run with the brand," they struggled with the fact that some of the ideas the adult users generated were too advanced for children. Designers had to translate the suggestions for its broader market. At the same time, they wanted to find a way to serve their sophisticated fans. That led to the creation of a service that allows users to design a 3-D model of their project in virtual bricks with software they can download for free from LEGOfactory.com. Users can then have LEGO produce a customized kit they can build themselves, or they can simply display their creation in an online gallery. Many do; by mid-2007, more than 2 million users had downloaded the software, and more than 150,000 creations had been uploaded for display.

CONSUMER LED, NOT CONSUMER DECIDED

Regardless of which segment or target your product may appeal to, innovation must be consumer led. That is not the same thing as consumer decided. As Henry Ford put it, if he had listened to the marketplace, he would have built a faster, cheaper horse. But he understood that what people really wanted was a way to travel that was easier and faster and gave them more freedom.

A good example of the difference between consumer-led and consumer-decided innovation comes from Febreze. Launched in 1998 as a product to take odors out of fabrics, its excellent performance made it dominant in a category it pretty much created. Says then marketing director Martin Hettich, "I never worked on a brand where consumers had this much deep emotion and deep love for the brand."

The key business challenge was that there just wasn't that much occasion to use it. In 2001, the Febreze business in North America was only $140 million in sales. When the team went into people's homes to talk about it, they would ask to see where consumers kept the Febreze bottle. Inevitably, it was stuck in the back of a shelf, sometimes dusty with disuse. People loved Febreze, but found a need to use it only a few times a year; the average repurchase time was eighteen months. The total market for fabric refreshers was about $300 million, and P&G had about half of it. There just wasn't much room to grow. So the innovation team began to talk to the bosses. They found that the most committed consumers were spraying Febreze all over the place, not just on their clothes and furniture. "The consumer," Hettich notes, "thought of Febreze as a freshener long before we did."

The team tested three options to grow the brand: add more laundry benefits like stain removal ("Care for where you live"); expand the brand to work on hard surfaces like kitchen countertops ("Just cleaned freshness"); and enter the air-care market like air-freshening sprays ("Breathing life into your home").

And then—the crucial point—they didn't just go with the winner. Instead, the team chose to focus on the "breathing life into your home" concept although it came in second place. This concept better addressed the business challenge of increasing consumers' frequency of use, as consumers indicated they would choose more products and use them more often based on the "breathing-life" concept compared to the other two ideas.

The team was led by consumers' thinking, but it did not let consumers decide for it. In addition, it changed the original "breathing-life" positioning to "breath of fresh air," in large part because this was the term consumers kept using.

Starting in 2004, Febreze extended into the air-care market. The team has since expanded its offerings to things like air freshener sprays, scented candles, and plug-ins. Further, Febreze has been added to other brands like Tide and Bounce. By listening to the bosses, Febreze has become a $750 million brand in North America alone and the team aspires to hit the billion-dollar mark before the end of the decade.

WHAT DO CONSUMERS WANT? 360-DEGREE DELIGHTFUL EXPERIENCES

The P&G definition of innovation focuses not just on the benefits a product provides, but also on the total consumer experience—from purchase (the first moment of truth) to usage (the second moment of truth).

The consumer doesn't just want clean hair or shiny floors; she wants to feel beautiful and have more time on Saturday morning. P&G needed to develop a broader understanding of what consumers really wanted beyond the functional benefits of clean teeth or an effective diaper, and design products to deliver a total experience that is different, memorable, preferable, and a better value.

To get there, P&G had to think in broader terms. For an analogy, look at the Apple retail stores. Of course, they are selling branded products that do specific things; but the stores are also an experience in and of themselves, and are all designed to promote a vision of Apple as an experience and a style that consumers literally buy into.

For P&G, the key was to think more holistically. A brand is a product that creates an experience and ultimately a relationship. It needed to work harder on delivering the promise that is the essence of a great brand. Game-changing innovation works through the whole cycle; it creates the kind of loyalty that makes consumers reach for the same product time and again.

The differentiated content of the product—the chemistry that makes Tide great, the scent in a Hugo fragrance—is necessary in the innovation experience. But it is not sufficient. Innovating to create a holistic 360-degree delightful experience involves many other aspects the consumer may interact with—functional, emotional, and experiential—from the packaging she sees on the store shelf to the brand or product's website, from what the product dispenser looks and feels like to how the product smells and how easy it is to use.

A good example is SK-II, the prestige skin-care brand that originated in Japan. When P&G acquired it, SK-II sales in Japan were approximately $50 million, and had earned a reputation for offering superior products and delightful experiences to its discerning consumers. SK-II contains Pitera, a secret ingredient for beautiful, clear, translucent skin. Inspired by the chance observation that the hands of older workers in a sake brewery appeared incredibly young and smooth, Pitera was discovered after more than five years of research into yeasts and fermentation processes.

SK-II has created a holistic consumer experience based on its unique Pitera ingredients, the fermentation legend, and its distinctive skin-care regimen. SK-II has used new innovation models for consumer bonding, beauty counseling, and creating delightful in-store experiences. SK-II marketing surrounds its consumers with a high-touch, highly personalized approach, consisting of exclusive burgundy-red counters in department stores that showcase powerful timeless Japanese beauty and include sophisticated beauty-imaging computer systems to assess and monitor the skin's condition (for example, microscopic skin lines, wrinkles, texture, and spots). Consumers receive personalized recommendations from highly trained beauty counselors who have a passion for service and a desire to work with their consumers to help them achieve their ideal skin beauty. Consumers experience best-in-class, high-end packaging and aspirational testimonial advertising from beautiful women with clear, flawless skin. SK-II creates an ongoing relationship with its core group of users through personalized touches, like sending women roses on special occasions.

This highly innovative, 360-degree experience has enabled SK-II to develop a loyal group of women who are fanatics about the brand and its ability to give them a totally new skin-care experience—the miracle of reborn skin. In fact, it is not uncommon for these women to spend more than $5,000 a year on SK-II products—a phenomenal testimony to their loyalty to a brand and a unique line of skin-care products.

Today, SK-II has more than a half billion dollars in annual sales and a growing group of millions of loyal users around the world. In fact, sales for the brand have increased tenfold since acquisition—a track record few brands ever achieve. SK-II aspires to become one of P&G's billion-dollar brands in the years ahead. Using 360-degree holistic innovation to draw on unique sources that surround consumers with delightful experiences at every touchpoint is a key contributor to consistent, reliable, sustainable brand growth.

EARNING THE LOYALTY OF OUR BOSSES

The most important element in innovation is the consumer closing the loop by buying the product. Then the challenge is converting a onetime buyer into a repeat buyer and a loyal user. Loyal users are less price sensitive. They use more products in the line and often become ambassadors for the brand. Loyal consumers are what drive P&G's innovation engine.

Consider the humble tampon. Feminine protection has been a checkered category for P&G. It pulled the Rely super-absorbent tampon off the market in 1980 because of toxic shock syndrome concerns that were eventually vindicated. Three years later, Always and Whisper sanitary napkins were introduced. These became market leaders very quickly, in large part because they were innovative, featuring a patented topsheet that provided a cleaner, drier feel. P&G built on this success by introducing Wings—patented side extensions that improved coverage and thus cut down on staining. And then, in 1990, it introduced another innovation in ultrathin pads. In each case, P&G proved it had a grasp of what women wanted—protection, comfort, and a clean dry feeling when wearing the pad. Always and Whisper were hits; both remain big earners. This success was a strong foundation when P&G decided to get back into tampons, with the acquisition of Tambrands, maker of Tampax.

The Tampax tampon was a disruptive innovation, if there ever was one. Debuting in 1936, it was the first tampon to have an applicator. Other than some tweaks to packaging, when P&G bought the brand in 1997, it had hardly changed in sixty-plus years; Tampax was very much your grandmother's tampon. P&G's competitors had not been so diffident—Playtex introduced the plastic applicator, for example. Tampax was almost exclusively cardboard, and was losing market share—more than eight points between its acquisition and 2001. The remedy for winning was clear: a dose of innovation.

Beginning in 2000, P&G stepped back and made an effort to understand the market, asking the bosses (i.e., menstruating women and girls), "What do you want? How can we improve your life?" Their answer—comfort, protection, and femininity. The result was Tampax Pearl, which launched in 2002. Tampax Pearl was conceived with the objective of introducing a fit and finish to the tampon that women would appreciate for more than functionality. Instead of regarding the tampon strictly in terms of performance, the Tampax Pearl team took a broader view, making it their mission to try to make the experience of having a period and using a tampon a more positive one. "The product," says Melanie Healey, then the president of Global FemCare (she has since added health care to her portfolio) "wasn't just about better protection, which was a given, but also about delighting her in every way."

The words *delight* and *tampon* are not often found in the same sentence. Nevertheless, with "delight" as its goal, the team set about reimagining every aspect of the tampon. For example, on the old Tampax, it was not obvious which end to open; moreover, upon opening, the package crackled loudly—a source of embarrassment to some women, particularly teenagers. We know that tampon choice is often established early on; once about two-thirds of women choose a form of protection they use it forever. A silent package could help us appeal to younger women—and perhaps get a customer for life. "Teens," as Healey says, unself-consciously, "are the lifeblood in this category."

The thing is, teens don't necessarily want to talk about their periods to a bunch of suits in a conference room. Ohmigod, gross! So P&G turned to its Home Lab, a series of rooms designed to look like a middle-class American home. One of the rooms is decorated to look like that of a teenage girl's room—feminine bed coverings (messy, of course—this is supposed to be realistic) and pictures of horses. Then the P&G team brought in a group of girls, fed them pizza, and got them talking with a youngish, female moderator. And the team listened.

The team also hosted a poetry jam for teenage girls who had recently started using tampons or were about to. They asked them to write either a poem or a short essay about their periods and feminine hygiene—and then to perform it. No one to bias what they had to say, no one to make them nervous about what they were saying, because they had the chance to think it through before they came to the event, which we held in a space converted to look like a club. While much of what they said was familiar, it became much more real: "When in need, tampons are a friend indeed," one fifteen-year-old wrote. "I think without a tampon / My life would not be the same. I'd be handicapped for a week / Letting bulky pads drive me insane," noted another. Perhaps nothing for the anthology books here, but it helped the team understand the boss.

The same kind of thought went into the design of the Tampax Pearl applicator; it is rounded, with a contoured grip that makes it easier to hold. The fact is, no one looks for long at a tampon applicator, but Tampax Pearl is smooth and pearlescent; the team wanted a quality look because if it looks comfortable, it becomes more comfortable because women feel more confident. And the absorbent material itself was redesigned. Instead of a tubelike shape, it expands inside the body into something that looks more like a butterfly for better coverage. The string is braided, capturing any overflow. Both features reduce leaks. And the packaging itself was enhanced, with a see-through window so the consumer can actually see the product, and some other features that give the package a touch of class.

Tampax Pearl debuted in 2002 and demonstrates how innovating for a target WHO results in closing the loop at the end of the innovation cycle. The Pearl brand is now the market leader with sales of more than $200 million per year and is the number one plastic applicator tampon, passing the Playtex brand, which had created the segment. Tampax Pearl is priced above Playtex Gentle Glide and almost double above store brands. Consumers willingly pay for this price premium because they get both a superior product and a superior experience— one that is attentive to the nuances of women's needs. And women will pay for Tampax Pearl's better value—month after month. Impressively, once women buy Pearl, they become loyal. More than one in two women who buy Pearl once have bought it again.

While it sounds painfully obvious, innovation will not be successful unless and until you know WHO the consumer target is and WHAT she wants. Find out who she is, find out what she wants, and then give it to her. There is no deep dark secret here. The formula for innovation success is as simple as that.

Of course, the hard part is pinpointing the WHO. There are, for example, few mass markets left in consumer products. Most consumer products have segmented and even begun to fragment into a dizzying complexity of niches. In this situation, the key is to understand who the primary prospect is for your new innovation—for your new brand, product, or service. It's critical that you know as much as possible about her and him; that you know how to connect with, communicate with, and reach her or him; and that you can attract enough hers and/or hims to create a viable going business.

P&G does after-action reports on failed innovation initiatives. The single biggest reason for failure is either an inability to pinpoint or segment the target consumer or an insufficient number of target consumers or primary prospects to make a viable business. Sometimes P&G gets the consumer right, but misses the real need or real want. Sometimes persistance will get it right on the second or third try. But, this is always more costly.

Tide laundry-detergent users are different from all other laundry-detergent brands. Dawn dishwashing-liquid users are different from users of all other dishwashing brands. Bounty paper-towel users are different from users of all other paper-towel brands. Pantene and Olay users are different from other hair-care and skin-care brand users. Hugo Boss and Lacoste fragrance brand users are different from other fragrance brand users. Understanding how they are different and understanding the different WHOs are the keys to successful game-changing innovation.

ASK YOURSELF ON MONDAY MORNING

• Do you know your WHO—your consumer or customer? Do you understand your marketplace dynamics, and the broader WHO for your product/service/brand?

  *What are your WHO's beliefs, needs, aspirations, and desires—both articulated and unarticulated?

  *Where are the biggest gaps in what consumers currently perceive they get (from your product/service and those of competitors) and what they want?

• Within the broader WHO, can you identify and prioritize which WHO subgroup(s) your innovation will most appeal to and design for that primary target?

  *Do you deeply understand each precise WHO subgroup?

*How does your brand, product, or service fit into her or his life?

*What aspects of consumers' lifestyle impact how they purchase? How do they use the product?

• Can you identify how to engage your WHO in cocreation and codesign so your innovation is game changing—i.e., meaningfully improves her/his life?

• Can you convert onetime buyers and irregular users into loyal consumers who buy and use more often?

*Why do some consumers try but not buy your product/ service again?

*What do you need to do to make your business more customer- or consumer-centric?

CHAPTER FOUR

WHERE TO PLAY, HOW TO WIN

How Goals and Strategies Achieve
Game-Changing Innovation

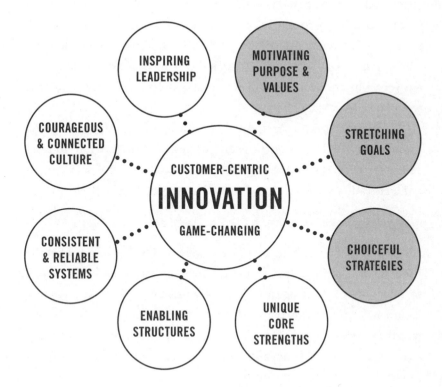

During the first six months of 2000, newspaper headlines were giving P&G a good swift kick in the pants for the first earnings miss in fifteen years. A couple of examples:

P&G INVESTOR CONFIDENCE SHOT

TROUBLE IN BRAND CITY
WE LOVE THEIR PRODUCTS BUT IN A TECH-CRAZED MARKET, WE HATE THEIR STOCK

By far the most painful one was:

DOES P&G STILL MATTER?

At 6 p.m. on my first day as CEO, I stood in a TV studio in the basement of one of the local Cincinnati television stations. I was a deer in the headlights, being grilled by CNN and CNBC about what had gone wrong and how we were going to fix it. Everyone was looking to me for answers, but the simple truth was that I did not yet know what it would take to get P&G back on track.

My instincts, though, pointed me toward two things: first, the foundation of P&G, its purpose and values; second, the need to reset external expectations about growth goals and the business and financial results we would have to deliver to put P&G's performance back among the leaders in the fast-moving consumer products industry.

P&G leaders were lying low. Heads were down. The mind-set at the time was that our big, mature brands were not particularly responsive to major innovation or capable of sustainable growth. The balance had tilted from creating demand and better value that consumers preferred to cash maximization, cost reduction, cycle time, and productivity improvement. Innovation was reserved for the creation of new brands and new product categories.

P&G business units were blaming headquarters for the earnings falloff, and headquarters was blaming the business units. Competitors were on the attack and forcing P&G to play their game. Employees were calling for heads to roll. Retirees who had just lost half their retirement nest eggs were upset. Analysts and investors who had been surprised were angry and understandably critical.

The way out of this funk was to get the company back on track *and* to create opportunities by starting down the path that would deliver sustainable long-term growth. Once people at P&G were shown the way, they could then use their well-known capabilities.

As important was redirecting the prevailing psychology from distrust and recrimination to moving forward so that P&G could come out of its shell, regain its self-confidence, and begin to play to its strengths. (See chapter 5 for more perspective on core strengths.)

Where to begin? I started with purpose and values because they unite P&G employees across all businesses, functions, geographies, and levels. They resonate across businesses and cultures and drive high levels of trust in a world where work is increasingly done across time and space without as much opportunity for high-touch interaction.

Trust is critical in a company that must have world-class innovation and world-class execution to grow sustainably. Innovation and execution are team sports. They demand high levels of collaboration. Collaboration requires trust—trust in management, trust in one another, and trust that what is at the core of P&G's business model and company culture will remain unchanged.

I knew that rebuilding trust in management and among P&G employees would take time. Those of us in management would have to earn trust with our actions and results. Intramural trust mainly needed to be reaffirmed; the organization's confidence had taken a hit, and we needed to remind ourselves that P&G remained one of the best companies in the world.

It went a long way with P&Gers when I assured them that our purpose and values remained as rock solid and relevant as ever, and would not change. Our purpose to improve the everyday lives of consumers is our common cause. It transcends all of our businesses, uniting us in our work across businesses, functions, and geographies. Simply put, it's who we are; and it's what we do.

I wanted, though, to make sure the emphasis was right—that everyone at P&G was externally focused; that everyone understood that the consumer is boss, not the CEO; not the business unit or functional managers, but the consumer—and that we were going to focus on winning the loyalty of more consumers by winning at two critical moments of truth: purchase and usage.

Being clearly and firmly externally focused was critical in 2000 because employees and management were under significant pressure and criticism. Criticism has a tendency to turn inward, and people are tempted to put their needs, wants, and concerns ahead of consumers. This is a natural but extremely dangerous inclination.

I urged more P&Gers to get out with consumers and tried to set the example by doing so myself. I asked them to think about two things: WHO their consumers were and what their unmet needs and wants were. I also asked them to think about what the growth opportunities with key customers (i.e., retailers) were. This helped us focus on the consumer and the shopper. It gave clarity and meaning to our business strategy—supersimple but surprisingly powerful. It pulled us together. It was crystal clear, compelling, and inclusive. Everyone at P&G had a role to play and a responsibility to deliver more and more loyal consumers of P&G brands and products.

With the purpose reaffirmed, clarified, and focused, I could turn to getting growth goals right and then to strategies of where to play.

SUSTAINABLE GROWTH GOALS . . . STRETCHABLE YET REACHABLE

The challenge at P&G—as at many companies—is to get the right balance between internal stretch goals that could deliver game-changing results through bigger and bolder business unit strategies, and external goals that commit the company to meeting specific growth and financial targets that, when delivered, would place P&G among industry leaders.

What P&G needed was clarity and focus. What were the one or two critical choices it needed to make? What would be the one or two or few key priorities? What was the clear end in mind? Where should it begin? What was the right *balance?* The simple choice made was to focus first on achievable external goals that are commitments to meet specific growth and financial targets, and then to set high expectations internally to inspire bolder innovations and plans.

Goals are the building blocks for growth; strategies are choices based on those goals that determine where you are going to play and how you are going to win.* Strategies include not only what you will do, but also what you won't do—the businesses you'll be in and the businesses you won't be in.

Innovation enables leaders to conceive more imaginative choices about "where to play," helping to reconceptualize the marketplace and competitive dynamics in new and unexpected ways. Take a well-known example, the Prius. Innovation played a central role in creating new demand, in driving differentiation, and expanding the size of the market. The result: amazing growth for Toyota in the segment it created.

Specifically, P&G set external goals that, when delivered, would over time make it the growth leader in the consumer goods industry. These goals could not be reached without consistent execution of industry-leading innovation which was at the center of P&G's growth strategy. In addition, internal goals were set that would force the organization to stretch. These would help sharpen and make more productive existing capabilities and define new ones. Three external goals were set.

1. Grow twice as fast as the industry; grow one-and-a-half to two times GDP. Each global business unit at P&G sets its own growth target, so, for example, fabric care is different than health care, which is

---

* The concept and terminology of "where to play, how to win" was initially developed by the Monitor Group.

different from feminine care. Paper products—such as bath tissue and paper towels—are slower growth, so their sales goal might be low-to-mid single digits in developed countries while demand in developing markets is brisk enough that double-digit growth is a plausible goal. These goals are not made up from thin air; they are derived by looking at industry scenarios and at historical and projected category growth rates. The impact of innovation and technology and a range of competitive moves are also looked at. Sustainable growth goals are not optional; business leaders are expected to set them, and to deliver them, or have a good explanation why not. By aspiring to grow at a sustainable rate, P&G focuses on making the right choices to get it there.

2. Innovate to drive strong, top-line growth and focus on gross margins and productivity to deliver double-digit earnings growth. In 2000, capital spending, R&D spending, and company overheads were way too high. P&G had built an infrastructure and made investments to support a $50 billion company—when it was still short of $40 billion in sales. That forced it to make some painful decisions.

A stretch earnings goal puts pressure on productivity while encouraging the innovation that leads to better relative pricing, higher margins, and revenue growth. P&G aspires to 10+ percent annual earnings per share growth for a *decade*—something neither it nor any other consumer goods company has ever done. To achieve this earnings growth goal, clearer, more robust strategies and stronger core strengths would be needed. P&G would need to make innovation a game-changer.

Operating total shareholder return was adopted as the primary internal *measure* of business performance. Operating TSR is simply cash flow return on investment. It is focused on value creation. Sales growth, margin improvement, and asset efficiency are the three primary drivers of the value creation that drives operating TSR.

Operating TSR is an excellent aid to judgment because it measures more dimensions of business and financial performance than less-holistic measures. This is important because it helps make choices. Operating TSR helps define business unit goals; it encourages strategic choices; it helps discriminate among plan options; and it's a criterion for top-management compensation. It brings the shareholder's perspective to important business decisions.

3. Focus on organic growth first, then acquisition for long-term strategic growth. Investors value organic growth more than acquired growth. More important, a management that prioritizes organic growth leverages current company and brand assets and core strengths, and is more intentional about building innovation capabilities and the innovation portfolio that are sustainable drives of organic growth. Acquisitions—like Tambrands, Iams, Clairol, Wella, and Gillette—play an important but longer-term role. These acquired brands become platforms for future innovation and engines for future sustainable growth. They broaden, for the most part, P&G's household and personal-care portfolios, and they strengthen some of P&G's core strengths. Most important, these acquired brands and categories are beneficiaries of future business model, business process, and new-product innovation.

STRATEGIES: THE FOUNDATION OF WHERE TO PLAY

The power of the right goals can be leveraged to make the choices required for transformation and sustainable growth. Strategies are the choices required by clear goals—choices that result in winning *with* consumers and customers and *against* competition.

Strategic clarity frees up and focuses the entire organization. It reduces complexity and confusion. It enables more-consistent, more-disciplined, and more-predictably excellent execution. Consequently, strategic clarity leads to more reliable and sustainable business and financial results. Strategy is about choices—about deciding which business or businesses a company should be in and should not be in. It is, as Peter Drucker said, "the most fundamental choice every company must make." It's a question that demands a continuous, strategic assessment of the company and its core capabilities, and of the industries in which a company competes or could compete. With this understanding, P&G made a few simple and clear strategic choices at the beginning of the decade—choices about which businesses it should be in and should not be in.

1. Focus on growing P&G's core   P&G started with four core categories in which it was already the global leader in sales and profits—fabric care, hair care, baby care, and feminine care—and ten leading brands that each generated a billion dollars or more per year in sales. These were brands that were already leaders in their category with loyal consumer following and high levels of trial, purchase, and usage. These were businesses it knew and understood well. Tide in the United States and then Ariel in Europe had revolutionized the laundry category. In fem care and hair care, new brands (Always and Pantene) and new products (a sanitary pad with a Dri-Weave topsheet and wings for superior protection, and a conditioner in a shampoo for healthy, shiny, beautiful hair and salon conditioning at home) had propelled P&G to leadership.

Keeping P&G's core businesses healthy and growing was and remains critical. It got in trouble in 2000 because P&G took its eyes off these leading and well-established businesses; profit and cash were taken out of these core businesses (rather than managing them for growth) to invest in new brands and categories.

By refocusing on and revitalizing the core, the company was returned to steady growth. P&G's core is healthy today. For example, the fabric-care business—one of the oldest and most mature businesses—grew double digits in fiscal 2007. In the early 1990s, P&G was the number two laundry company in the world, with a 19 percent global share. Today, P&G has a 34 share of this big global category—nearly double the next competitor. And share has grown for six consecutive years.

Feminine care is another good example. P&G was the last major player to enter this category in the 1980s and has since leapfrogged the competition becoming the global category leader. On average, a global share point a year and, on average, 2 share points a year in the United States since the beginning of the decade have been added. Today, P&G has a 50 share in the United States and a 37 share globally—double its closest competitor.

In 2000, the ten billion-dollar brands accounted for about 50 percent of net sales and slightly more of profits. Today, there are twenty-three billion-dollar brands, and they account for two-thirds of net sales and over 70 percent of profit.

The key point is this: Where it is focused strategically and operationally on core businesses and leading brands, P&G is widening the market share gap. It is adding new consumers, increasing consumption, and growing sales and profits ahead of category growth leaders . . . *and* it's delivering growth sales and profit at or above the top end of P&G's long-term targets.

2. Migrate P&G's portfolio toward faster-growing, higher-margin, more asset-efficient businesses This choice got P&G focused on winning big in beauty, health, and personal-care businesses by using core strengths to change the game. Winning in these categories complemented the focus on P&G's core businesses and turned out to be very important. Generating disproportionate growth in beauty, health, and personal care provided a balance of consistency *and* growth that's unique in the industry. By focusing on P&G's core strengths, it was able to stay close to consumers, continuing to build brands and slowly but surely transform innovation into a game-changer for more and more of its businesses.

This clear strategic focus is paying off. Beauty, for example, was about a $10 billion business just five years ago. Today, it's a $23 billion business and profits have more than doubled.

Olay is now the number one retail skin-care brand in the world and has doubled sales in the past four years. P&G is now the number one hair-care company in the world, and Pantene the number one hair-care brand. P&G now holds the number one position in the mass fragrance market with nearly $2.5 billion in sales. And, with acquisitions like Gillette, Wella, and Clairol, beauty, health, and personal care represent more than half of total company sales, up from about 30 percent a decade ago.

Success in these first two strategic choices provided P&G with the resources, capability, and courage to invest in its third choice.

3. Win with lower-income consumers, particularly in the fastest-growing developing markets Historically, P&G brands served largely middle-class consumers in developed markets. Even in developing markets, where it began making a push in the early 1990s, the most affluent consumers were primarily reached.

This was changed by making the strategic choice to win with more of the world's consumers. P&G added about a billion people to the total served since the beginning of the decade, and it expects to add a billion more by its end. There is the confidence to win in countries such as China, India, Russia, and Brazil—all of which are challenging—without sacrificing TSR goals.

Developing markets were less than 20 percent of total company sales at the beginning of the decade; that figure is expected to hit 30 percent by the end of the decade. This growth has been achieved with greater household penetration; broader and deeper retail distribution; a wider mix of brands and products targeted to consumers at a range of income levels; and strong local P&G organizations. Being clear about where to play—about which businesses P&G should be in—made an enormous difference.

Equally tough and clear choices were made about what P&G would *not* do. Underperforming businesses and nonstrategic businesses were shut down. Product lines such as Olay Cosmetics were discontinued. Geographic expansions such as the tissue and towel category move into Asia were stopped. A huge investment in Olean, the fat-substitute product, was written off. P&G brand icons like Comet, Crisco, and Jif, and major businesses like Sunny Delight and P&G's European bath tissue and paper towel businesses were sold. And capital spending was cut in half without foregoing any investments in capacity to grow, or in important new innovation.

P&G's entire corporate strategy now fits on one piece of paper. Every conversation at P&G begins with goals and strategies. It's a fundamental discipline that focuses leadership and expands the capability of the organization. Clear and simple strategies are easy to deploy and easier to execute with more consistent, more sustainable results.

More important, P&G has built strategic discipline into the rhythm of the way it manages its business. Clear where-to-play choices are made not only at the company level, but also at the business unit, brand, market, and customer team levels.

Choices cascade throughout the business. Annual strategy reviews for each category and geographic business unit are conducted, as are annual brand and customer reviews. The innovation pipeline is reviewed every year to ensure it's sufficient to meet growth goals. Operating plans and budgets are reviewed throughout the year. And at each review, choices are made and priorities set and reset. P&G tries to be decisive and clear about every single choice made.

DISRUPTIVE AND INCREMENTAL INNOVATION

As noted above, one of the three strategies was revitalizing P&G's core categories and brands through innovation. Adding a few market share points to big leading brands can translate into hundreds of millions of dollars in revenue and profit. That is clearly worth doing on a regular basis; in fiscal year 2007 alone, net sales were up 7 percent for the billion-dollar brands. Finding and keeping up this rhythm of growth in core categories and on leading brands is central to P&G's innovation strategy. The pace of innovation has doubled in the past decade. Brands need to be improved and extended on a regular basis.

P&G, as does other companies, looks at innovation in two ways— disruptive and incremental. Disruptive innovation changes the game by creating entirely new consumption, making obsolete and/or transforming current markets. For example, Tide was the first synthetic detergent technology and made soap powders a thing of the past. These kinds of disruptive innovations don't happen every year, whereas incremental innovation that adds value to the customer (for example, new benefits, new versions, new sizes) can happen much more frequently.

Since World War II, P&G has had a total of seventeen disruptive innovations. The value of these disruptions continues to be substantial. Brands created by disruptive product innovations still account for more than half of current revenues. But P&G would be a much smaller and much-less-successful company without a steady stream of incremental innovations. While always actively seeking the next killer product, incremental innovation drives P&G's sustainable growth model. There has to be a balance between disruptive and incremental innovation.

The table below shows seventeen P&G brands with disruptive innovations that helped drive significant sustainable sales and profit growth. As of fiscal 2007, the combined sales of these seventeen brands account for over half of P&G's sales. Most of these brands have become either the number one or number two market leader in their respective category.

P&G BRAND	DISRUPTIVE INNOVATIONS
Tide/Ariel	• Revolutionized the category by introducing a synthetic detergent technology that obsoleted soap powders
Pampers	• Created the first mass disposable diaper that replaced cloth diapers
Gillette Blades and Razors	• Reduced the level of consumer skill required to achieve the best shaving performance and improved safety via game-changing shaving technology

Pantene	• Provided first-ever "salon level conditioning" at home and reframed the hair-care category by positioning the brand with a higher-order, more aspirational benefit—hair so healthy it shines
Always/Whisper	• Transformed the feminine care category with Dri-Weave technology and new product designs, such as pads with wings
Fine Fragrances (e.g., Dolce & Gabana, Hugo Boss)	• Transformed business model by focusing on consumer "pull" vs. manufacturer and retailer "push"
Bounty	• Changed the product design and the cost structure in a highly commoditized category
Olay	• Brought department store skin-care benefits and products to the mass marketplace
Downy/Lenor	• Created the first mass retail fabric softener
Head & Shoulders	• Reframed the antidandruff care category—providing no trade-offs between beautiful hair and scalp care
Crest	• Obsoleted previous toothpastes by providing cavity protection enabled by fluoride technology; enabled professional-quality teeth whitening at home
Actonel	• Introduced first offering that provided osteoporosis treatment *and* protection
IAMS	• Created animal-based protein for the dry dog food market. Increased consumer access by expanding distribution into mass retailers
Dawn/Fairy/Joy	• Transformed category by creating true performance-based products and benefits (grease removal)
Prilosec OTC	• Dramatically broadened consumer access by switching from pharmacy to over-the-counter

P&G BRAND	DISRUPTIVE INNOVATIONS
Febreze	• Created new category of fabric odor elimination and freshness
Swiffer	• Created "quick surface clean" category

REVITALIZING THE CORE: THE STORY OF TIDE

Based in Cincinnati, the city that hosted the first professional baseball team, P&G has this to learn from the national pastime: Good teams do not depend exclusively on the home run; they seize all available opportunities. You can score a lot of runs with singles and doubles. Similarly, a continued accumulation of modest innovations over a period of time can change the game. With this in mind, P&G decided to put greater emphasis on its biggest markets, biggest customers, and, most important, biggest brands.

Look at Tide. It's a great example of how P&G is winning from the core using a balance of disruptive and incremental innovation. In its sixty-plus-year history, Tide has seen precisely three disruptive innovations: the original heavy-duty synthetic laundry detergent in 1946; Liquid Tide in 1984; and Tide with bleach in 1988. That's three disruptions in sixty years. What P&G has done is introduce a series of incremental innovations so that Tide is always the best laundry detergent and overall value in America—in fact, an average of one innovation per year for sixty years!

Bringing innovation to Tide was not an easy task, precisely because it was already so big and successful; and there's obvious risk when you change a popular brand and product line too often. But it became essential in 2001. The brand wasn't growing, in part because the price gap versus the competition was widening. Consumers were saying, "Yes, Tide is better, but is it *that* much better?" Immersing ourselves in the real-world lives of consumers, we realized that many of them used Tide as a premium product, buying the brand occasionally and keeping it on hand for the tougher loads of laundry. P&G wanted to move these people up the commitment ladder, to turn them into more-loyal, more-regular, and more-frequent users. The answer was innovation as the means for having consumers reconsider their laundry habits and the value of Tide.

Tide created an Innovation Leadership Team, composed of people from different functions (sales, brand, finance, etc.), that screened at least ten new Tide ideas every quarter. Their job was to decide which were most promising. There was an urgency to their work, but one informed by an enormous amount of in-depth consumer-immersion observation and understanding.

P&G learned that Tide could serve a wider variety of consumer needs through a series of incremental innovations, such as improved fabric softening, improved deodorizing/freshness, and improved cold-water cleaning performance—Tide with a Touch of Downy; Tide with Febreze; and Tide Coldwater.

There is particular pride in the last one; Tide Coldwater is a technically superior product that delivers great cleaning while consuming less energy. More than 7 million American households have now used Tide Coldwater and saved significantly on their monthly energy bills. And, even though they are washing their clothes in cold water, they still get the superior performance expected from Tide.

In essence, P&G has restored the virtuous circle. It can continue to sell Tide at a modest premium, and continue to attract new users. Once they try Tide, they see that the product proves itself in the only place that matters—on clothes laundered in the washing machine. If users like it, they will buy it again—the beginning of a beautiful relationship that is nourished through more innovation. In the early 1980s, Tide's market share was barely above 20 percent. Today, Tide's share is comfortably above 40 percent. In North America alone, this brand has added almost $1 billion in annual sales in a category notoriously hard to grow. Far from being commoditized, Tide laundry detergent is a value-added brand and a star innovation performer. This cumulative, persistent practice of innovation has changed Tide's competitive game and enabled sustainable growth. This relentless focus on innovation— one new-product innovation per year for more than sixty years—has clearly been a game-changer. Longtime laundry competitors have decided to withdraw from the U.S. laundry market in the face of relentless Tide innovation.

The Tide story illustrates the value of consistent, incremental innovation. The steady flow of product innovation creates a combination of benefits that are meaningful to consumers, develops and improves the brand's promise, and builds the brand's business—even for an older established business such as Tide. When the innovation dynamic is really working, the result is rewarding not only financially, but also organizationally. To change the metaphor, incremental innovation is like weight training. Done regularly, it builds both strength and flexibility.

DEVELOPING HIGHER-GROWTH, HIGHER-MARGIN BUSINESSES: THE STORY OF OLAY

Peter Drucker said, "Changing demographics is both a highly productive and a highly dependable innovation opportunity." He was, as usual, right. When P&G began to consider the matter, it saw an aging, increasingly prosperous world for which new products could be offered. Changing demographics was one of the motivations for going into beauty, health, and personal care in a much bigger way. These are higher-growth, higher-margin businesses that are not that capital intensive, and thus more attractive financially. And the thinking was that P&G could win with product and technology-based innovation based on satisfying unmet consumer needs and wants, and on creating more delightful brand and product purchase and usage experiences.

Take facial care. P&G did not invent the category, but bought into it, with the purchase of Olay as part of the Richardson-Vicks acquisition in 1985. It might seem an unlikely area for an innovation success story.

And yet the transformation of Olay is exactly that—from about $200 million in global sales on acquisition to more than $2 billion today.

When acquired, Olay was a respected brand, an effective product line, but, unfortunately, a little tired—the brand's all-too-common nickname was "Oil of Old Lady." The decision was made to reinvent the brand. The question was how. The place to start was by figuring out what P&G knew, what it didn't know, and, most important, who the "WHO" was.

P&G knew chemistry; there was much less clarity about how to make chemistry work for women. So by going to the bosses, P&G worked with thousands of women around the world to understand what they felt about their skin. On the basis of these conversations, the "WHO" was pinpointed: women who were noticing the signs of aging on their faces—wrinkles, age spots, etc.—and wanted to invest the time and resources to improve their skin. With that in mind, seven different areas of concern were identified: lines and wrinkles, texture, tone, dullness, spots and blotches, dryness, and visible pores. The bosses told P&G researchers where to look. Only then did the innovation team go to the laboratory, where a trademarked vitamin complex, VitaNiacin, was developed; this was the critical active ingredient for Olay Total Effects, a game-changing innovation that launched in June 2000. These "signs of aging" were confirmed with an international panel of dermatologists who helped benchmark performance versus best-in-class products in the industry—many of which sold for two to three times more than Total Effects. This huge new, superior product revitalized the brand as profoundly as it did women's skin. After seven years, the Total Effects line is larger in sales than the entire Olay brand at the time of acquisition and is still growing year after year.

Total Effects was rolled out in a single test market with a new package that looked and dispensed better, and with a prestige-inspired marketing campaign. It took off. Even better, the product worked so well that women came back for more. Repurchase is an infallible sign of success. P&G has followed up with Regenerist, an antiaging line with amino peptides, providing dramatic results without women having to resort to the more drastic cosmetic procedures that are becoming more and more prevalent, and Definity, with glucosamine, to improve skin tone. Olay was successful—because Total Effects, Regenerist, and Definity were all well-differentiated and superior-performing innovations of department store quality and therefore significant consumer value. In 2007, *Consumer Reports* tested Olay Regenerist among many other brands and products, and Regenerist was named the best skin-care product line, regardless of price. Olay's market share is now above 40 percent, the leading skin care with a strong position in the high end of mass distribution and a very strong brand equity. The brand has been introduced into adjacent categories, such as hand and body lotion (Olay Quench). Olay facial and body wash product lines (e.g., Olay Ribbons) have been reinvigorated. Olay has also been cobranded with Cover Girl makeup and Secret antiperspirant. And it all started by pinpointing the Olay consumer, then formulating well-differentiated products with the right technologies from P&G labs, and delivering a series of innovations targeted like a laser at important consumer needs. Looking at the big picture, in fiscal 2007, P&G beauty sales reached $23 billion, almost a third of P&G's total revenues, and profits are a beautiful $3.5 billion.

The first lesson of Olay is using demographic trends to help identify skin care and specific unmet antiaging needs as areas of focus. Second is doing the deep consumer research to understand the target consumer's life-stage skin-care needs and what would truly delight her. These became the "promises" that needed to be delivered, and then P&G identified the technology to fulfill the promises made with Olay. Third is defining a full consumer experience that would delight this consumer, from the store shelf through product use. An elegance was provided that was found previously only in department stores at a much higher price. This allowed P&G to better delight target consumers, reframe the mass retail market with higher-priced, better-performing products, and create a highly attractive business for P&G. Success stories like Olay are evidence of how P&G can win in higher-growth, higher-margin beauty businesses through game-changing innovation.

INNOVATING FOR LOWER-INCOME CONSUMERS IN LOWER-INCOME MARKETS: THE STORY OF NATURELLA

In 2000, P&G served about 2 billion consumers; that figure is up to 3 billion in 2007, and with a billion more that could be added. The vast majority of these new consumers are outside the United States, Europe, and Japan. While they are generally poor by Western standards, their incomes are growing fast, and their needs, desires, and aspirations are the same: to take care of their families, their homes, and their health.

Sure, P&G had a presence in developing countries; what it didn't really have was a strategy. Typically the same products were sold in much the same way they were marketed in developed markets. That meant that while the upper class in the biggest cities were reached, the great majority of the middle class was not.

So the process of innovation based on consumer is boss was used: What is her need, what can she afford, what does she value? Designing and innovating directly for lower-income markets began, reformulating products like Tide and Ariel, and creating new brands and new products to fit specific consumer needs. In a world in which billions of people are moving from subsistence levels to a better life, this is simply good business. Sales in fiscal 2007 from developing markets rose from $8 billion in 2000 to $21 billion, accounting for 27 percent of total sales. That proportion is certain to grow—to 30 percent or more by 2010. After-tax profit margins are generally comparable to those in developed markets. One unexpected benefit is learning things from the developing world that can then be applied to developed markets. And work in developing countries has also focused attention on lower-income consumers in North America, Europe, and Japan by developing versions of Pantene, Bounty, and Charmin that provide these consumers with quality at a good value.

The story of Naturella, a sanitary pad, illustrates that identifying the "WHO" and delivering innovations that delight the consumer works just as well in a developing country as a rich one. In the late nineties, Always was our only entrant in the sanitary protection market in Mexico (tampons are unpopular in Mexico for cultural reasons). But the lower-income consumer was not being reached. Cost was one factor; Always is on the high end of the price spectrum. Learning from previous failures in low-income markets such as Mexico, a cheaper version of an existing product wasn't just created. Instead, P&G asked what will it take to delight these consumers? And then it asked them, through home visits, shop-alongs, and one-on-one interviews.

Here's what was heard. Lower-income Mexican women cannot afford to change their sanitary pad as often, so they need to be able to wear it comfortably for longer periods of time. And because they wear it longer, they wanted a pad that was comfortable and could also actually soothe their skin. Many lower-income women spend large chunks of their time on public transportation and in crowded public situations. Odor control is important. They are extremely skeptical, and unlikely to give a flawed product a second chance. Finally, they have a strong preference toward products they perceive as natural; everyone seemed to have a story about a special herbal remedy handed down from a grandmother.

It was, therefore, decided to develop a new, lower-cost product that emphasized odor control, skin care and feel, and natural ingredients. The desired consumer experience were defined this way: "Take care of my skin during menstrual days in the same natural, healthy way I take care of my other needs."

As the process moved along, it was realized that this product profile was in many ways the "anti-Always," a product sold on the basis of superior protection. Tweaking Always, then, to add these additional benefits was not going to be the answer; its brand equity couldn't be stretched that far. The development team suggested creating a whole new brand. The decision was discussed and agreed to by the feminine care leadership team because a new brand is a much bigger investment, and a much bigger business risk, than a new product based on an established brand. But the logic was compelling; the leadership team gave the go-ahead. They were persuaded, despite the costs, because the team had done its homework. It knew who they were innovating for, knew what was needed, and figured out how. Everything was designed to create a better experience for the consumer. The attention to detail and execution was exemplary.

Once the commitment was made to create a new sanitary pad, one of the next steps was figuring out the financial framework—both in terms of price to the consumer and rate of return to P&G. This helped us to make decisions on the product itself. "In a sense," says Carlos Paz Soldán, vice president of P&G in Mexico and Central America, "we reverse-engineered the process, asking: 'What price does it need to be in this category?' Having that clarity in terms of the price target allows us to be affordable and to meet consumer performance and quality needs."

Early product designs that featured the effective but costly Dri-Weave topsheet couldn't deliver the numbers. That was a hurdle to be overcome. Lower-income consumers are more demanding than richer ones; they cannot afford to waste money on products that don't work. Quality was crucial. But the impasse also forced priorities to be set. Instead of using the state-of-the-art Dri-Weave topsheet, another proprietary substrate technology to provide a high-performing pad with better absorption was used that could be manufactured affordably. The savings were used to include a chamomile fragrance for odor control and a proprietary lotion technology for skin comfort. In essence, things she didn't care about were swapped for things that she did, while ensuring that there was always sufficient protection—the primary benefit.

The key to innovation for lower-income markets is to deliver what the consumer values. To put it in P&G language, the aim is to delight, not dilute. This was a critical insight that enabled changing the innovation game for low-income consumers. The point of any new product is to create something that addresses a consumer need, articulated or not—and different women rank different attributes differently. Superior technology *per se* is meaningless; it has to be technology that suits. Every consumer, rich or poor, has a price in mind that represents good value; the company that understands that price point has the better chance of succeeding. P&G, in its consumer research, digs into "weighted purchase intent," measuring what factors matter most. By analyzing what specifically drives the buying decision, a product can be created that is likelier to suit, regardless of the price level.

Naturella costs less than Always but it is not inferior—only different. When it comes to sanitary pads, the scientist might look at the data on absorption ratios and conclude that Always is superior. But many Mexican women would argue that odor control or skin comfort is a form of protection, too—and that is why they prefer Naturella. By listening to the bosses, P&G was able to innovate in ways that delivered what was most important to them at a price they could afford.

ALTERING THE COMPETITIVE SPACE AND CREATING NEW CONSUMER DEMAND THROUGH INNOVATION

The traditional portfolio approach to strategy—analyzing the attractiveness of the space in which the businesses in the portfolio are positioned and the expected rate of growth—misses the point. Through mental gymnastics, using financial analytic tools, the leaders try to figure out which businesses to keep and get rid of and how to do resource allocation. All of this has its place, but it is not enough. This kind of thinking does not take into account what a sustained process of innovation can do to alter the space itself—its scope, composition, rate of growth, margins, and profitability. The value of innovation is that it provides the courage to make the commitment to make these alterations, particularly when you see that the market will decline in the near future.

That was quite literally the case with Shimano, the bike components manufacturer. Thanks to "the Lance Armstrong effect," the company was doing nicely earlier this decade. But Shimano knew that at some point Armstrong was going to retire. When that happened, the bike industry was going to be in a world of hurt. What to do?

Shimano had a great reputation with the bike makers who used its products and excellent relationships with the bicycle dealerships who sold them. While it is not all that common for a parts manufacturer to take the lead on product innovation, if Shimano could come up with something interesting, the manufacturers and dealers would listen.

The answer came by listening to consumers and then using those insights to reframe the landscape. What we mean by this term is to see not only the market as it exists, but to imagine and develop ways to serve it that do not as yet exist. The classic example is the container, which revolutionized shipping. There was nothing technologically interesting about the original container, which was just a rectangular metal box. The difference was seeing the ship not strictly as a big boat, but as a piece of capital equipment whose job was to move stuff. The faster things are loaded and unloaded, the more efficient the ship. As Peter Drucker noted, the solution, in retrospect, was obvious: Do the loading and unloading on land. That keeps the ship at sea, where it belongs, rather than stuck in port, eating money. Thus the container, which could be rolled on and off the freighter with dispatch.

In 2003, Shimano was comfortable, with profits increasing nicely. But it realized something important. It was prospering because bike enthusiasts, inspired by Armstrong, were upgrading; there were few new converts to the sport. At the same time, the baby boom generation was edging into late middle age and retirement; this demographic bulge was about to have considerable time and money on their hands. Interesting, but where to go with this? To Palo Alto, specifically to the offices of IDEO, a renowned product development and design consultancy. Shimano asked IDEO to help define the real consumer need so that it could tailor its expertise in technology to create growth.

To discover where the unarticulated need might be, Shimano and IDEO inverted the idea of "consumer is boss" by talking to some of the 161 million American adults who didn't ride bikes. What they found was intriguing. Many adults had rose-colored memories of cycling as children, but had been put off the sport. It was too complicated, too expensive, too intimidating to walk into a bike store and have to deal with Spandex-wearing ectomorphs who spoke of incomprehensible things like climbing ratios and carbon cranks.

"These people were not interested in a bells-and-whistles, feature-laden solution," recalls Dave Webster of IDEO. "Biking is not their chief hobby. They want something simple that they can roll out of the garage and use." Shimano is a company based on biking bells and whistles; this is not particularly what it wanted to hear. But it did listen. The conclusion was hard to dismiss, since Shimano people were part of these conversations and reported the same thing.

Working with IDEO, Shimano developed the platform for the "coasting" bike. Equally important, it defined what the coasting experience should be. The seat is wide, and positioned so that riders can plant their feet on the ground when seated. The handlebars are upright and hold no controls. The innovation is that the gears are hidden in a box on the rear hub; this changes gears automatically, depending on terrain. The front hub has a microprocessor hidden under the crankshaft that makes the gearbox work. Shimano developed this technology, which is highly advanced—but the result is that riders can be determined bike novices and still use the gears. It takes away some of the fear factor. Along the same lines, the brake is applied using the backward kick familiar from childhood. The frame is sleek and simple. As a reviewer in *Bicycling* magazine put it, the coasting bike "is not for type A's, people in a hurry, or triathletes."

Shimano showed the prototype to its three biggest customers—Trek, Giant, and Raleigh. The three bought the idea, then created their own distinct models, using Shimano parts. Trek, for example, has a flip-up seat and "Lime Peels," which allow owners to change the bike's color—not the kind of thing a die-hard cyclist cares about. Raleigh has a front rack to hold a basket, Giant a cell phone holder and a back rack that can hold a laptop. The coasting bike went on sale for $400 to $700 in a select group of bike-friendly cities and was an immediate hit, selling out faster than anyone expected. Seven more manufacturers are joining the category in 2008, for a total of ten.

Furthermore, the three manufacturers worked with bike dealerships on how to sell the bikes to this new class of consumers. Shimano even identified the most "bike-friendly" cities in America to lobby for more safe places to ride and let people know about them. Dealers report they often sell coasting bikes in twos, as couples come in together, and the feedback Shimano has been getting is just what it was hoping for. "I can ride wearing normal clothes," wrote one woman, "and have lost ten pounds," because she now feels comfortable bicycling at more times in more places. *Bicycling* magazine, which might be considered the reading of choice for those scary ectomorphs, also gave its blessing, choosing to give away coasting bikes in its annual Biketown promotion.

IDEO thus helped Shimano tap into deep, emotional lifestyle needs, such as losing weight and having more opportunities for social interaction.

What is interesting about this process is how all three links in the value chain—Shimano, bike manufacturers, and bike distributors—benefit from the innovation, by turning a stagnant market into a growth one. Second, the coasting bike is to a large extent a social innovation. That is, the idea emerged by considering broader trends in society—a rich source of ideas, particularly in the developing world, where billions of people are forming new habits of consumption.

Shimano did not reinvent the wheel; the features of the coasting bike all existed before. What made it distinctive is the way all of it was integrated. The coasting bike is the end product of imagination, consumer insight, and technology. The most important thing, though, is that Shimano identified a problem while it was still coasting economically. On its own initiative, the company *reframed* the competitive landscape; it did not sit back and hope the landscape would change to suit the company. It identified new where-to-play choices so that its innovative products would appeal to a new consumer segment. That is true innovation.

ASK YOURSELF ON MONDAY MORNING

• How can you translate the purpose of your company or your business so that it is meaningful to both employees and consumers? How can your company's purpose become the foundation for creating and capturing growth?

• Do your company's goals lead to and result in sustainable growth in your industry? Are sales, profit and margin, and cash and return goals balanced and realistic?

• Are your company's strategies choiceful and crystal clear? Do they declare what businesses you *will* play in, and what you *will not* do or *stop* doing? Are the strategies measurable?

• How could innovation factor into your business goals? Is innovation a potential strategic choice for your company or business? Could innovation be or become an enabling capability? How could innovation open up game-changing possibilities for strategic and sustainable growth?

• Are you applying innovation to imagine what your industry landscape could be, not following conventional wisdom that you play only in the landscape as it now exists? Are you using your innovation capability to imagine and conceive new strategic alternatives about where to play?

CHAPTER FIVE

LEVERAGING WHAT YOU DO BEST

Revitalizing Core Strengths with Innovation

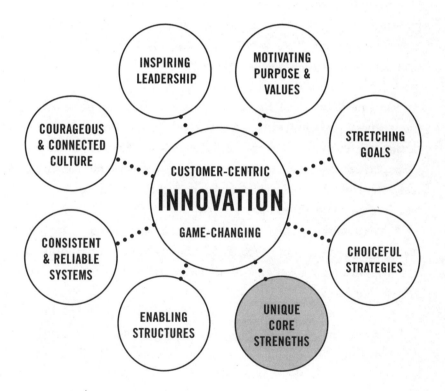

What is your company best at? Which capabilities are best suited to deliver sustainable competitive advantage for your company in your industry? How can innovation enhance or transform your capabilities to be a growth driver—even a game-changer—in your industry?

Asking and answering hard questions about what your real strengths are can help you decide where your business can play to *win,* and whether an innovation-driven strategy could be decisive for you. Identifying weaknesses is important, too, but these can take time to sort out. Knowing your unique core strengths can get you started.

Just as P&G decided in a very deliberate way where it planned to play—growing core household and personal-care businesses; migrating into more strategic and structurally attractive beauty, health, and personal-care businesses; committing significantly more resources to growth in developing markets—it was also decided to play to P&G strengths of consumer understanding, branding, innovation, go to market, and global learning scale.

From an initial list of 100 to 150 potential strengths, provided by the businesses and functions, P&G worked long and hard to reduce the list to a few capabilities and competencies. They would, it was believed, be decisive in the consumer products industry *and* constitute real advantages that P&G could continue to build and measure versus best-in-class competition.

It is very important to not only understand what each core strength really means, but also how very specifically each links to innovation and helps ensure innovation-driven, and therefore more-sustainable, growth. For P&G, they are the following:

1. A deep understanding of the consumer. P&G invests in consumer research—more than $200 million a year (more than $1 billion since the beginning of the decade) to understand the "whole" person—who she is, what she does, what are her aspirations, her needs, and her wants. While continuing to build capabilities and strength in traditional consumer research, P&G is also creating and developing new research methodologies—including more experiential and immersive techniques like in-store shopping and in-depth home usage, for example, *Living It* and *Working It*. These more immersive techniques unlock insights into consumer attitudes, beliefs, behaviors, habits, and practices that deliver more delightful shopping and usage experiences through innovation. This gives confidence to understand both articulated and unarticulated needs—and helps identify game-changing innovation that meaningfully improves her life.

P&G is developing proprietary consumer research methods that not only enable deeper understanding, but also broader understanding across forty consumer product categories in more than eighty countries. What is learned in one category (or country) is transferred across all categories and countries to get a more complete or "holistic" understanding of the consumer P&G serves.

2. Creating and building brands that endure. Products have life cycles; brands don't. Tide is more than sixty years old. As of fiscal 2007, P&G has a portfolio of twenty-three billion-dollar brands and eighteen other brands with sales between $500 million and $1 billion. These are trusted brands with strong equities in the hearts and minds of consumers. These are brands that retailers want and need in their stores. They are platforms for innovation. Innovation on these leading global brands can be commercialized far more effectively, more efficiently, and more profitably than could be done on smaller, less successful ones. There is an annual assessment of the strength of each brand's equity in consumers' hearts and minds to ensure the innovations and other connections made with consumers continue to resonate and build their trust and loyalty. P&G brands are kept strong with sustained investment in brand equity—more than $8 billion per year in advertising—more than twice any other consumer products company. Scale enables market approaches unaffordable by the competition—for example, a captive 15 million household direct mail network in Western Europe. It also enables significant investment in what is called the Brand-Building Framework and best practices that have been taught and trained every

P&G BILLION-DOLLAR BRANDS AND UP & COMERS
(AS OF FISCAL 2007)

BILLION-DOLLAR BRANDS	$500 MILLION+ BRANDS
1. Actonel	1. Ace
2. Always	2. Asacol
3. Ariel	3. Bold
4. Bounty	4. Cascade
5. Braun	5. Cover Girl
6. Charmin	6. Dash
7. Crest	7. Eukanuba
8. Dawn	8. Febreze
9. Downy	9. Fusion
10. Duracell	10. Herbal Essences
11. Folgers	11. Hugo
12. Gain	12. Mr. Clean
13. Gillette	13. NyQuil
14. Head & Shoulders	14. Prilosec
15. Iams	15. Rejoice
16. Mach 3	16. SK-II
17. Olay	17. Swiffer
18. Oral B	18. Tampax
19. Pampers	
20. Pantene	
21. Pringles	
22. Tide	
23. Wella	

year around the world to more than seven thousand brand builders in P&G.

3. Jointly creating value with customers and suppliers. Go-to-market advantage comes from the strength of P&G's retailer relationships, supply chain network, and an organizational structure that enables global scale *and* local responsiveness. P&G seeks a "partnership" with retailers by setting joint business goals, aligning respective business strategies, and creating joint value—sales and profit growth, cash flow, and returns on respective investments. It works because both partners focus on the consumer. The retailer's shopper or customer is P&G's consumer. Both focus on shopper-based business growth—attracting more shoppers to their stores and P&G brands and products, converting more shoppers to loyal usage of their stores and P&G brands and products. P&G dedicates account teams with all the necessary functional resources—consumer research, finance, marketing, IT, logistics, in addition to sales—to provide full and unique service and support to retail partners. This ability to partner with retailers to create value together results in making the "pie bigger."

4. Global learning and scale. Size in and of itself does not yield scale; it can result in complexity and even become a liability. P&G thinks about scale more broadly and at all levels—global, regional, country, as well as retail channel and customer, consumer segment, and product category. Scale is a source of competitive advantage through a unique way of being organized and the collaborative way people work together. There are considerable scale advantages from selling and distribution, from advertising and consumer research, from purchasing, manufacturing, and R&D. In addition, knowledge scale, transferring learning across different businesses, functions, and geographies, is also an advantage. Knowledge sharing is the big scale driver when we have done it right. Crest Whitestrips, for example, learned bleach technology from P&G's laundry business and film technology from P&G's paper business. An insight about lower-income consumer needs in Russia may be reapplied in China or India or Brazil.

5. Innovation is P&G's lifeblood. It's the "core" of core strengths. For 170 years, innovative new brands and products have been the engine of P&G's growth. P&G consistently introduces more new innovative household and personal-care products than any other competitor.

Innovative new products and technologies have propelled new brands and established brands to market leadership. As important as product and brand innovation has been and will continue to be in the consumer products industry, P&G is working to innovate more broadly—in its business models, its organization, and its management methods and work systems to ensure innovation stays at the center of its strategy and culture. To gain access to even more sources of innovation and to evolve the company's culture, P&G has moved to an open innovation architecture that encourages connection with third-party innovators to collaborate and bring better and cheaper and faster innovation to market to improve more consumers' lives in more ways.

While each individual core strength is important and provides a source of competitive advantage in its own right, the real power and the biggest edge comes from combining P&G's strengths in ways that deliver more consumer, customer, and shareholder value. Deep consumer understanding enables big brand creation and unleashes game-changing innovation. Leading brands and leading innovation enable more productive partnerships with leading retail customers and suppliers. Scale can be built and competitive advantage gained across consumer segments, a portfolio of brands that, together, deliver category leadership; a portfolio of technologies that provide a palette for formulating novel and superior products; and a portfolio of businesses that represent meaningful growth and profitability for retail customers and suppliers. Combining P&G's core strengths enables entry into new markets, categories, and segments—and sometimes into entirely new businesses.

Consider the move into beauty (see pages 77–78 and 84–86). There were some interesting arguments about whether this was a good idea, in part because more than a few people thought, based on traditional portfolio analysis, that it did not fit into P&G's core strengths, which were more adapted to the kitchen and the laundry room. This was a plausible argument, but it also missed the point.

P&G's unique combination of core strengths would, in fact, provide competitive advantage to win in the beauty marketplace. That would also prove to be the case for a business that in 2000 seemed to be an unlikely candidate for success.

USING THE DYNAMIC COMBINATION OF CORE STRENGTHS TO INNOVATE A BUSINESS MODEL

Leveraging the combination of core strengths enabled P&G's fine-fragrance team to turn a small, underperforming business that it easily could have walked away from into a global leader.

P&G got into the fine-fragrance business in 1992 with the acquisition of Max Factor. The business includes Hugo Boss, Le Jardin, Laura Biagiotti, Otto Kern, and Ellen Betrix. But with slow growth of 2 percent to 3 percent a year, low margins, and weak cash flow, fine fragrances was hardly an attractive business for P&G. The fine-fragrances team needed to innovate and build a business that played to P&G's strengths in strategic, structural, and financially more attractive ways. If not, then there would be an exit from the business.

This wasn't an easy proposition because P&G's strengths didn't play to the prevailing fine-fragrance industry model, characterized by:

- An attitude that consumer research would not yield fresh insights and would, in fact, be destructive of the "fashion magic" of the business; traditional competitors relied heavily on the "eye" of the fashion designer and the "nose" of the perfumer.

- Manufacturer and retailer push versus consumer pull.

- A costly and complex proliferation of brands and product lines, and annual new-product launches.

- A great deal of competition, with no real barriers to entry.

• The belief that all efforts should focus on the consumer's initial purchase, resulting in sales peaking at launch. Sales would then steadily decline until the product died.

• High costs; in fact, a disregard for costs that characterizes many so-called prestige businesses, based on the belief that all costs can easily be passed on to the consumer.

Instead of calling it quits, the fine-fragrance team went to work. It determined how the unique combination of P&G's core strengths would create competitive advantage and then flipped the industry model on its head. Specifically, the business model was innovated in several ways:

• Using a *deep understanding of the consumer* to drive the business—beginning with clearly and precisely defining the target consumer for each fragrance brand (and even identifying subgroups of consumers for some brands; see pages 53–55 in chapter 3, "The Customer Is Boss"). P&G's fine-fragrance brands and product innovations were driven by consumer pull instead of a manufacturer push.

• Emphasizing *big global brands* with well-differentiated brand equities and promises that reflected the aspirations of the consumers they were designed for.

• Focusing on a few, big launches driven by *consumer-inspired innovation*—with emphasis on creating holistic propositions that included fresh new fragrances, distinctive on-equity packaging, provocative marketing, and delightful in-store and usage experiences.

• *Working with retailers* to provide shoppers in their stores with a steady stream of commercial and conceptual "news" and innovation to entice new users to try and buy P&G's fine-fragrance brands and products year in and year out, not just during the first few weeks following a launch.

• Leveraging a global, *scale-enabled* organization structure and supply chain to reduce complexity and enable a significantly lower cost structure that results in industry-leading margins.

The team got the business model—from consumer insights to product innovation to launch to repeat purchase—right. They've altered the industry permanently and changed the old beliefs of its various players. P&G (as of 2007) is the largest fine-fragrance company in the world—with more than $2.5 billion in sales (twenty-five times its size only fifteen years ago). The credit for creating this winning strategy goes to the P&G leadership team running the business.

Game-changing innovation comes not just from disruptive, "big-bang" product innovations but also from leveraging what your business does best to create competitive advantage. Revamping a business model is not easy; it requires visible, consistent commitment from the top. It takes time. First, the more established an industry's norms, the more difficult it is to innovate business models. Everyone has a big stake in preserving the status quo, but it is critical to resist the temptation to do so. Next, keep 80 percent to 90 percent of the organization focused on driving the current business model for growth while reserving a small segment to create and qualify the new model. Finally, reject false trade-offs, compromises that people assume must be taken but, in reality, present issues that should be addressed head-on. Use them as a catalyst for identifying opportunities to innovate the current way the industry does business.

USING DESIGN TO AMPLIFY THE POWER OF YOUR STRENGTHS

I was in the laundry business when I began to understand the power of design. We were launching Liquid Tide in 1984, the biggest change in what was then P&G's biggest category since we'd introduced Tide Powder in 1946. We had a better product and a well-designed package. But it turned out that one of the most critical elements for our success was the cap. It measured. It pre-treated. It had a self-draining device built into the package so it left no mess. We thought the cap was a small thing, but the women who used Liquid Tide thought it was a big deal. They didn't always appreciate Tide's cleaning efficacy because they didn't always have stains or particularly tough cleaning problems. But they appreciated that little cap every single time they did the laundry.

That stuck with me.

The roots of my being a "design believer" actually lie when I lived in Japan from 1972 through 1975. I ran retail and service operations (the Navy Exchange) for a community of several thousand Navy airmen and their families. Years later, I moved back to Japan in 1994 to lead P&G's Asia business. Japan was an incredible experience. Design is important in Japan—not only outstanding product design, in everything from automobiles to electronics and exquisite packaging, but also the design of everyday experiences.

The P&G business in Japan was no exception. Take three examples. The first was a small, niche skin-care brand, acquired with Max Factor, called SK-II (see pages 62–63). The other two were new-to-Japan P&G brands: Vidal Sassoon hair-care and styling products and Joy hand dishwashing liquid. While Vidal Sassoon and Joy had established businesses in the Western world, all three brands used the power of design to elevate and improve the total experience for Japanese consumers. Each resonated with Japanese women due in part to the uniqueness of the brand, the package, the product, and the design of other key consumer touch points.

SK-II designed a unique in-store consultation and product shopping experience to go with a standout burgundy and silver package, and a unique natural ingredient (Pitera) in simple frosted glass bottles. SK-II became the number one superpremium prestige skin-care brand in Japan.

Vidal Sassoon stood out from a design standpoint with its signature geometric hairstyles, unique red packaging, and salon-quality products. Vidal Sassoon himself introduced the product line to Japan, an important factor since many Japanese professional salon hairstylists had been trained at his London or Los Angeles academies. During my tenure in Japan, Vidal Sassoon became the number two hair-care brand.

Joy was an ode to clarity and simplicity. We introduced one size in a clear bottle with a no-drip, easy-to-open-and-close cap. The product was a unique green color and concentrated three times into a small, simple, easy-to-use cylindrical package. One drop of product cleaned a pan or plateful of grease, the number one dishwashing problem for Japanese women. No other brand was addressing grease cleaning. Joy went to number one versus two big, longtime market leaders in a matter of weeks and has held market leadership for more than a decade.

I learned a lot while I was in Japan. When I returned to the United States, I was passionate about the need to make design an important new innovation strength for P&G. Good design is a catalyst for creating *total experiences* that transcend functional benefits alone and *delight* consumers. It is a catalyst for moving a business from being technology-centered or product-myopic to one that is more consumer-experience-centered.

I believed design could become a game-changer for P&G in the consumer packaged-goods industry, where design thinking and design practice had not yet been broadly applied by leading manufacturers. Design could create unexpectedly delightful experiences that build stronger bonds and relationships because they are more intuitive and simple. When done correctly, consumers often respond with "Wow!" or "Why didn't someone think of this before?" or "Using brand X or product/service Y is a small, but meaningful improvement in my everyday life." From the consumer's point of view, *design is about form and function, about emotion and experience.* Ultimately, consumers will pay more for better performance, better quality, better value, better design, *and* better experiences.

Design was a missing ingredient in our quest to achieve superior organic growth. Design enabled our teams to think and make decisions differently about product ideas and new business models.

The real power of design is that it differentiates brands and product lines. The orange Tide bull's-eye package is a brand icon, a graphic design that is unique, ownable, and, once established, an equity that cannot be taken away by competition.

The Pringles chip shape, canister, and Mr. Pringle character are unique and ownable—and clearly separate it from all other chips, including the market leader, Frito-Lay. This designed brand and product uniqueness enables Pringles to lead with the launch of Minis, Select, and Rice Infusions product offerings.

Pampers creates a differentiating design experience through its unique brand name, mom-and-baby-bonding package graphics, and Stages of Development product line—beginning with Swaddlers and ending with Easy-Ups versions.

In the end, it's the holistic design of the brand and the brand equity, specific product lines, unique packaging, and the elements of in-store execution that create a totality of experiences that delight consumers and result in leading market shares, strong organic sales growth, strong margins, and consistent returns.

I believed the design thinking approach could open up new innovation possibilities for P&G. Design thinking is a methodology for problem solving or identifying new opportunities using tools and mind-sets taught in design schools. While business schools tend to focus on *inductive* thinking (based on directly observable facts) and *deductive* thinking (logic and analysis, typically based on past evidence), design schools emphasize *abductive* thinking—imagining what could be possible. This new thinking approach helps us challenge assumed constraints and add to ideas, versus discouraging them. Design, in addition, could amplify and connect with P&G's core strengths in the following ways:

• Reorienting and significantly improving P&G's *consumer understanding*. Design shifts the focus to understand who the consumer is and how he lives his life. It helps us focus on behavior and on experiences. It requires a more anthropological, ethnographic, and empathetic approach to consumers.

• Design enables us to build stronger bonds—trust and passion—between consumers and our *brands* by consistently creating holistic, delightful experiences.

• Design dramatically changes the way we *go to market* with retailers and distributors. We've redesigned the first moment of truth in the store—when the consumer decides which brand and product to buy. For example, the launch of Iams pet food when distribution moved from pet specialty stores into mass retail, the Prilosec over-the-counter launch that "painted the store purple," and the Gillette Fusion razor launch that infused stores with orange are all great examples of design at work to transform the in-store shopping experience.

• Great design is *scalable*, globally. SK-II, Pantene, and Olay are each one brand with one brand equity and one design execution in a lot of countries and for a lot of customers and consumers around the world.

• Finally, design unlocks and unleashes new sources of brand, product, and business-model *innovation*.

In 2001, in order to significantly improve P&G's design capability, I asked Claudia Kotchka, a CPA who had worked in brand management and marketing and who was heading P&G's package design department, to create and lead P&G's design capability. I gave her a direct line to me. Believe me, everyone noticed. Over five years, we hired about 150 midcareer designers. This was a deliberate choice to add new capability. It came as a bit of a shock bringing so many midcareer designers into P&G. Midcareer hires are considered disruptive in a P&G culture built on hiring recent college graduates and promoting from within. Moreover, designers think differently, act differently, and tend to be more intuitive and less linear thinkers. They were different than biochemists, chemical engineers, and marketers with deductive and inductive thinking skills. The mix wasn't easy, but it was powerful. Our objective was to integrate design into the innovation process right from the beginning.

In addition to bringing in fresh, experienced design talent, we also enlisted design experts from outside P&G. Three times a year, we convene a Design Advisory Board. Its brief is to look at innovations in various stages of development and to evaluate marketing strategies; because its members do not have a "dog in this hunt," their judgments are not clouded by who is in the room and how it will affect their career. I attend every one, but Claudia Kotchka moderates the meeting.

P&G isn't the only company whose eyes are opened wide related to the power of design. Over four years, SAMSUNG doubled the size of its design organization and created a new position of chief design officer, which enabled inspired designers to "go straight to the top" with their new ideas.

Can design really create value? Yes. Swiffer is a designed experience. Working with Massachusetts-based Continuum, a team of P&Gers watched women perform their number one most hated cleaning task—mopping floors. The team noticed consumers' frustration with current mops, as they only pick up dirt, and then slosh it around. The result: a prototype that looked like a "diaper on a stick" with a motor that sprayed liquid on the floor. This prototype eventually became Swiffer Wet Jet. It provides, if there is such a thing, a satisfying floor-cleaning experience; you can see the dirt coming up on the pad, and then you toss the pad away. Swiffer Wet Jet was designed in a way that made the mopping experience easier—and, therefore, actually increased consumption because consumers now mop more often. Consumer response to the entire Swiffer brand has been huge; it racked up $355 million in 1999, its first year, and is now an $800-million global brand, well on its way to becoming a billion-dollar brand.

Febreze is another case in point for design. As Febreze began extending into the air-freshener market (see chapter 3, pages 60–61), the team faced two challenges. First, the category was already very established and crowded; and, second, Febreze's air-freshening product offering needed to provide differentiated benefits of actually capturing odors versus masking them with perfumes like the entrenched competitors.

The team decided to approach these challenges with a design mind-set—one with an intent to learn instead of a desire to confirm a preconceived solution. Great designers seek great understanding of their user and the context. They do not limit their considerations to what can be quantifiably proven. In fact, designers are known to "listen with their eyes." The Febreze team spent countless hours in stores and in homes "listening" to consumers. After watching shoppers shop the air-freshener shelves, the team discovered the shopping experience was wrought with confusion—countless canisters that all had the same shape, but came in a rainbow of colors. They also learned about consumers' dissatisfaction with the effectiveness of current products to really eliminate odors.

Based on these learnings, the team developed physical and virtual prototypes against the following design criteria: improved visibility on the store shelf, differentiation versus competition, and better communication of air freshening versus odor masking. Based on consumers' involvement along the way, the final product and package delighted consumers in each of these areas, and included an ergonomic spray handle design that was different from the competition and easier to use. In fact, consumers liked Febreze Air Effects so much that supplies ran short during the launch.

Technology innovations are necessary, but not sufficient to create profitable innovations that consumers buy, experience, love, and improve their lives with. The Japanese invented MP3 players in the early 1990s. But the Japanese had an *invention*, not an *innovation*. It wasn't until Apple got the illustrious iPod right that the category exploded. The iPod was all about design, the consumer interface, and the experience—from iTunes to user-friendly spin wheels, an array of colors, and countless other accessories that have become must-haves.

USING DESIGN AS A MECHANISM TO IMPROVE COLLABORATION AND CULTURE

I also decided to apply design to the way P&Gers work together. Over the course of several years, we have moved to open offices and open workspaces around the world. Why? To encourage connection, collaboration, and conversation. Open spaces encourage human interaction and, we believe, more creativity and better problem solving. No office change was more important or more symbolic than the executive floor at corporate headquarters in Cincinnati.

Senior executives work on the eleventh floor of the P&G global headquarters built in 1956. What they do is serious business, and the look of the place when I became CEO clearly reflected that. There was a lot of oak. Security guards kept a close watch on the comings and goings. The offices were dark, and most executives worked behind closed doors. Communication was by memo, even to the person next door. I wanted to open P&G up in every way, starting with the executive team. Again, the Japan experience was useful here. When P&G rebuilt in Kobe after the 1995 earthquake, we moved to open offices everywhere—even for executives—and I liked how it changed the way we worked together and the impact it had on business and organizational results.

Broadly at P&G, I wanted to integrate design with the innovation process, and the executive office redesign was an unmistakable, highly visible marker of what I wanted P&G to be—open, collaborative, mutually supporting. So back in Cincinnati, I had the administrative staff and the executives codesign the layout and their workspace *together* (not something that would have happened in the old P&G). We opened up the corridors, raised the ceiling, and removed the walls and doors. There are places all over with comfortable couches and coffee machines where people can sit down and swap ideas. The whole building has a new look. The executive offices are next to the learning center, where a lot of training takes place. P&G executives are actively involved as teachers and facilitators. Now, every time we open a new office, we make it an open plan; the idea is to create a physical ambience that fosters creativity, collaboration, and connections.

And we didn't stop there—we've redesigned other P&G venues where we bring consumers and retail partners together to foster innovation. We've created innovation centers around the world—in

Kobe, China, Geneva, Singapore, and Cincinnati—that are designed to represent real-world home and shopping environments. This enables us to iterate and innovate with consumers and shoppers and with retailer partners at the first moment of truth to ensure we create the most desirable shopping and usage experience. For example, we will put different package designs on the store shelf and observe shoppers making their brand and product selection. Which brand do they prefer? Which version of Pantene shampoo is best for them? Were they confused trying to find the right type for their hair? Did the package have stopping power? Was the package information clear?

EXPANDING OPPORTUNITIES IN A SHRINKING WORLD

Innovation used to be a one-way street, with new products or modifications of existing products traveling from the big, developed markets out to the rest of the world. The reality though is that it is a two-way street with the opportunity to learn from everywhere. Just look in your grocery basket—there are likely items from four or five different continents. It is hardly possible to go through a day without touching on the realities of the global marketplace—your shirts or sheets are Egyptian cotton; your gas is from Saudi Arabia; your phone is from Finland; your baseball cap is from China; your car is from Ohio; your iPod is from the United States (with components from everywhere); your house was built by locally based workers, many of them immigrants. This is not going to change. For companies, the goal must be to recognize, and use, the best, most-productive capabilities, wherever they are. It is not sufficient to only identify a business's core strengths— you must also work at enhancing these strengths on an ongoing basis so that they continue to provide an advantage. This means opportunistically looking throughout your organization and identifying where capabilities are best in class—where they are delivering game-changing results—and shamelessly reapplying them in other parts of the world. That means going borderless. Intellectually, this is obvious. The challenge is how to do it.

The stereotype is that small companies are better innovators because they are nimbler and have a more coherent sense of purpose. There is an element of truth to that, but the fact is that big companies also have advantages—scale, management capability, and the resources to take risks.

So why don't big companies do better? Two reasons: They don't have a growth process in place (a problem in many small firms, too, where the leader *is* the process); and second, because the layers of management stretch out cycle times. There is a paradox here—the curse of not enough organization, or too much. But this is not that surprising. Big companies are complicated entities; it is all too possible for a large firm to get the bureaucracy wrong, in different ways, in different places. But it is not impossible to get it right—as Toyota does with its knack of applying the right resources on the right pressure points at the right time.

Big companies are likely to have operations in different countries. That gives them a built-in innovation edge—if only they use it. Cross-cultural diversity is a great driver of ideas and innovation. Still, there is great opportunity to work more globally, as is the case with supply chain networks. Pantene, for example is one of P&G's most global businesses and has been run this way for nearly two decades.

Pantene became part of P&G in the 1985 acquisition of Richardson-Vicks; at the time of purchase, it was small (in P&G terms), with annual sales of $40 million. A few years later, the Taiwan office was looking for a way to score bigger in the local hair-care market, where its market share was languishing. The Taiwan brand manager decided to reframe Pantene as a high-end beauty product versus just another shampoo. The team created a new brand equity of "shine through health." To give the positioning meaning and differentiate it, the team members did several things. First, they introduced this new positioning at the same time they launched a new, disruptive product innovation: the first shampoo to provide salon-level hair conditioning at home. They also added provitamins to the shampoo formula to reinforce the hair "health" benefit and redesigned the bottle to make it look more cosmetic, upscale, and salonlike. Finally, the advertising agency developed a provocative way to dramatically showcase the new equity by using the now well-known "hair-drop shot" of a woman lifting and dropping her healthy, shiny, and beautiful Pantene hair. This shot was used for over a decade in a myriad of TV commercials that ran around the world.

After some tweaking, the brand took off and the new, improved Pantene spread throughout the Pacific region, then eventually to Latin America, Europe, and the United States. "What Pantene did was turn shampoo from a commodity to a beauty product," says Sonsoles Gonzalez, the Pantene global-brand franchise leader. "That was almost a revolution in the category." By the mid-1990s, Pantene was a billion-dollar brand; now it is close to $3 billion—and it all started in Taiwan. The fact that a brand repositioning could be successfully launched from outside the mother ship in Ohio helped open eyes and minds to the larger possibilities of truly global innovation.

In an age when knowledge workers can work from anywhere, companies are missing the boat if they do not tap the diversity that exists across cultures, geographies, boundaries, and time zones. The value is in combining creativity that comes from anywhere and everywhere. Intellectual capital is global; the innovation-oriented company creates an ambience that permits ideas to flow from outside in and all around.

P&G has always known how to create well-differentiated products with unique attributes and benefits. It didn't have a design capability or a broad game-changing innovation culture that excelled at creating a delightful shopping or usage experience. An innovation capability that drew on all available sources of innovation enables the consumer to experience and, in a real sense, actually "feel" the design, not the underlying product technology. The technology is important— because it underpins the distinguishing product benefits. But design brings the benefits to life, and the feeling is often the differentiator for the consumer. In the marketplace, P&G brands and products stand for election hundreds of millions of times a day; design is an important part of winning consumer votes. P&G's ambition is to become a top design company as part of becoming the innovation leader in its industry, because world-class innovation supported by world-class design is a game-changer. It is a powerful combination in the journey to be a consistent and sustainable growth company.

The concept of core capabilities or core strengths is easy to understand, but the practice of choosing the few potentially decisive strengths that can create real, sustainable advantage is hard to do. Why? Because too many companies get caught up in consultants' "capability du jour" or chase what other competitors or industries are doing. Choosing core strengths requires deep thinking and hardheaded choices about what it really takes to win in your industry or market, and then playing to your few real strengths—core capabilities where you already have competitive advantage or can acquire or build competitive advantage. The work of selecting core strengths takes careful analysis, real objectivity, and tough-minded discipline. It is the work of decisive leaders.

Without clear goals, choiceful strategies, and consensus about a company, business, or function's core strengths, the important work of making innovation happen—organizing for innovation and integrating innovation processes into other everyday work processes—cannot, or at least should not, begin.

ASK YOURSELF ON MONDAY MORNING

• Are you disciplined in identifying your business's few unique core strengths (not just developing a laundry list) that will give you sustainable competitive advantage?

• How does the ongoing combination of strengths either create new opportunities for growth, outwit the competition, and/or change the game in the marketplace?

• Are you intellectually and honestly identifying gaps in core strengths that need to be filled and by when? Do you have the openness of mind required to fill in the gaps in core strengths so that you challenge old cultural assumptions?

• For new strengths to be effective, what is required—a shift in organization structure, a change in culture, new leadership?

• How does the lens of innovation keep your combination of core strengths and help you make better choices about where to play?

• Is there an opportunity to incorporate design as a way to enhance the capabilities of your business?

PART TWO

MAKING INNOVATION HAPPEN

So far we have shown why and how the consumer is boss must be at the center of all key decisions of your business. We have also illustrated why choosing the right goals and strategy (where to play and how to win) and revitalizing core strengths chart a path of future sales and profit growth.

So far, so good, but then something happens. The intent and the flow of innovation gets bogged down. "That's just the way we do things around here" is the way many people sum up the bottlenecks or impenetrable walls between functions peculiar to their business. It often explains why expectations of innovation are not met.

What follows in this section are tools for creating organization structures that develop the ability to actively seek outside ideas and then channel them effectively inside the workings of the organization. Such structures change culture and enable you to open your mind to seek new ways to change the game.

This section also describes in detail the practical framework for *operationalizing innovation*—from generating ideas to go to market. This process can help you bust the silos of the organization and make the flow of ideas seamless. It is through this process that "the rubber meets the road." Managing such a process in its *totality* is an imperative for you to continue to build your personal capacity and capability to shape and confront the future.

Making innovation happen is not the mechanical process of project management often used in many companies. It is a social process. We illustrate the social tools that are effective in cooking ideas, monitoring their flow, and deciding when ideas need to be killed.

Many people have an inherent fear about innovation: that it's too risky, sporadic, and doesn't pay. We have made real breakthroughs from both practice and research to take out this fear. We show the sources of risk and provide tools to manage it, such that through practice and learning you can improve your batting average. For example, over a seven-year period the success ratio of products at P&G increased from 25 to 50 percent. At the same time, fewer resources were used.

We have used these tools and ideas. You, too, can use them Monday morning, without waiting for a command from the top, whether you are an innovation project manager, a business unit manager, the head of a function, or the CEO.

CHAPTER SIX

ORGANIZING FOR INNOVATION

Building Enabling Structures

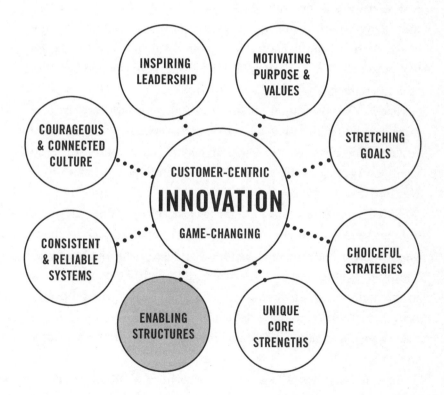

The decision to drive organic growth by placing innovation at the core of your business impacts how you structure and organize your business. The structure of an organization aligns the energy of people. It can stimulate creativity or stifle it, depending on the organization. It can be inward oriented or it can be opened up to fresh ideas from the outside. In this chapter we take you through the journey of various organization structures that are enablers of innovation in various settings and types of businesses.

Just as there is no single model of innovation, no single organizational structure will work for everyone. One-size-fits-all just doesn't work. That may not sound all that helpful; the point is that you need to design and install the right organization structures to suit the business strategy and the innovation model. We observed many companies attempt to make innovation happen through enabling structures of one form or another. Where they often fall short, surprisingly, is that most people in the company don't understand what, in fact, these structures are and how they actually work.

The mix of innovation initiatives can range from short-term and incremental to high-risk, high-reward, long-term breakthroughs. Different organization structures within the same corporation are needed to respond appropriately to the challenges and opportunities of specific initiatives.

Often, companies make the mistake of going to one extreme or another when organizing for innovation. For example, creating a structure in which the team is totally isolated from the business— "out in the wilderness"—rarely interacting with the people who are in the mainstream of the business. Or, members of the innovation team have full-time, highly demanding responsibilities and are expected to make game-changing innovation part of the routine of their "day jobs."

Innovation is about "just-enough structure." While some level of structure is needed, there is a balance that must be achieved between structure and creativity. The leadership skill is finding the right balance.

The following six criteria can be used in designing and selecting the appropriate organizational structure.

1. Whether the innovation opportunity is inside a core business, in a business adjacent to a core business, or in an entirely new business.

2. The level of risk and opportunity and the level of investment.

3. The degree to which the innovation opportunity leverages existing strengths or requires the creation and development of new capabilities and strengths.

4. The time horizon of innovation development.

5. The type of experience and expertise required on the innovation development team.

6. The phase of innovation development—ideation and prototyping, development, qualification, or commercialization.

These six criteria above help you consider the following questions.

• To what degree should the team be separate from or integrated into the current business (both from an organization design standpoint, as well as physical location)?

• Should people be fully dedicated or involved as part of their "day job"? If fully dedicated, do all team members need 100 percent dedication, or only a few?

• What experience and expertise should you go outside of your business and company to find?

• What is the most effective way to fund the innovation to ensure it gets the resources, attention, and nurturing it needs, while also ensuring it delivers the required business growth?

• What connections and interdependencies between different organization structures can ensure a given innovation has the best chance of being successfully commercialized in the marketplace?

Getting an innovation organization of any type and of any size up and running takes time. The idea is to test and learn which approach(es) works best for a given mix of innovation in your business.

One reason why innovation doesn't take place on a sustained basis is lack of enabling structures to consistently fund different kinds of innovations with different kinds of mechanisms. In addition to a lack of or erratic funding, a second reason is that managers are responsible for meeting day-to-day operational and financial commitments and innovation gets shunted aside as something to do when they find the time.

We describe ways to overcome these hurdles. First, we look at the structures that P&G and Hewlett-Packard have set up to fund innovation. Then, we look at additional structures used by P&G and DuPont to find and develop promising innovations for the business units of their respective companies. Next, we show how to tap into the world's talent pool, one that is, of course, orders of magnitude larger than that of even the biggest corporation. P&G calls it "Connect and Develop," and it has been the source for many new products, some of which are now billion-dollar brands. And, finally, we show how to multiply your ability to grow through joint innovation with competitors, retailers, suppliers, and other partners.

STRUCTURES FOR FUNDING INNOVATION
P&G'S CIF

The P&G Corporate Innovation Fund (CIF) specializes in high-risk/high-reward ideas and is an organizational structure with some resemblance to a venture capital firm. It is led by the chief technology officer and supported by the CEO and the chief financial officer. Its primary objective is to provide "seed money" to either create totally new businesses and/or create major disruptive innovations.

These ideas can come from any organization within the company or even outside of P&G. The CIF funds projects led by innovation teams that reside in different organizations throughout P&G. But the CIF budget is completely separate from that of the business units. It does not, therefore, burden the business unit's P&Ls, thereby enabling them to focus spending on innovations that are closer in and more specific to a given category and/or brand.

Take, for example, Crest Whitestrips. In 2000, the Crest business consisted primarily of toothpaste and toothbrushes. A team from the corporate and oral care organizations, with CIF funds, explored the idea of combining the film technology from P&G's corporate R&D organization and bleach technology from the laundry organization to create and prototype Crest Whitestrips, the first at-home professional teeth-whitening treatment. This corporate team did the initial concept, design, and engineering work, and when they qualified the initial product prototype, and its potential with consumers, they handed over the early-stage innovation to the established oral care business unit to bring Crest Whitestrips to market.

HP'S INNOVATION PROGRAM OFFICE

Hewlett-Packard has a structure similar to Future Works. Its Personal Systems Group (PSG) created the Innovation Program Office, or IPO, to meet two common problems around innovation: funding and speed.

Speed is crucial since technology and the competition make PCs quickly obsolete. Todd Bradley, who heads PSG as its executive vice president, believes those challenges are the result of a disconnect between the business units and PSG's group headquarters. The business units *wanted* innovative new products, but developing products that were a significant departure from existing ones was a cultural challenge. Headquarters was concerned that if they provided funding and drove development, the business unit leader might not embrace the project and fail to commercialize it properly. To support the need for developing innovations that result in products, Bradley and Phil McKinney, the chief technology officer for the Personal Systems Group, created the IPO. It's charter is to work with the business units to create new products and services that would become the new growth engines for PSG.

The IPO has specific targets, processes, and methodologies to jump-start projects that would be difficult to pursue within a business unit. It has a clear measure of success for the projects it launches. Every approved project must meet a targeted hurdle—a ratio based on total estimated gross margin divided by the R&D expenditure associated with the development of the product.

IPO's first target, set in 2006, was to launch one major new product. That was the Blackbird 002, a gaming PC introduced in September 2007 to rave reviews. The Blackbird was the work of a team drawn from people in the business units who dedicated their time and emotional energy to the project. IPO provided the funding, nurturing, executive protection, and oversight.

For IPO to take a project under its wing, it first has to pass the scrutiny of a review board, which uses five questions it has devised to judge the project's prospects as a game-changer. One such question is: "If the breakthrough is made, does this project have the potential to fundamentally change the competitive landscape or create new consumer demand?" But the project also has to meet another crucial condition: The business unit has to sponsor it, not financially, but in terms of making the commitment to take it to market when IPO is ready to hand it off. IPO commits to providing sufficient resources to make it a reality, providing the project meets the criteria at each of four stage gates.

For the 2007 calendar year, IPO had a target of developing two new products, and the same conditions applied: The business units submitted projects they were committed to, the IPO review board decided which ones to take on, and the projects were subjected to the rigor of a stage-gate process. IPO spent about $100,000 on each of twenty projects to get them to the point of "customer qualification." Of those twenty, only about eight will pass to the next phase to become prototypes that can be put in customers' hands. Only about four of the eight will make it from prototype to limited launch, and only two will be scaled up. When the project is commercialized or when the project is ended, the team members go back to jobs in the business unit, with no negatives around having tried and failed, if that's what happens. "How do we get to work on that cool cutting-edge stuff?" some people ask. The response of Phil McKinney, the leader of IPO, is to come up with a great idea in the first place. "We want true project champions, people who are passionate enough about their vision to drive it," he says. "Every market success in a new category has been the result of having a passionate champion behind it."

IPO's nurturing, oversight, and financial support are central to a project's success. McKinney reviews the teams' progress and ensures adherence to the discipline of the process. IPO thereby delivers the best of both worlds: it gives promising, ambitious projects the chance to come to fruition and protecting the organization against projects that could languish for lack of sponsorship.

STRUCTURES FOR ORGANIZING FOR INNOVATION
FUTURE WORKS

P&G's Future Works is an organization consisting of multidisciplinary teams, led by a general manager. Its primary objective is to *seek out innovation opportunities that create new consumption*, which can be used as the basis for creating new businesses, thereby resulting in net extra sales and profits. Unlike innovation teams that reside in the business units, Future Works is not constrained by existing category paradigms. Rather, it explores discontinuous ideas that might create a new category or segment, cut across existing categories, or create an adjacency to an existing business. This includes new business models and partnerships, such as P&G's joint venture with Swiss Precision Diagnostics for at-home consumer health-monitoring devices. Given the disruptive nature of Future Works innovations, they are primarily funded via the CIF.

Importantly, while Future Works is a separate organization from the business units, its innovation efforts are not off in "never-never land." A business unit "sponsor" is identified early on for each Future Works project to provide pragmatic business input up front and, more important, take responsibility for the commercialization phase of the innovation project after Future Works qualifies the initial concept and prototype. This sponsorship is critical to ensure there is a "home" and a "nurturing sponsor" for the disruptive innovation after the initial idea and prototype have been evaluated. For example, the exploration of at-home health-care diagnostics was done in Future Works; the P&G management of the joint venture is done entirely by the P&G health-care business unit.

NEW BUSINESS DEVELOPMENT STRUCTURE IN A BUSINESS UNIT

The New Business Development (NBD) organization in each business unit is another organizational structure that helps P&G innovate. The NBD organizations focus on creating both disruptive and incremental innovation for a specific category, like laundry, home, or skin care. Innovations led by NBD are usually based entirely on new ideas, products, and technologies that are developed inside the business, for example, Downy Single Rinse fabric enhancer (see pages 38–40).

NBD innovations can also be partially or entirely sourced from external sources. For example, P&G's home-care NBD team led the development of Mr. Clean Magic Eraser, based on a product sold in Japan (see page 134 for more details) and a sponge foam technology produced by supplier BASF. NBD projects are primarily funded by a specific business unit. Sometimes, when exploring adjacencies, or new segments, some initial seeding funds may be provided from the CIF to enable initial prototype development.

Innovation Project Teams embedded within the established category and brand businesses, focus on developing a pipeline of incremental and commercial conceptual innovations that better serve existing consumer needs. The Olay Total Effects, Regenerist, and Definity innovations (see pages 84–86) all came straight out of the Olay business team. Most of P&G's sustaining and incremental innovations come out of the business units, as they should; these are the people who best know their business and their consumers. Not surprising, given the nature of these innovation projects, they are usually funded within the business unit.

EXTERNAL BUSINESS DEVELOPMENT

Another enabling structure for a corporation with two or more business units or functions is the creation of a "brokerage house" for innovation. Instead of each business unit doing its own outside search for innovation opportunities, such a structure facilitates speed and interconnections of business units with outsiders, as well as between different business units within the company. At P&G it is called External Business Development (EBD). EBD gets involved with all business units with initial connections to lead the deal-making process, and to help identify and close deals with external parties. It accelerates the flow of the right kind of ideas by actively searching for innovations from the outside, assessing them, and bringing appropriate ones inside and linking them with the appropriate parts of the organization. While EBD may send relatively low-risk projects to the business units, it parcels out higher-risk innovations to Future Works.

A few companies have structures similar to P&G's EBD. At DuPont it is called DuPont Ventures. In existence for many years, it has been reinvented and given a new purpose—to focus on one key question: "What can come from external sources through venture-capital-funded and early-stage companies to help us innovate?" Previously, corporate venture investing at DuPont had never played more than a marginal role sniffing out small acquisitions, most of which the company passed up. In its new incarnation, the group—four people plus director Michael Blaustein—actively searches externally for technology opportunities through a variety of networks. It is also the first filter for opportunities that people inside DuPont come across or that small outside companies propose. The Ventures people are explicitly charged with developing a feel for what the business units are working on. Each of the innovation centers in DuPont's business units is hooked up with someone in DuPont Ventures so they know exactly whom to talk with. That's especially helpful given that DuPont's innovation centers are spread across the globe.

The Ventures group stays in constant touch with people throughout the company. Since all team members have worked in the businesses and have a technical background, they don't have to ask a lot of questions to understand the issues. They not only field opportunities to enhance DuPont's innovation projects, they also have the acumen to do the due diligence and design the business arrangement. "We're often trying to work out special rights or concessions," Blaustein says. "If a smaller company is pursuing a particular application of a technology, DuPont might negotiate to use the technology for other applications, or in geographic regions that are beyond the scope of the smaller company and don't interfere with the ongoing mission of their business. We try to think creatively to make strategic connections. With experience we learn and our ability to connect improves."

Establishing DuPont Ventures as a separate structure allows it to maintain a broader, higher-level perspective. The group is able to spot ways to change the game that people in the business unit might miss; that perspective helps ensure that the various technologies work well as a portfolio, not just as one-off opportunities. "The business people tend to be focused on today's problems, while the Ventures people have their antennae out looking for the next opportunities," Blaustein says. "And because our group gets exposed to upward of a hundred and fifty deals a year, we're in a position to recognize when something is really special."

INNOVATION HOT ZONES

In addition to its more structured organizational approaches for innovation, P&G also has innovation hot zones that can be used to identify and begin to develop ideas. Their purpose is to test an idea through the eyes of the consumer: what she actually experiences as a shopper, thus improving the chances of success before the innovation is launched.

Innovation centers are located around the world and contain simulated in-home and in-store shopping environments. Innovation teams use these centers to partner with retailers (Carrefour and Costco, for example) to identify opportunities that will create value for the shopper once the product makes it into the store and faces the first moment of truth. The innovation centers are not laboratories with scientists and test tubes, but a place where shoppers lend their wisdom and retailers and P&G learn from it.

The innovation center just outside of Cincinnati includes a small, five-aisle grocery store, complete with checkout counters and cameras and microphones for observation. Shoppers are asked to look for certain items, do their regular shopping, or buy a certain amount of goods from a couple of specific aisles. The P&G and retailer teams watch the shopper go through her paces.

For a store to change its layout—specifically, the sections that are adjacent to each other—is a very big deal. Many retail stores place the pharmacy in the middle, often flanking it with beauty care. By watching and talking to shoppers, the team learned that when shoppers are thinking about their health, improving personal appearance is pretty much the last thing on their minds. So, based on research conducted at the innovation center, P&G identified a better store layout innovation that clusters the over-the-counter products (for example, aspirin) next to personal care (toothpaste and deodorant) and close to the pharmacy. It may sound obvious, but it isn't. Actually watching and hearing real shoppers explain their choices in a real setting is a powerful way to identify actionable insights that result in meaningful innovation.

Another hot zone is Clay Street (see chapter 9 for more details). It is a unique, experimental place where P&G teams isolate themselves for several weeks to solve tough innovation challenges—from repositioning a brand's equity to developing a pipeline of product innovations for a new target consumer group. At Clay Street, an innovation team goes through an array of creative and immersive experiences that enables it to uncover innovation opportunities in different ways.

While there are a variety of approaches P&G uses to enable innovation, most all of these structures are part and parcel of everyday work. And in every case, they follow two principles: first, to encourage and to build connections, both within and outside of the company; and second, to get closer to the consumer as "shopper" and as user of prototype products and services. These are the best ways to get an organization to open itself up to potential new ideas and innovations.

The effectiveness of these enabling structures can be multiplied by regularly and consistently tapping into the huge pool of external ideas and talent in the world. The methodology for achieving this is an open architecture for the flow of ideas.

THE CASE FOR OPENING UP

Open architecture is the organizing principle that enables a business and its people to *open themselves up to get ideas from anywhere at anytime*. The advent of the Internet and inexpensive communications makes it possible for any company, whether small or large, to take advantage of the best brains in the world, cutting across industries, countries, and age groups. P&G knew it was going to get its fair share of ideas—but nothing more. *So it wanted to improve the odds by opening up what is referred to as the "fragile front end" of the innovation process.* P&G wanted to become the first choice of everyone from the eccentric inventor to other multinationals for collaboration and innovation; and it wanted to be the best at spotting, developing, and leveraging relationships in every nook and cranny of its businesses.

An insular company that believes that it has all the answers is missing out. For a long time, that was the case at P&G, a proud company, with a proud past. It has been an innovation pacesetter for more than a century in the consumer products industry. The challenge it faced was to keep true to its inventive history, while coaxing people to become more open to outside ideas. The problem was that P&G's usual practices were not working well enough. Its innovation success rate—a metric derived from analyzing how many new products met their financial targets—was flat at about 15 percent to 20 percent. That wasn't good enough. It was, frankly, no different than the industry average. Some researchers were more focused on the research itself, instead of how the innovation connected with the consumer. The idea of "the consumer is boss" was not translating throughout the company. Something different had to be done.

As Gil Cloyd, P&G's chief technology officer, puts it, "We have moved from a marketplace with slow change whose dynamics favored internal focus, insularity, and vertical integration to one characterized by very rapid change, elimination of geographical boundaries, remarkable global capabilities, with constant focus on lower costs. This favors vertical disintegration and a very open corporate business model."

Said another way, we are now in the era of the open, networked corporation. This is a radical change in any company's culture, not only in the way people work day to day but also their mind-set for being open to and searching for new ideas. To make this concept operational, the first step for any leader is to set measurable goals that form the foundation for the evaluation of their performance.

Shortly after becoming CEO, I knew the only way we would dramatically step up our approach to innovation was to establish a measurable target. I set an ambitious and unprecedented goal: "We will partner 50 percent of our innovations with outsiders." Why 50 percent? It seemed like an ambitious but possible goal; it was specific and easy to remember. (At the time, the figure was more like 15 percent, so there was a lot of hard work to be done to meet it.) More important, it was measurable and had milestones. It was specific, something managers could easily relate to and focus on delivering.

Accomplishing this goal meant ditching "not invented here." Now P&G collaborates with anybody, anywhere, anytime. P&G likes *un*usual suspects. It will even compete with a company on one side of the street, and cooperate with it on the other. In an open innovation system, anything out there is fair game, even if competitors are sitting on it. And that's fine with both partners because it works.

CONNECT AND DEVELOP

Enter Connect and Develop. The single characteristic of C&D is the willingness of all people at P&G to be psychologically open and to seriously consider new ideas, whatever the source, thus building a truly open, truly global innovation network that can link up—and be first in line—with the most interesting thinkers and the best products to "reapply with pride."

P&G opened up to enable it to connect. Larry Huston, a former P&G vice president of innovation and technology, liked to say, "Creativity is really the process of making connections."

C&D is a form of relationship building that enables P&G to stay slightly ahead of the game. It is a new approach for sourcing innovation, not a new strategy. What it is *not* is a form of outsourcing. It is better understood as a way to insource the creativity of the world and therefore allow P&G to leverage creativity beyond organization boundaries. It's a way to connect internal business units with outside intellectual capital.

Connect and Develop, in geographic terms, means everywhere; in human terms, everyone. But a brief that says "everywhere, everyone" isn't that helpful. P&G narrowed it down by emphasizing products, packages, or technical ideas that are "pretty well cooked"—needing only a few steps for completion, or that may already be in the market in some form. At the very least, there needs to be a working prototype.

Moreover, P&G is not looking so much for brand-new categories, but more for "adjacencies"—things that can fit into one of P&G's existing category or brand portfolios, particularly things that speak to one of the top-ten needs every P&G business unit identifies each year.

Initially, many people at P&G thought this was the fad du jour. Some were defensive about what C&D could mean to their positions. Some were fearful—was this outsourcing in disguise? Some were worried—does my technical expertise still matter? Over time, they came to realize the opportunities—getting innovations faster to market and allowing them to do higher-value work. But part of the leader's job is to make people take such pronouncements seriously, to follow through on execution and to make delivering the goal part of everyday work.

For every one hundred ideas found on the outside, perhaps one will make it into a store. That sounds like a pretty poor batting average, but consider this: Of the products we do take to market, over 50 percent succeed.

So far, Connect and Develop has closed more than five hundred deals; two a week is now the average. All told, more than two hundred new products have been launched as a result of this relentless networking. The goal set back in 2001 has been surpassed. Over 50 percent of P&G initiatives in 2007 involved at least one external partner. In short, P&G is well on its way to achieving its aspiration: to become the world's partner of choice. And in the process P&G is creating an agile and flexible way to organize for innovation.

THE PROOF IS IN THE PUDDING

While there are many success stories from Connect and Develop, here are a few that bring the idea to life.

• *Buy a proven ingredient: Olay Regenerist.* Like Ponce de Leon, P&G scientists traveled extensively to find a fountain of youth—or more precisely, an antiwrinkle technology. At a technical meeting, Sederma, a small French company, presented data on an ingredient that had clear benefits in cell regeneration and wound healing. P&G scientists hypothesized that, in combination with some proven antiaging ingredients, it might also have significant benefits for wrinkle reduction. Clinical testing proved this hypothesis, and so P&G bought this penta peptide, a key ingredient for Olay, from Sederma, did some tweaking, and launched it in Olay Regenerist, an antiaging cream. In its first four years, Regenerist reached over $250 million in annual sales. The ongoing relationship with Sederma continues as an innovative scientific partnership that will lead to future ingredients and consumer benefits.

• *Use established technologies in new ways: hair products.* P&G wanted to improve hair color retention between major color treatments. One opportunity was to improve color retention with conditioning technology. UK Dow Corning's functionalized silicones expertise fit the bill. The expectation is that three-quarters of P&G hair colorant products will eventually use some variation of this technological innovation. A second opportunity was to create a way to touch up roots in between colorings. Based on Clairol's proprietary brush technology to apply color to men's facial hair, Tin Horse, a British design firm, developed a root touch-up brush for Nice 'n Easy. During its first year in the market, Nice 'n Easy Root Touch-Up received more awards from beauty magazines and associations than any other haircolor, including *Allure* magazine's recognition of it as a "Big Beauty Breakthrough," an award that recognizes products presenting new solutions to age-old problems. Nice 'n Easy Root Touch-Up was also identified by *Marie Claire* magazine as one of twenty-five products that have changed women's lives.

• *Observe parallel products and consumer behavior: Mr. Clean Magic Eraser.* Cleenpro was a household sponge product sold in Japan. P&G's Connect & Develop team noticed Cleenpro and sent samples to Cincinnati for consumer evaluation. After more in-depth consumer research, the P&G innovation team found people used it more as a spot eraser, not as a cleaning sponge. Intrigued by the possibilities, and backed by more consumer testing, the team confirmed the sponge removed all kinds of spots from hard surfaces such as kids' dirty finger marks on walls and shoe skid marks on floors. Consumers really wanted this kind of product. In fact, one woman who lived on the U.S. west coast was so enthusiastic, she wanted to import the sponge from Japan herself. Based on the strong consumer appeal, P&G licensed the sponge technology from BASF, the German chemical company that is a major supplier to P&G. This Connect & Develop innovation on the Mr. Clean brand went from initial consumer testing to production in only seven months.

• *License innovation from competitors: Swiffer Duster.* In Japan, P&G and Unicharm compete head-to-head in the diaper and feminine care categories, but not in home care. They began working together to understand the consumer appeal of Unicharm's "curly fiber" technology. Based on their relationship,

Unicharm also shared with P&G their latest innovation—a new duster. Consumer research conducted by both companies in Atlanta, Georgia, revealed an overwhelmingly positive response to the new duster. Recognizing both companies would benefit, P&G negotiated the sales rights outside of Japan. P&G took the product "as is" and named it Swiffer Duster. To reduce costs and time to market, P&G asked Unicharm to use their same production lines and help start up production in P&G's Canadian plant. P&G even used a dubbed version of Unicharm's advertising. Swiffer Dusters are a winning innovation and have exceeded the original forecast estimates many times over. Success was driven by the team's ability to follow the mantra, "If it ain't broke, don't fix it" as they reapplied Unicharm's innovation "as is."

While many of the C&D successes described above are drawn from technology and product development, the same approach can apply to innovation in conceptual marketing ideas, logistics, and innovating new business models.

THE HUNTERS AND GATHERERS OF INNOVATION

The three ways P&G has operationalized C&D as part of its innovation culture include technology entrepreneurs, connections with Internet-based engines for finding solutions to problems, and tapping the expertise of retirees.

Technology entrepreneurs P&G has about eighty-five hundred researchers; outside the organization there are another 1.5 million similar researchers with pertinent areas of expertise. Why not pick their brains? P&G needed a process to make this happen routinely.

That is the role of technology entrepreneurs (TEs). They are the "connect" half of the equation for new technologies. TEs are linked with specific P&G businesses and are rewarded for innovation that drives business results. These senior scientists develop relationships with researchers, whether in academia or business (including suppliers and competitors), and then make sure the P&Gers in the business units know these links exist. TEs are also hunters, using advanced search methods—via the Web, patent offices, and scientific literature—to find answers to questions.

P&G has C&D "hubs" in the United States, Europe, China, India, Japan, and elsewhere that collect and distribute innovation questions to "nodes"—companies, academic institutions, government labs, suppliers, and so on. According to research done by professors at Harvard Business School, roughly 29 percent of the problems submitted to the likes of C&D external networks get solved within three weeks. Interestingly, most solutions come from fields not directly related to the researcher's primary area of expertise.

For example, P&G wanted to print pictures and trivia questions with edible dyes onto Pringles potato crisps. To do so, it needed a system that could deliver 340 million drops per minute, without duplicative images. The choice was either to develop it on its own, or to find it in the outside world. So a technology brief—a one-page statement describing the technical challenge that needed solving and the technical parameters or requirements—was sent out to P&G's internal technology network. A TE dove into a database of thousands of small- and medium-sized companies. He identified a small bakery equipment company in Bologna, Italy, with the technology that provided a lead approach. He then identified external vendors who had technology that was applicable for the development and integration of edible inks and printing equipment. This allowed the Pringles innovation team to do what they wanted faster, better, and cheaper, with a higher degree of certainty and at a lower risk. In fact, Pringles Prints went from concept to launch in less than a year (versus at least two years if the traditional P&G way was used) and at a fraction of the cost. It also resulted in double-digit sales growth for Pringles over the next two years.

Internet-based engines There are exciting new areas of research outside P&G's technical areas of strength, such as 3-D prototyping, math algorithms, and biosciences. But many of the connections P&G people were making—for example, with universities—were sporadic, ad hoc, and often constrained by excessive confidentiality. In short, P&G was not leveraging all the possible connections it could. That has changed.

Now connections with global brains are made through several Internet-based engines. NineSigma, which P&G helped to create, links a company with a problem with a company that can solve it. P&G also uses InnoCentive, a private, for-profit company spun off from Eli Lilly in 2001. InnoCentive links what it calls "Seekers" (companies with problems) and "Solvers" (experts with solutions).

Here's how it works. Companies contract with InnoCentive to become Seekers. This allows them to post an anonymous challenge on the confidential forum—for example, how to synthesize a particular chemical at a specific cost structure. Each challenge includes a detailed description of the problem, a deadline, and the amount of the award. Solvers register to solve challenges. If a Solver (also anonymous) devises a solution that the Seeker accepts, the Seeker pays the award. These can be significant. In November 2006, Prize4Life, Inc., offered a $1 million incentive to identify a biomarker associated with Lou Gehrig's disease; typically, the figure is under $100,000. But it is the company that sets the award, so the Seeker can ensure that the service makes economic sense, in terms of paying for itself in time and effort saved. With a global network of 110,000 Solvers, from 175 different countries, Inno-Centive offers companies a way to tap into a world of brains on a need-to-know basis.

Retirees   Another approach P&G uses is connecting with a different group of external technology experts from an underused demographic: P&G retirees and retirees from other companies. These people worked decades in their specialties and certainly didn't lose their brain cells when they packed up their offices. P&G created a new, separate company, YourEncore.com, to utilize the expertise of retired technical specialists. We not only use P&G retirees but those from other companies—Boeing, for example. Likewise many other companies utilize the services of YourEncore.

Connect and Develop has been a very important driver in the success of the integrated process of innovation at P&G, accelerating the building of both intellectual partnering and intellectual property. C&D requires an "info-structure" that guides the right information to the right people at the right time, and P&G continues to invest in it. This approach, however, should not in any way be interpreted that P&G will not continue to build intellectual property internally. It continues to invest in R&D and the worldwide infrastructure of people, labs, and buildings. And P&G will of course continue ferociously protecting its 38,000 patents. But with this dual approach P&G now has both the internal infrastructure to generate intellectual property and C&D info-structure to generate intellectual partnerships.

MAKING THE PIE BIGGER

The first section of this chapter provided ideas for developing the structures that enable innovation. Then we showed, through Connect and Develop, how to radically shift the way your business finds and develops external ideas that convert into new products and services for organic growth. Here we show how to increase revenue growth by working with external constituencies to increase the size of market demand by creating new customer needs, thereby making the bigger pie for all.

The strategies and structures of a company and its businesses have to be designed so they can innovate with organizations not under their direct or full control, including customers, suppliers, competitors, and an array of interested third parties.

IBM has devoted serious resources to its InnovationJam, an online brainstorming session it has done several times. In 2006, the Jam was devoted to the identification of new ideas. Although the Jam was limited to employees (and their family members), clients, and business partners, it drew in 150,000 people from 104 countries. The goal, according to the corporate website, was "to move beyond simple invention and idea generation. We want to identify new market opportunities and create real solutions that advance businesses, communities, and society in meaningful ways."

Before the Jam, IBM built an interactive website with sound clips, virtual guided tours, and video snippets with background information. Two moderators got the Jam going on four topics: transportation, health, the environment, and finance and commerce. The first phase was a brainstorm; in the second, the participants weighed in on a couple of dozen of the most promising ideas. After the Jam, IBM analyzed the output and decided to invest $100 million in the ten most promising ideas (out of forty-six thousand generated). These ranged from smart health-care payment systems to real-time translation to branchless banking to 3-D Internet. Will any of these make Big Blue see green? Who knows? What is interesting is how IBM is seeking out its customers to figure out new directions. As CEO Sam Palmisano put it, "Collaborative innovation models require you to trust the creativity and intelligence of your employees, your clients, and other members of your innovation network. We opened up our labs and said to the world, 'Here are our crown jewels, have at them!' "

The key, of course, to "connect and develop," or any networked or partnered innovation initiative, is that everybody wins. The customer must win in any case for the innovation to be successful. But, as importantly, each partner in the innovation venture should realize results and returns that are satisfactory in the absolute and better than what any single party could achieve by going it alone. This is a critical point. The pie must be made bigger so that everyone gets a bigger slice.

INNOVATING WITH RETAILER CUSTOMERS

Another important way P&G innovates from the outside is working with customers, namely key retailers such as Carrefour, Metro, Tesco, Wal-Mart, and Target. By jointly creating value through innovations for shoppers both the retailer and P&G build organic growth. The best innovations meet specific, important retailer business challenges in which P&G can add unique value by leveraging its core strengths and its leading brands and products.

Wal-Mart accounts for about 15 percent of P&G's worldwide revenues (and 30 percent of U.S. sales); Target accounts for about 7 percent of U.S. sales. P&G needs Wal-Mart and Target; Wal-Mart and Target need P&G. The mutual recognition of this reality has profoundly changed how they deal with each other. P&G has become a partner, not just a supplier.

Today, the P&G team working with Wal-Wart is multifunctional, consisting of marketing, finance, supply chain/logistics, and market research experts. This change in the business model began in 1987 when P&G and Wal-Mart set out to change how they work together. The premise was simple. Working against each other would:

- better meet the needs of the consumer
- take cost out of the supply chain
- accelerate the growth of both companies

This innovation to the buying-selling model is called "Inverting the Pyramid." Historically, companies worked and communicated with one another through one point of the pyramid—buyer to salesperson, salesperson to buyer. Inverting the pyramid created a flow of communication and planning between the functions of each company—expert to expert, speaking a common language with joint goals and measures.

The first area of focus was product flow and logistics. In the past, the Wal-Mart buyer would read the scanner data and issue an electronic purchase order to a P&G order clerk. He in turn sent it to the manufacturing site. The product was then shipped to the right Wal-Mart distribution facility. The process worked, but there were a lot of human "touches." As a first step, P&G and Wal-Mart took the touches out. For a high-turn business—that is, buy-as-you-use things like laundry detergent and toilet paper—P&G now has real-time access to Wal-Mart's information, monitoring the sales of its brands and products and placing orders directly. This "continuous replenishment" increased sales, reduced costs on both ends of the transaction, and took five days of inventory out of the supply chain.

The next evolution came when the two companies decided to automate all the daily ordering decisions. Wal-Mart and P&G partnered to set up the replenishment parameters, and the orders "write themselves." Another four days of inventory were removed from the supply chain.

Innovation in the supply chain continues. It is more shopper-centric, focuses on shelf availability, and ensures the products are in stock. Using real-time point-of-sale data, eight retail analysts process more than 7 million store-item-level combinations every day, looking for opportunities to improve availability on the shelf. They send targeted shelf in-stock corrections to the operations staff of stores, thereby maximizing shopper satisfaction. The result, says Jeff Schomburger, who leads P&G's relationship with Wal-Mart, is that the consumer "gets the product she wants, where she wants it, when she wants it." Instead of a supply chain with a lot of small links, one long seamless chain is being created.

Partnering with retailers to better understand their shoppers is another way to create demand. Through retailer-specific marketing programs, such as "Speaking of Women's Health," research by P&G and Wal-Mart revealed that women were broadening their definition of health to include wellness, nutrition, exercise, and beauty. A holistic marketing program was developed to meet these health needs of women, Wal-Mart's target shopper.

A second example of collaboration was the joint Wal-Mart and P&G campaign to increase Wal-Mart's sales of cough, cold, and flu products. When people needed them, they went to the nearest, most convenient shop, not Wal-Mart. The P&G–Wal-Mart joint-marketing strategy centered on preparedness by the consumer, and Wal-Mart's share of spending on these products increased by over 30 percent.

A third marketing program to increase awareness of P&G brands at

involved an interactive display of Swiffer products. It in-
sales threefold over previous displays and, as a result, Wal-
increased its Swiffer share-of-market by 5 share points.

Retail partners are also great sources of product innovation ideas
that P&G ultimately brings to market. It was Wal-Mart that saw the
Swiffer duster, and suggested that P&G put it on a pole to clean blinds
and ceiling fans. And it was also Wal-Mart that pushed P&G to develop a Crest mouthwash. It had been looked at for years, but Wal-
Mart's early and strong commitment helped the new product generate
trial and purchase among consumers.

The sustainability movement will create potential for P&G and its
retail partners to innovate by reducing packaging and developing
products that are more environmentally friendly. In a speech on October 10, 2007, Lee Scott, CEO of Wal-Mart, said, "We will drive sustainability and reward suppliers' sustainability innovations. There should
be no trade-off between sustainable profit and sustainable products.
We all have creative, innovative people to make this happen." In the
liquid laundry category, for example, a Wal-Mart–P&G collaboration
resulted in P&G taking 32,000 tons of packaging out of the environment and saving 230 million gallons of water every year.

The partnership with Target illustrates another dimension of P&G's
relationships and partnership with key strategic retailers. In the late
1990s, top on P&G's agenda was to work with Target to redesign its
hair-care aisles. P&G spent several years making this case, with no success. For good reason: Target's main concern was to increase the number of times consumers shopped in their stores. On average, shoppers
visited only seven times a year. Revamping the hair-care aisle was way
down their list of strategic priorities.

Eventually, P&G understood and decided to try and solve Target's
problem. It was done in a very P&G way, starting with a database of
twenty-seven thousand shoppers, then doing specific research among
eight hundred "guests" (Target's term for their shoppers), and finally
in-depth research with more than one hundred of them. It is very
much the same process P&G uses to understand its own consumers.

The team developed a profile of the Target guest—mapping her attitudes and behaviors—and found guests tend to be better educated than the norm, above-average-income women with families, who were confident, individualistic, and had time-pressed high expectations; they shop for more than price. They valued the time-saving aspects of shopping at Target; they also went to places like Kohl's and Bed, Bath & Beyond, and other specialty retail outlets, but not so much to Wal-Mart. A typical comment was "I love Target, I'm a Target person."

At the time, Target's core guests (those spending more than 50 percent of their mass market dollars at Target) came to the stores on average about once a month. Good, but Target figured it could do better, and so did the P&G team. The average guest tended to think of Target primarily for those categories she wanted on occasion, such as gifts, home decor items, and seasonal offerings, but not everyday items such as laundry detergent, paper towels, personal-care products, or diapers. These "need" items have more frequent purchase cycles than discretionary categories which can often be put off.

Research showed Target's very best guests shopped there every week. This group thought of Target in terms of both "wants" and "needs"—a major reason for their more-frequent attendance. Based on this research, P&G recommended that Target focus on high-repurchase-frequency categories as a way to build a "Target-first" mind-set for their guests for products they need every day. A joint team of Target and P&G employees was formed to flesh out the strategy and plans.

Research also revealed that shoppers enter a store with a set amount of time mentally allocated; they start by going for what they need first. If they finish this quickly enough, they may invest the remaining time browsing for things they want. Given this insight, the Target/P&G team worked together to make it easier for guests to buy things they needed most. If it worked, both Target and P&G would be better off. Target would increase revenues and margins, while P&G brands and products would benefit from more frequent "need" trips. High-repurchase, "need-based" categories were put together and moved to the front of the store, making it quick and easy for the shopper to get her beauty, health, and household needs taken care of.

A "Target baby world" was created that grouped all baby products—which had previously been scattered across as many as seven locations—into a one-stop baby shop. The team redesigned the beauty and health department based on research around how guests wanted to shop these categories. The plans were tested, Target's guests loved the changes, and both Target and P&G loved the results.

By 2005, Target had picked up one incremental shopping trip per average guest (up to eight) and had done even better among the best guests, whose frequency increased from twelve to nineteen visits. In 2006, Target picked up yet another trip (to nine) across all guests. How did the team know the in-store innovation worked? Because sales in total and for P&G brands and products increased significantly faster in stores that had the guest-preferred store layout than in those that did not. The intangibles can't be measured, but there is no doubt that P&G's partnership with Target deepened. Today, Target and P&G work together in ways that would have been unimaginable in the 1990s when all P&G worried about what was important to itself.

When innovating with retailers, the focus should be on what matters most to the shopper. What are her unmet needs and wants? How can the frequency of her visits increase, or how can the amount she spends in-store be more like the retailer's best shoppers? How best do retailers and P&G work together to create a delightful shopping experience at the first moment of truth? These innovations should focus on an area that delivers on the retailer's strategic priorities and goals, not just the manufacturer's. It's important to test, measure, and track—and once proven, expand.

Innovations should help retailers differentiate themselves from their competitors. Throughout, it's essential that manufacturers and retailers focus on joint value creation, joint business goals and plans, and joint responsibility for executing with excellence and delivering better business and financial results while delighting the shopper in the process.

Innovating with retailer partners can take on several shapes and sizes, including innovation that is based on an idea that does not involve new products or technology. For example, working with Metro, the international retailer based in Germany, P&G leveraged the scale of its portfolio of brands to drive shopper loyalty to Metro and brand loyalty to P&G. Metro and P&G cocreated the "I love Metro" in-store campaign. It featured an array of P&G brands to draw small shop and business owners for their everyday business needs.

The global retailer, Carrefour, worked with P&G to target families with children to make the family shopping experience easier and more pleasurable. The combined team created and executed a plan that included grouping P&G brands together in places throughout the store and providing information for moms and entertainment for kids.

Manufacturers and retail customers can also work together to develop commercial innovation that supports social causes. In the UK, ASDA's "Tickled Pink" program raises awareness of breast cancer and raises funds for this important cause. Participating P&G home-care brands not only convey their support of doing good, but they also build loyalty and share among their target female users. In the United States, P&G partners with CVS drugstores in key markets to support Special Olympics and CVS's "All Kids Can" causes. This program includes sponsorships of local Special Olympic programs and in-store merchandising to build awareness and support of the cause and drive purchase of P&G brands.

Innovating with retail customers not only creates value for both trading partners, but also builds and strengthens both brand and store loyalty. Moreover, the best innovations build differentiation for both manufacturers and retail customers and improves their respective brand equities.

INNOVATING WITH SUPPLIERS

Suppliers are another rich, often underutilized source of innovation ideas. P&G realized that its suppliers have a combined R&D staff of fifty thousand talented people located around the globe and eager to work with it. Most businesses keep their suppliers at bay for competitive reasons; adversarial relations are common. Suppliers want higher prices; customers, lower ones. It's a prescription for conflict and unending negotiation. P&G turned past practice on its head, creating a secure IT platform to share technology briefs. The response to this proprietary network has been tremendous: P&G has seen a 30 percent increase in innovation projects jointly staffed with researchers from our suppliers.

For example, in Ludwigshafen, Germany, P&G and BASF scientists work together as one seamless team to develop breakthrough polymer technology used in P&G laundry detergents, like Tide and Ariel.

Innovating with suppliers is not just an opportunity but practically a necessity in technology-driven industries that have long lead times and require big investments. Innovation can happen faster and with lower risk. When, for example, a business unit of Cisco Systems needs to develop a unique integrated circuit for a specific application, the upfront investment can be in hundreds of millions of dollars, with the return on it materializing over several years. By not going it alone but working with suppliers, the circuit can be developed faster and at lower investment for Cisco. This process of joint innovation requires a far-reaching, trusting, long-term relationship between the technology developers at the supplier and the product developers in Cisco's business units.

Angel Mendez, Cisco's senior vice president of supply chain, has made his organization the bridge for joint innovation. He has transformed the traditional function of a supply chain. It is not just manufacturing, logistics, and delivery at the lowest costs and least inventories but making innovation with suppliers a vehicle for enhancing organic growth for Cisco through discovering emerging technologies across the globe.

Mendez has commercially trained technologists who embed themselves in the product teams of Cisco's business units. He has a systematic way to search these technologies and related opportunities, linking them with the business units on a routine basis. As a result, the technologists know what the business units are working on and what their current and future needs are. Simultaneously, they search for suppliers with new technologies the business units can use to develop their products. The managers of the business units then can see new opportunities not previously imagined. Suppliers, then, don't just ship product to the business units but actively coinnovate with them to create new business opportunities. Similar to the technology entrepreneurs of P&G, Cisco's technologists create links between the business units and the suppliers. The benefits of this new relationship between Cisco and suppliers include lower investment in new products for revenue growth and getting a lead over the competition.

INNOVATING WITH COMPETITORS

When it comes to bringing innovation to the marketplace, P&G will do almost anything—including partnering with competitors. One example is a technology and promising prototype called Impress. It's a plastic food wrap with tiny adhesive-coated dimples that seals surfaces rather than just covers them, preventing the awkward clumping so characteristic of competitive products. In test markets, consumers loved it. The first thought, naturally, was to invent a new brand and build a new manufacturing process. That, however, would take too long and be far too expensive. The second approach was buying a related company and adapting their manufacturing. P&G was outbid twice, and a third company didn't want to sell.

The innovation team working on this project rethought their approach and took a different tack. The food-wrap category was new to P&G, and was strongly defended by imposing competitors of long experience. "Ultimately, it came down to practical economics," says Jeff Weedman, P&G's vice president of external business development. "How can we get the best return on our innovation investment? And since we ultimately wanted to retain a stake in the business, we also had to consider: Who can get the products to market faster?"

What previously would have been unheard of at P&G happened: a joint venture with Clorox, the maker of Glad household products and a key P&G competitor for decades. P&G took a 20 percent stake in the business by contributing proprietary technology and cash. In addition,

P&G placed two managers on Glad's operating team, and P&G employees made up nearly half of Glad's R&D team. A P&G vice president was placed on the Glad joint-venture board of directors. P&G agreed to funnel any related innovations Glad's way. Glad did everything else. The result was Glad Press'n Seal wrap and Glad ForceFlex (stretchable, stronger trash bags). Today, Glad is a billion-dollar brand, up from $650 million. While Glad is technically a billion-dollar brand for Clorox, P&G is proud that it is the innovations that came from the joint venture that catapulted it to this level of sales. It is called P&G's twenty-fourth billion-dollar brand.

INNOVATING WITH NONRETAIL CUSTOMERS

Industrial companies, such as 3M, invest time and money doing research that can result in real technological breakthroughs. It's often the case, however, that the technology has no clear link to customer need. Only after it is developed do they begin to search for an application.

In the very early stages of research, they usually need to "go it alone" in the lab, but if, at the appropriate point in the development of the technology, companies like 3M started working with customers, then applications could potentially be developed faster and more effectively. That is, in fact, how 3M Optical Systems has been able to help its customers (companies like HP, Samsung, Sony, and Sharp) compete in the fast-changing consumer electronics market.

Optical Systems developed its approach to innovating with customers in its early years, when it was just a dozen or so people on a small business development team searching for a big market opportunity for a kind of film 3M had developed. The film, best described as having many closely spaced micro-louvers, like mini–vertical blinds, could direct and manipulate light in various ways. The team and their leader, Andy Wong, were sure it had market potential. The question was, for what market?

Eager to find their big market opportunity, the team visited company after company in industry after industry, listening to the business and technology challenges those potential customers described. Just about everybody on the 3M team, from the engineers to the manufacturing manager, talked directly with customers. They'd go back home and tackle the problems, then get back together with people in the customer shop with ideas for how 3M could help. As the team explained how their technology worked, the ideas began to flow back and forth between the two companies.

In the automotive industry, the team explored whether 3M film could manage light in the passenger compartment of a car so it wouldn't distract the driver. Could it make the dashboard instruments brighter without creating glare on the windshield? That exploration helped 3M unearth some small market opportunities. The big break came when the team explored possibilities in the nascent PC notebook industry and discovered that their films could be used to improve the brightness and efficiency of the PC notebook display. The timing couldn't have been better: As the PC business took off in the 1990s, so did Optical Systems. By 1998, its films were standard in the PC industry, and revenues exploded.

3M Optical Systems now has a huge network of customers with which it does joint problem solving, and to this day it's not just salespeople talking to purchasing agents. Technology people and manufacturing people from 3M talk directly with a range of people in the customer shop—and often. As Jeff Melby, the business director and former technical director of Optical Systems, puts it, "Nobody here says 'Hey, wait a minute, you're a chemical engineer, you can't be out talking to customers!'" Exchanging ideas with customers is an everyday activity even for Marc Miller, the head of manufacturing for Optical Systems. That's how Optical Systems discovered that many of their customers used several different 3M films, each of which had a protective film attached. Customers spent a lot of time removing the protective film, which is tricky because even the tiniest particle of dust will ruin the film. Miller and his team asked customers, "What if we could supply two or three of these films already stacked?" Customers were interested, and the team went to work to figure out how to accomplish it.

By being steadily alert to opportunities and always on the offensive to meet customer and consumer needs, Optical Systems continues to differentiate itself against the competition and ensures a steady stream of new revenues.

While much of this chapter has focused on opening up and bringing in ideas from the outside, don't neglect the obvious: your internal research-and-development organization. AskMe is a feature on P&G's own internal intranet. If a P&Ger has a problem, he can send out a query to ten thousand fellow technical employees to solicit their experience and thoughts on how to approach a specific innovation challenge.

Establishing research centers in different locations is another way to leverage the world's talent in your own company—and at this point lots of companies are doing it. A survey by the Boston Consulting Group found that of new R&D centers being planned, 75 percent were in China and India. Although the developed world (chiefly North America, Western Europe, and Japan) still accounts for the great majority of R&D, spending is rising much faster in the developing world. Toyota supports a small-truck design center in Thailand; John Deere, a technology center in India. More than half of IBM's research facilities are outside the United States—one in Europe, three in Asia, and one in Israel. And 80 percent of Siemens's 150 facilities are outside Germany.

Such centers are, of course, only one link in the chain of innovation; still, the trends are suggestive. By mobilizing global R&D 24-7, companies can create better products and bring them to market faster. But that is not enough; the point is to use the different capabilities of workers around the world to decide where to focus your energies and to choose what strategies to pursue. One approach is the contract model: to buy brains, and with them speed and cost efficiency. A study by Booz Allen Hamilton estimated that current global spending on offshore engineering is $15 billion; that figure could rise to as much as $225 billion by 2020, with most growth coming from emerging markets like India, China, and Russia.

The complexity of the work being produced is also rising; while price is clearly part of the equation, this trend is also about expertise and time of delivery. P&G, for example, contracts with Axiom, an Indian partner, to supply lower-cost computer-aided design and engineering. P&G is also working with Indian government labs to identify high-efficacy botanical actives and technologies for use in beauty, baby, and oral-care products. This is an expertise that P&G just doesn't have.

Another strategy is to build in-house networks with complementary strengths. Take Microsoft's research facility in Beijing. Founded in 1998, Microsoft Research Asia exudes a certain pseudo-California cool—it has foosball tables and massage chairs—but it is best seen as a whirlpool sucking in talent from all over Asia to create global solutions. The techies based here do some work directed at specifically regional problems, such as speech-based systems for Chinese speakers; mostly, though, this is a collection of brains that storm difficult problems.

Microsoft figures the Beijing lab is responsible for more than a hundred innovations that have embedded themselves into such products as Office XP, Office System 2003, Windows XP, Windows Server 2003, Windows XP Media Center Edition, Windows XP Tablet PC Edition, Xbox, Windows Live, Windows Vista, and Office 2007. The lab is also developing expertise in computer animation and digital arts that the entire company taps into.

Making this work requires a high degree of internal integration. Whirlpool has speeded up its innovation process by developing a software platform that allows its engineers to work off the same technical information. "The broader benefit," IBM notes in a case study of the project, "is flexibility to rapidly deploy new capabilities on a worldwide basis to seize opportunities and sustain competitive advantages in the global marketplace."

Organizing for innovation is not easy. One size does not fill all innovation circumstances. When deciding how to organize, think through a number of criteria and variables. And, be willing to experiment with organization structures until finding one that works best for your company, business, function, or project. Finding the right organization structure can make a big difference in the effectivness, efficiency, and indeed the ultimate success of the innovation effort.

Opening up and partnering for innovation can be successful and can work at the company, business, function, or project level, as was the case with P&G's broad Connect and Develop program. Innovation centers and joint innovation teams can productively involve customers and suppliers. Networking is the broadest sense, through Web communities like Nine Sigma or Your Encore, or via communities of common interest or practice, can identify innovation opportunities and solve innovation problems. Connecting and collaborating are critical to the innovation process. Once the organization design is decided, then people can concentrate on taking an idea to full commercial execution and ultimate business and financial success.

ASK YOURSELF ON MONDAY MORNING

• Are you experimenting with different organizational structures to enable and support different kinds of innovation teams?

• Are you multiplying your internal capabilities through open-source innovation or a connect-and-develop–like program? Are you using this approach not only for products/technology innovation, but also other innovations like commercial/conceptual innovation, supply chain/logistics, new business models?

• Have you set an explicit goal to track the effectiveness of your connect-and-develop program, and are you tracking your progress against it?

• Are you assigning accountability for the connect-and-develop program, selecting the right person to put "meat on the bone," and then making needed changes in methodology to execute it?

• Are you making sure that you are not reinventing the wheel? Before green-lighting a new innovation idea, are you first searching whether anyone else in the organization is doing anything related to it and scanning through a connect and develop network to see whether it is being done elsewhere on the outside?

• Have you appropriately modified your reward-and-recognition program to showcase those employees who "walk the walk" and use external partners for innovation?

• Have you prepared your people to actively search for ideas and insights? Are they looking whenever they go to trade shows, association meetings, and conventions and sharing their findings in a useful, constructive way when they return? Are they leveraging their social networks outside the company for new ideas? Have they created an Internet-based network, starting with suppliers, consultants you have used or might use, and academics or researchers who will be willing to participate?

CHAPTER SEVEN

INTEGRATING INNOVATION
INTO YOUR ROUTINE

From Generating Ideas to Go to Market

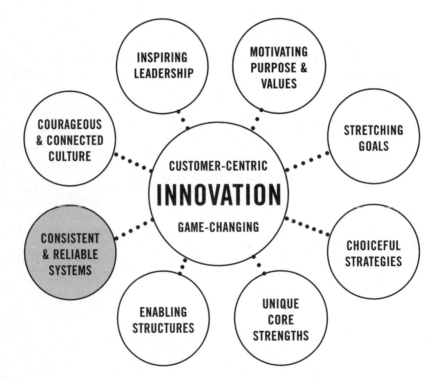

As you read this book, you may be thinking, "There are some good ideas here . . . for someone else. In my shop, we can barely keep the trains running on time. How am I supposed to do all this?"

For starters, while it isn't easy, it can be done through an end-to-end flow process of innovation for converting ideas into profitable offerings. Innovation doesn't just happen. You have to work at it. It requires deliberate practice, consistency, rhythm, discipline, and continuous learning from success and failure. Doing innovation right means developing a repeatable, scalable, and consistent way of converting ideas into results. It requires a degree of standardization so that others can imitate the model, and improve on it.

And all this has to happen seamlessly. It cannot be piecemeal, or by jumping from silo to silo; it has to be integrated with the mainstream of managerial decision making, particularly the strategic choices of where to play, revenue growth goals, margin improvement goals, reprioritization of resources, and annual review of performance and rewards. It's akin to a basketball team practicing and developing seamless teamwork, since almost all ideas are nurtured through cross-functional teams. The selection of the team leader, the composition of the team, how well it functions formally and informally, the interaction of the team with higher management, how well higher management conducts reviews—all are pivotal.

We'll show first how the routine process of innovation works at the business unit and functional levels at Honeywell International. Then we will illustrate a critical tool for operationalizing innovation: the 5-building-block framework for converting an idea into a commercial winner.

INNOVATION AT HONEYWELL

When Dave Cote became CEO of Honeywell in February 2002, his challenge was to increase organic revenue growth to drive bottom-line earnings growth. The processes to drive revenue growth should be as rigorous as a production process or supply chain, he reasoned, and would help make organic revenue growth sustainable.

Cote set the overall corporate goals and asked the leaders of each business unit to develop their own top- and bottom-line growth goals, which he then discussed with them. He didn't want to set the specific targets without their input because he wanted to be sure they bought into the plans. He did, however, make it clear that they had to be aggressive. "I asked each business to explain their top-line growth goals. I knew that if the goals were aggressive and they achieved them, they'd be doing the right things around developing new products," he explains. The goals set a clear agenda for the leader of each business: figure out where to find new sources of growth, define the markets you want to pursue, learn about those customers, create profitable new offerings for them, and get them to the market quickly. Innovation became the job of each business leader, not the exclusive domain of their chief technology officers.

Cote knew that setting goals and issuing an imperative would not ensure results. Honeywell had to develop the infrastructure and tools to make innovation—and growth—happen. On the marketing side, it had to beef up its capabilities to segment markets and extract insights from customers. People in Honeywell's Automation and Control Solutions (ACS) business, for instance, thought they did a good job listening to customers, but in many cases they were listening to "the voice of the last sale we lost," meaning salespeople could tell you very specifically what a customer had wanted that Honeywell didn't provide. But they had no methodology for evaluating whether that missing ingredient was something the company should pursue. Was the lost sale a major long-term marketing opportunity that might mean hundreds of millions of dollars in future revenue or just a onetime missed opportunity? Consequently, people worked on lots of technology projects with little information about the real nature and relevant size of the market opportunity they represented.

Cote gave Rhonda Germany the challenge of building Honeywell's marketing capability. As head of strategic planning and business development, Germany established a training program in which a mix of marketing, engineering, and sales and service people from across Honeywell's four main business areas—Aerospace, Transportation Systems, Specialty Materials, and Automation and Control Solutions—came together in a workshop-type environment for a week at a time to put marketing rigor behind ideas from technical people. They started to get a sense of how to think like a marketer, learning techniques for segmenting the market, and listening to the voice of the customer. While the transformation to being more customer focused was by no means complete after just one session, it was a turning point, as people started to see that knowing more about customers led to new ideas and better decisions about what to do with the technology.

GETTING THE FLOW OF IDEAS MOVING

People throughout Honeywell took the message to heart, but in ACS, the focus on customer segmentation, and data-driven marketing was something of an epiphany. Seeing their revenues decreasing, leaders at ACS *had* to do something. Bringing a better understanding of how and why customers buy into their decision making opened new horizons.

Dan Sheflin, vice president technology for ACS, had the idea for an innovation workshop that would bring people together from disparate parts of the company to discuss what they were working on and to see how it matched up against the market opportunities. Sheflin knew wireless technology was important to many ACS customers; he also knew there was lots of work being done on it across Honeywell. He invited fifty people involved with developing wireless technology or who understood customer needs for it to meet for a day and a half.

The format was simple: First, the marketing people talked about what they were seeing in the marketplace and what they believed the opportunities were. Then technologists spent six hours describing their projects. As is often the case, many of the engineers were unaware of what their colleagues in other pockets of the company were working on. The dialogue that ensued was electric as engineers and marketers spontaneously swapped ideas and began brainstorming ways to use technology being developed in separate businesses to meet customer needs.

For example, the environmental combustion control teams were looking at the people in security systems saying, "I didn't know you were doing that," and people in the security systems business were saying, "We've already built twenty million of these products. We can show you how to solve that problem." The thermostat engineers were saying, "Why do we have to create our own if we can just use your wireless device?" And during one of the breakout sessions, one said, "You know, wireless can be a significant game-changer for the industrial space. Honeywell provides controls for seventy percent of the critical infrastructure on the planet. We're already serving those customers. Some of them measure their plants in square miles. There's a real need for wireless in these big facilities. I was with a customer just yesterday following this guy walking around with a clipboard and getting in and out of his truck. WiFi for these plants would be huge."

The group broke into smaller teams to put together product concepts with rough estimates of potential revenues and resources needed and a description of the value proposition. The idea was to make the ideas more concrete and to tie them to the market opportunity, so it was easier to judge which ones were most appealing.

By the end of the workshop, it was clear that the opportunity for wireless was immense, and that ACS should have one engineering team designing a wireless platform, or common technology base, that all six of its business units could use as the basis for their own applications. Using wireless technology for systems to help industrial facilities operate was clearly a huge opportunity, and the leader of that business, who was participating in the workshop, was more than happy to take ownership of it. The first wireless industrial systems product was launched in 2004, and a complete system was launched in 2007 with outstanding adoption by industrial customers.

ACS quickly followed up with innovation workshops geared around other technology platforms (they ultimately identified four). The workshops, now routine, cover a range of opportunities. But they always have the same basic purpose: to get technology and marketing people, along with industry experts and customers, together to move from the vague outline of an opportunity to a clearer definition of actual projects with numbers tied to them. Then, business leaders can get their arms around projects and make decisions about whether to pursue them. It proved to be a breakthrough in solving the biggest cultural problem companies have with innovation—getting marketing and technology to work together to create a seamless flow of ideas and convert them to commercial offerings.

One example occurred in the Building Solutions business unit when it focused on the security badges that employees scan when they enter the workplace. People in the Building Solutions business unit, which sells hundreds of access control systems annually, knew that it was possible to use smartchips in new plastic ID cards, but thought the extra cost would turn away customers. Getting people with different perspectives and knowledge in the same room wrestling with the issue led to an aha! The group discovered that with the smartchip technology there was a way to vastly reduce the cost of installing the security system, which would more than offset the expense of putting chips in the cards. "That was a deep idea that we wouldn't have come up with in the usual course of running the business," says Daryll Fogal, chief technology officer of the Building Solutions business. "It took a combination of lots of pieces of information, lots of different kinds of technical expertise, and outside stimulation."

There are many other sources of ideas in addition to the workshop. ACS uses an online tool to collect them. Anyone can enter an idea into the Innovation Portal, and there's a person at the other end who ensures that it is channeled to the right people. But it's up to a business leader to turn an idea into a project that is shepherded through the remaining distinct development phases of planning and specification, development, validation, and delivery and support. Business leaders are open to new ideas because they have growth and new product goals to meet, but they don't always bite because they also have profitability goals. Sometimes there's just too much uncertainty for them to want to make the investment required to bring an undeveloped idea to market. Most of Honeywell's products are heavily engineered and require significant verification and validation, which consumes the lion's share of development resources. As Sheflin says, "Innovation is hard because by definition the people running the businesses have a very operational focus. You have to bring them something that is detailed enough that they'll believe they will make money from it." Fogal says the question he hears repeatedly from the heads of the business units is "Will this pay me back?"

SELECTING AND GREEN-LIGHTING IDEAS

Sometimes a concept simply needs a bit more refinement or market research to appeal to a manager with P&L responsibility. In the past, some innovation projects stalled because there were insufficient resources to develop good business plans to sell to P&L leaders. As Sheflin says, "Cash is gas," and frequently there was insufficient cash to develop compelling business plans. ACS projects can now get funded from one of two sources created to push opportunities across that threshold: the Honeywell Growth Board or the ACS Venture Fund. (The Growth Board is similar to P&G's Corporate Innovation Fund that funds new businesses that cut across categories, such as Swiffer and Crest Whitestrips. The Venture Fund is similar to P&G's New Business Development groups, which reside in specific categories of business units.

The Honeywell Growth Board has $20 million set aside at the corporate level to fund projects that cross over several of Honeywell's divisions, such as putting controls from the Automation and Controls Solution division on the turbochargers from the Transportation Systems business. The ACS Venture Fund has about $1.5 million, which it dispenses in grants of about $100,000 to help people in a division go from "I have this cool idea about wireless networking in an industrial facility" to "We have this idea, and we've talked to a hundred customers, we've done the segmentation, done the profitability analysis, and we think wireless networking in industrial plants is a $100 million business." When business unit leaders hear something like that, then they're willing to spend some money and make it part of their business plan.

When a business unit leader assumes "ownership" of an idea that emerges from one of the workshops, he engages his entire leadership team, the Product Action Council (PAC). The PAC includes the business unit president, and his sales, finance, technology, and marketing people. Once the PAC decides a project is promising, the president incorporates it in the budget and makes projections of profit and revenue. A core team is then chosen to develop and bring the project to market. It can be as few as two people—typically an engineer and marketer—or as many as thirty and include people from supply chain management, R&D, sales and operations.

At its most basic level, the process of innovation is universal: Start by generating some ideas (this is often the easiest part, although the quality and diversity of ideas can vary); select the ones that show the most promise and best fit with the company's goals and strategies; nurture those ideas, or, as some say, develop those ideas into products; and take them to the marketplace, not just to the point of introducing the product or service, but to the point at which you achieve your profitable peak market share, or widest adoption. Along the way, kill projects that no longer show promise to free up people with expertise. Many companies have created some version of a stage-gate process, by which they track the progress of innovation projects through the nurturing and taking-to-market phases. The vocabulary is not what matters. The exact number of phases is not crucial, either. What does matter is how well you adhere to the process, simultaneously stimulating creativity and maintaining discipline at those critical junctures. There is inevitably a psychological tug-of-war between championing a project to overcome obstacles and being willing to end one that is not meeting its hurdles and will drain resources. There is also the risk that the market need will shift before a project is fully ready. Honeywell's ACS business has found that the PACs are an effective way to balance those tensions and reduce those risks.

NURTURING IDEAS

The online tool that helps keep ACS projects on track was developed in 2003 when a small group of technical people concluded that the off-the-shelf software did not give them the information they needed. They put their heads together and created their own for about $40,000. They've continued to refine it, and the Velocity Portfolio Manager (VPM) has become a central tool in making new product development faster and more efficient. It is transparent: All its information is online and available for anyone in ACS to see. And one of its main virtues is that it links individual projects to projections of revenue and profitability.

The screens on the Velocity Portfolio Manager contain essentials such as:

• Basic information about each project: who is leading it; the technologies involved; market segments it is aimed at; whether the idea is "major" or "platform"; what needs to be done to move it forward—making sure, for example, that promises to customers are being met.

• A list of all innovation projects under way and the total amount of revenue they are expected to deliver in the next one to five years, thus enabling a business unit leader to see how her entire portfolio of projects links with her budget and business plan and see whether and when there are revenue shortfalls. Decisions can then be made about accelerating projects to meet any gaps in revenues and profits.

The tool provides an overview of the entire portfolio of projects so they can prioritize and allocate resources accordingly. Roger Fradin, the head of ACS, can look at the portfolio across all of the business units. When there are bottlenecks, the problem is usually not enough engineers. So the leadership team might decide to end some projects that are proceeding on schedule but are less promising strategically or financially to free up the engineers. In the past, ACS typically had one engineer working on as many as five projects; now they're more likely to have five working exclusively on one project. Needless to say, projects get developed faster.

The tool automatically brings to the top of the list individual projects that need attention: those that will bring in significant revenues, the ones behind schedule, or those entering the final phase. A project at the very top with symbols for all three of these issues next to it will surely attract a leader's attention and spur discussion.

The core teams input information to the VPM and use it as a guide; that information is combined with other relevant facts to make decisions about whether a project should proceed to the next phase or should end. Projected revenue and profit are weighed at each phase, because they may change for any number of reasons as the project proceeds. In 2006, for example, a huge spike in the cost of copper forced one PAC to reconsider whether its project would still be profitable. The core teams also have to ensure the incremental funding is available to continue and might at times have to advocate for it with the PAC. Another project in the portfolio might be competing for funds, and the PAC will have to decide. Most businesses have trouble cutting off projects; ACS has become pretty good at it.

An important part of what core teams do is to "socialize" a project, a term used to recognize that nurturing a project is a social activity. Members of the core team stay in constant touch with one another and with all the people who are working on the project to be sure everyone's concerns are being met and to avoid getting torpedoed at monthly PAC meetings. People are expected to reach out beyond their functional boundaries and talk often. The PAC ensures everyone is connected. How this plays out can be seen in the way that the R&D labs and the business units now work together.

The labs are more connected to the businesses than ever. It used to be a common complaint from Honeywell's businesses that they were expected to support the labs financially, yet the research was often disconnected from their customers' needs. That thinking has completely flipped. "We don't hear the businesses saying they want their money back anymore," notes Sheflin. It is not an overstatement to say that there has been a cultural revolution at Honeywell.

About six years ago, Honeywell's one large research operation was broken into four labs, one for each of the four businesses. Driven by a relentless focus on development cost and speed to market, the businesses started turning to the labs for help of two kinds: as a clearinghouse for solutions that might lie outside of Honeywell, and for common platforms the businesses can use. A platform ACS recently identified is user-based design, a need that came directly from a better understanding of customers. Across ACS, people found, design and ease of use were as important to customers as how the product functioned. The labs worked on it, and the business units tapped into it, often finding new ways to innovate that could bring stale product areas back to life.

Thermostats, for instance, do pretty much what they've always done—schedule your heating and cooling systems to keep you warm in the winter and cool in the dog days of summer—and had become a dull product to sell. Making them easier to use, easier to install, and nicer to have on the wall has generated twenty-seven new versions of thermostats and revitalized the market. Salespeople were excited about selling them again. The user-based design platform also contributed to new products for the life safety market, like a control panel designed to help firefighters who arrive at the scene of a burning building. The control panel shows where the nasty chemicals are stored and which parts of the building are affected in a way that is intuitively clear—a vital aid to first responders who have to make crucial decisions in less than five minutes.

Not too long ago there was a "Berlin Wall" that prevented functions and business units at Honeywell from collaborating. Now people have the processes, tools, and even the expectations that make it part of the normal way they do their jobs. The labs are better connected to the businesses, the businesses are better connected to each other, the various functions of the business are connected as well, and all of their efforts are connected to real customer needs. The infusion of marketing expertise and customer focus, the design of mechanisms to provide funding, and the creation of innovation workshops ensure a steady stream of relevant ideas.

Budgeting and resource allocation are tracked to projections of future revenues and margins. The discipline of fixed criteria at each stage of the end-to-end process, cross-functional teams for shepherding innovation projects, and the online tool to view innovation projects individually and as a portfolio are important in making the connection.

Behaviors have changed, too, and metrics reinforce them, especially when the business and function leaders revisit them during operating, budget, and strategy reviews. For instance, every ACS project is measured for speed—when development starts, when it's supposed to end, and when it actually does. The VPM tool makes it easy to do without a lot of extra effort. Discussions of annual operating plans and strategic plans always include the speed and number of new product introductions, and measures of their profitability. Fifteen percent of the chief technology officers' compensation is tied to meeting goals for the number of days it takes to introduce new products and platforms. There is no ambiguity about what people should be trying to accomplish, and there are tools to help them track it.

GO TO MARKET

Because people in manufacturing and marketing are part of the PAC, they start their work earlier and products move faster and more smoothly to commercialization. As soon as a product has been defined and has a solid business plan and schedule, manufacturing starts figuring out how to produce it. In the past, manufacturing ramped up slowly, working out the kinks over the six months to a year following a new product launch. Now Honeywell has a "new development shop," a manufacturing line identical to its regular production line that is dedicated to new products. Engineering and operations use it to work out the bugs in manufacturing ahead of a product's launch, so they can achieve their target yield of 95 percent at startup and 99 percent three months later. The new development shop process also builds supply ahead of the launch, so when sales and marketing are talking to customers about the new product, they can promise to ship high volumes in a matter of days and thereby build momentum. That's a stark contrast to the instant stock-outs that used to occur when some new products were released.

The ability to fill orders goes hand-in-hand with a new marketing approach designed to create buzz when a new product is launched. Honeywell puts on day-long shows, which distributors actually pay to attend using the bonus points they accumulate from selling Honeywell products. The shows provide fun entertainment along with demonstrations of important new Honeywell products. In fall 2007, for example, at an event in St. Louis, audience members were called on to compete in a contest onstage, demonstrating how easy it was to install and configure Honeywell's new system for controlling multiple heating and cooling zones in a home. Some five hundred people attended. The shows get people to see how the new product is differentiated and energizes them to get comfortable with it. The new marketing approaches and the ability to deliver high volumes fast have driven a dramatic uptake in initial sales.

What Honeywell's ACS business has assembled is an end-to-end process of innovation that is integrated with the business. It has processes to generate and shape ideas, select among them based largely on market opportunities, and tap Honeywell's combined expertise to take them to the market. And it has tools and incentives to do it fast. But developing innovation projects does not stand in isolation from normal business activities. Each project, regardless of its stage of development, is linked to revenues and profits in the short, medium, and long term, and is reflected in operating plans and budgets. Ideas that are too fragile to withstand the rigors of a budget review are protected, but even they are subjected to the discipline of prioritization and measured against other opportunities. And the need for growth from innovation is built into reward systems. Operating reviews, budget reviews, and even talent reviews have innovation built into them.

THE 5-BUILDING-BLOCK FRAMEWORK

The Honeywell ACS story illustrates the value of a disciplined process for generating ideas and either taking them to market or killing them. Without the discipline of a system that fully shapes, revises, and reshapes an idea through multiple iterations, a project rarely reaches full potential. A kind of self-fulfilling prophecy then takes over. People see the innovation for what it is: half-baked. As a result, the support needed to get maximum market share fast doesn't materialize. That gives competitors the opportunity to jump in and snag profits.

A disciplined process for going through iterations improves the chances of success. This doesn't mean putting an idea through the wringer of a slow-moving bureaucracy. In fact, some of the most successful companies in the fastest-moving industries are the most disciplined at nurturing and commercializing their ideas.

The conversion of ideas into profits is a matter of practicality. And it requires a well-engineered but flexible social process that glides the idea step-by-step into the marketplace (or oblivion if that is where it belongs).

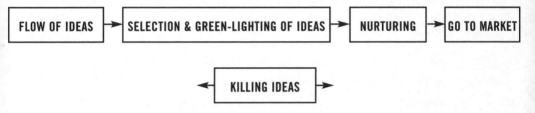

In many companies, innovation is a linear sequential process—starting with R&D and moving from department to department. The 5-Building-Block Framework, on the other hand, practices the principle of simultaneity, with different units working in parallel. Here in outline form are the key issues and questions that are part of each stage.

FLOW OF IDEAS

• Ideas can come from two sources: They are either internally developed from within the business itself; or they can come from outside sources—customers, suppliers, alliances, and joint ventures. Ideas from outside sources can be searched for on a regular basis as we discussed for the P&G program of Connect and Develop. Other companies with similar structures for sourcing ideas from the outside include DuPont, LEGO Group, and Nokia.

• These ideas can range from incremental to disruptive: the reinvention of a business model (such as Apple with the iPod and iPhone); totally redesigning the value chain from the business through the final user (such as Nokia in the Indian market); changing the cost structure as well as productivity of capital, that is, by getting 5 percent to 6 percent productivity of capital improvement through innovation in operating processes, as DuPont has.

• A transparent mechanism within the business is needed to both receive and deal with ideas, whether from internal or outside sources. The challenge is to have these ideas travel inside the organization to the right places so they get serious attention.

• Middle managers should not wait for an order to come down from on high to get a flow of ideas moving. Actively create the structures to ensure that ideas flow. It will expand the capability of both the leader as well as the people within the organization.

SELECTION AND GREEN-LIGHTING OF IDEAS

• There must be a clearly-defined social mechanism for selecting ideas to be green-lighted, after which a major dedicated effort is made to nurture the chosen idea to final fruition.

• The mechanism must operate on a disciplined, rhythmic basis. There must be a framework for people becoming part of the mechanism and improving the way decisions are made.

• The composition and leadership of this social mechanism must be explicitly considered and carefully chosen.

• The criteria the mechanism uses must be clear and link with the strategic selections of where to play and the desired revenue growth goals. There must be a balance of the chosen ideas from incremental to disruptive, low risk to high risk, and from internal to external.

• The mechanism must keep the "customer is boss" at the center and use failure productively, developing prototypes and observing customer reaction to them. If a prototype fails quickly try another iteration.

NURTURING

• The process of taking a selected and green-lighted idea to fruition requires someone "owning" and being accountable for its success or failure—usually a business unit manager—as part of his goals (particularly top-line growth, gross margin, preventing price erosion, and/or commanding premium pricing), budget, and performance.

• The "owner" is responsible for funding it; moving it forward or killing it; selecting both the team leader and the members of the innovation team; allocating resources, reprioritizing when necessary; doing reviews of the team's output, using milestones to measure the various phases; and rewarding success and dealing with failure.

• Decisions need to be made as to whether the idea requires a dedicated full-time team to nurture it to full fruition.

• Criteria need to be established for selection of the team leader and the members who make up the team. Do the leader and the team members have the necessary skills to carry the idea through the entire process or will mid-course corrections be necessary? (For example, someone skilled at idea generation may not have the right skills for commercialization.)

• The team needs to work together to shape the idea to prove whether—or not—the concept works in the marketplace ("proof-of-concept"). The team leader need not be a domain expert in either technology or marketing. Her job is to lead the team in its day-to-day working on the task, keeping it on target, dealing with emotional highs and lows, and helping the team be both creative and practical.

• The team leader (1) articulates early and often the most difficult hurdles to be overcome, not postponing coming to grips with tough issues; (2) searches for external and internal help for dealing with hurdles; (3) sets milestones in agreement with the business unit manager and has the discipline to deliver on the milestones (called the "stage and gate" process at many companies); and (4) continues to take the project forward by figuring out its commercialization, scalability, price points, margins, and the appropriate methodology to achieve revenue growth goals.

GO TO MARKET

• The process of going from the nurturing stage into the actual marketplace is not sequential, but overlapping. The managers responsible for actually taking an idea to market are engaged during the process of nurturing so that trade-offs and resource allocation are done with the scaling up, cost consideration, and reach to consumer in mind.

• Funding, until this point, has not been major. With go-to-market decisions, major investments are made and major risks and rewards ensue as, for example, manufacturing facilities, marketing and advertising campaigns, and new channels of distribution are developed.

• Throwing a nurtured idea "over the wall" from the innovation team to people in manufacturing, design, sales, and marketing to make it and bring it to customers will, in most cases, guarantee failure. Manufacturing, for example, might find that the product cannot be made at the required cost and tolerances. People in marketing might say that the design won't appeal to consumers. If they were part of the social process throughout, issues such as these would have likely been raised and dealt with, making final commercialization a more smoothly integrated process, not one with bumps and gaps. The business unit manager ensures that the consumer is the boss in making the right trade-offs between the innovation team, what marketing is asking for, and what is commercially feasible to achieve financial goals, ensuring that the consumer will buy it and come back for repeat purchases. All of this has to happen without compromising the integrity of the offering. This is a central skill of a leader in making innovation an effective end-to-end process.

KILLING IDEAS

• Not all ideas will succeed. That's the nature of innovation. As the process of nurturing goes forward and milestones are evaluated, the business unit manager and team leaders need to have intellectually honest conversations whether to proceed further; whether to assign a higher priority and possibly more resources; give the project a lower priority, possibly extracting resources; or kill the project. The skill is to reappraise the most critical hurdles and reevaluate the social process of dealing with them.

• Major causes of failure include the wrong choice of team leader, poor team composition, not searching for outside sources of ideas and help, not rigorously practicing the idea of customer is boss, bad timing, or simply a dysfunctional team. According to one estimate, a third of innovation resources are wasted because business unit managers let emotional commitment keep a project moving and don't kill it at the right time. However, just as there is a risk in funding ideas, so there is the risk of killing an idea and discontinuing funding, thereby possibly missing an opportunity.

WORKING TOGETHER TO COOK THE IDEA

While the 5-Building-Block Framework is a disciplined process, following it is half the story. The real cooking that leads successfully to the first moment of truth is done through human interaction among experts, team members, and the team leader.

The danger many fall into is managing each of the phases mechanically through traditional operating reviews that can have the atmosphere of "keeping feet to the fire." Far more productive is *organic* discussion and debate, nurturing and exploring issues involved in meeting the targets and *then* becoming decisive. Mastering the human aspects and social dynamics in each of the phases makes all the difference in successfully bringing innovations to market. It is as true, if not more so, in the overlap as one phase moves to another, as different people come into the process and constructive dialogue and continuity of communication can break down.

Especially in the process of nurturing, the team learns more about how to deal with hurdles involving the consumer, the market, and technology. As a result, the original plan often changes. There is nothing wrong with that. It is the job of the boss to say yes, no, or keep exploring. The key is to monitor the team, to solve problems, to bring in help, to frame the issue in a way that suits the overall strategy.

This must be done formally, but most senior managers who are good at nurturing find moments for informal interaction too. It doesn't take much—five minutes here and there to ask: How are you doing? What is coming in your way? *The purpose is not control but communication.*

The innovation leader needs information, but not all of this comes in a way that can be measured. It's important to try to develop a demeanor that tells people you are open to hearing from them. Walk the halls; keep the door open; hang out by the coffee machine; initiate conversations; pick up the phone; take off the headphones in the company gym.

Nurturing, then, is both systematic and episodic. It draws on both business skills and highly developed personal skills. And it is absolutely essential to building an innovation culture. Nurturing innovation takes place on two levels—the idea and the team—at the same time. It requires creativity and imagination. It is a matter of testing assumptions and considering variables and thinking ahead. Nurturing innovation means dealing with unknown challenges and uncertainty; this is not the time to analyze a spreadsheet or calculate return on investment.

And yet it is not without discipline. Nurturing means making decisions, not just once but many times—about whether to do more experiments; whether to change the team leader or the team composition; whether to give more resources (or not). Discipline matters, but too much emphasis on numbers and metrics can squelch creativity and enthusiasm. Creativity does not end with idea generation. The skill is to probe in depth.

The process of nurturing is at the heart of the soft skill of orchestrating human interactions that is required of an innovation culture. Nurturing requires discipline and tenacity; the art is in being able to connect the ideas from people in different disciplines—and also to put them in perspective.

How well the team functions as a social unit and keeps the discipline of the end-to-end process has a direct bearing on its output. However, the effectiveness of the outcome of the team can be enhanced or detracted in the ways a business unit manager and his management group interfaces with a team leader and his team. The central mechanism for such interfacing is robust reviews as the team progresses. The architecture of the reviews—the support of the business unit manager and his group, their decisiveness, and the coaching they provide—is our next topic.

USING INNOVATION REVIEWS TO KEEP A WINNING STREAK GOING

Innovation reviews enable the right people to align and strengthen the innovation playbook of a business. The playbook outlines the game plan for how they are going to win with customers in upcoming seasons in the marketplace. These discussions allow the team to identify which plays and players are working well and winning, which need to be improved to provide advantage, and which aren't working and should be cut from the plan. Innovation reviews can be for a total business unit (for example, at P&G, the fabric-care category), for a brand or product line (for example, Tide laundry detergent), or for a specific innovation project (developing and introducing compact sizes of Tide). A performance review looks backward; an innovation review looks in both directions.

At P&G, it seems that innovation reviews are happening all the time. Every business unit has one among themselves on at least a quarterly basis; and every year, they present their innovation program to senior management. The CEO goes to all of these reviews—it signals how essential innovation is to sustain P&G's organic growth.

Like any team, it is important that everyone have a common understanding of the plans, an assessment of what the strengths are and what gaps must be closed. However, unlike a sports team, the focus of an innovation review is longer term—say three to five years or more. Managing an innovation program is like steering an ocean liner. Many of the innovation programs require extensive resources and longer time horizons that can't be redirected overnight.

This next section provides suggested "nuts and bolts" to get innovation reviews started in your business in an effective way.

THE ELEMENTS OF AN INNOVATION REVIEW

There is an important prerequisite before beginning any innovation review—the business team must have already completed the hard thinking in two areas: clearly defined business growth goals for a minimum of three to five years out; and clearly defined "where to play" choices or business strategies (see chapter 4). Only after these areas have been fleshed out will an innovation review be effective. That's because the business goals and strategies ground and integrate the innovation program into the business. P&G has learned that without this context, the review would turn into a discussion among people who have a lot of disconnected ideas and would tend to become technology-driven, not consumer-centric and not business-connected.

After the essential business goals and strategies are clarified, an effective innovation review addresses three primary questions:

1. How robust is my innovation portfolio? Will it deliver my three- to five-year business growth goals? The leader needs to determine if the plan sufficiently provides key innovation building blocks that will deliver the required business growth. Judgments need to be made if there is the right balance of risk in the innovation portfolio. This can be assessed first by understanding if you have a big idea. Analyze the data showing how customers (the boss) respond to the idea. Is the proof data-rich or based on people's opinions and experiences? Understand the degree to which the team knows how to make the product at a given stage in the project. Innovations that are already in hand, of course, have a higher degree of certainty. Assess the sufficiency of proprietary information protection by looking at which patents have been filed. Determine how well the plans leverage your core strengths and technologies to improve chances of success and identify what types of help may be needed from outside of the business unit. Ensure the innovation plans are concrete, not just for the next couple of years, but also three to five years out.

2. How strong is my innovation plan compared to key competition? Answering this question requires benchmarking. Forcing teams to look externally at what's happening in the marketplace enables them to ensure they are approaching the innovation in a way that creates advantage. Assess key competitors' where to play and how to win choices. Understand in what areas they are filing patents that may impact the team's freedom to innovate.

3. How attractive is my innovation program from a financial and return standpoint? Innovation that creates value for the customer creates differentiation against the competition and creates value for the business and the company. It should never result in margin dilution. Of course, within an innovation portfolio there's always a range of profit margins. Can the innovation be commercialized with a cost structure that enables the right balance between margin enhancement while also providing the customer a good value? Does the innovation portfolio as a whole provide a good return on investment? This assesses the potential investment attractiveness required for commercialization.

YOUR ROLE AS INNOVATION COACH

Like any sport, the head coach plays an important role. It is important the leader (aka "coach") approach an innovation review using a very different mind-set than when reviewing budgets or operating plans. Innovation reviews are conversations that involve a higher degree of uncertainty than the more analytic approach needed to review a budget forecast. Importantly, using the appropriate mind-set will actually influence the culture and how the organization perceives and approaches innovation.

In a nutshell, the leader should do three things:

• **Be honest.** It is important the leader provide his candid overall assessment of the innovation program against the three questions above to help the team come to grips with reality. A senior executive is able to see where there are gaps and deal with them. Are there areas of the program that seem overly optimistic? Is the team crystal clear about the consumer or customer target? Has the team underestimated the competition in some way? Is the program focused too much on small incremental innovations instead of disruptive game-changing opportunities? Does the team have the resources it needs—both human and financial? Are there some projects that should be stopped or that should be accelerated? The leader and team shouldn't try to solve the problems at the meeting, but rather come to closure on the specific action steps required.

• **Be helpful.** Based on the leader's experience and broader vantage point both in and outside of the company, he can provide the team unique perspective and access to resources. The leader should feel a sense of responsibility to make big ideas bigger instead of head nodding through the review. Asking questions like, "Have you considered this approach" or, "This reminds me of a similar experience in business X or industry Y" opens up the team's mind to consider new possibilities for the innovation. The leader also helps the team identify and address killer issues. This may look like directing the team to connect with another group that overcame similar challenges. Or, help may require understanding and delivering on specific resource needs (for example, access to resources with skills not available on the team, increased funding, etc.).

• **Foster a free-flowing yet frank conversation.** This is not a grilling, but a dialogue; the idea is not to call out people, but to explore, explain, and to move ideas forward. The tone should be probing but constructive. The point is not to find error but figure out ways to keep going forward. This approach also demonstrates that the leader recognizes that not everything goes as planned. This dynamic enables the team to get excited about innovation and stretches their ability to seek out bigger innovation opportunities that may involve more risk. If the review feels more like a win-or-lose discussion, the team will begin to approach innovation more conservatively. Ask, "What are the hurdles?" "What could you do if you had more resources?" "What other alternatives did you consider?" "What help do you need—either outside or inside of the business?"

At GE, for example, Jeff Immelt makes it clear to the presenters that he doesn't want a pitch, but to see how the team is molding the idea. He wants an actual prototype, if not physically during the review then virtually on the computer screen. He then probes and pushes the boundaries using the broad perspective he has developed from GE's operations around the world and meeting with customers from diverse industries. Pushing the boundaries enables those participating in the reviews to see things through a new lens. They have their imaginations "dialed up" and often reframe their ideas. At the same time, he can get the team to see the most critical issues, questions, and hurdles that need addressing if the project is to succeed.

It is the job of the leader to say yes, no, or keep exploring. As a coach during the review session, he encourages certain behaviors, boosts morale, and imparts priorities. By trying out and going into the lab, the leader not only shows interest, but he also emboldens people and deepens his own understanding. On high-risk projects, this can make a big difference. Perhaps the most important thing the leader can do is ensure that "consumer is boss" stays at the center of decision making.

COACHING YOUR FIRST SCIENCE FAIR

Attendance at an innovation review should be broad enough to be inclusive of key team members, yet small enough to enable a productive and candid conversation. The attendance also depends on the scope of the review. At P&G's business unit innovation reviews, the CEO, chief technology officer, chief financial officer, and chief supply chain officer attend. In addition, key leaders from the business unit and multifunctional members of the innovation team are present.

P&G "does" posters—yes, posters—as a way to conduct innovation reviews. This approach could hardly be more low-tech. If anything, it has the feel of a grade-school science fair. Each team creates a single poster that simply lays out the key idea and technology for the innovation, relevant consumer research data, the business potential, key timing and milestones, and the key issues the team is facing. Why posters? Because these reviews are often full of scientists, and the posters force the scientists to speak in terms that the senior management can understand. If they can understand it, so can the business units and, eventually, consumers. They also drive focus and simplicity—to distill the innovation to a simple set of ideas. The posters are placed on stands around the room, so the group is on its feet and gathers around a poster to have a thoughtful conversation. One or two people from the team go through the data, and add their own remarks. Often, the discussion also involves show-and-tell—where people get to touch and use a product or key technology element. The leader can begin a dialogue with the team to help assess the sufficiency of the innovation plans and identify where the most value can be added. Over a period of a few hours, the group can go through a dozen or so innovation projects.

The science-fair analogy may sound like Little League baseball, but is actually very apt. The poster conversations are used as coaching moments, to let people know what priorities are and how senior management thinks. And just by walking around the room and taking it all in, the senior team can make connections that go beyond the specific projects, seeing something in Technology A that may be applicable to Business B or seeing a process that is working in one place that really should be replicated globally. It is an open-ended process, but one with a sense of direction and inspiration.

INTEGRATING INNOVATION WITH
THE MAINSTREAM OF DECISION MAKING

Budgeting is an important influencer of all management decision making and behavior. Never far from a business unit manager's thinking, when reviewing innovation projects, are the goals—such as revenue growth and improving margins through innovation-driven differentiation—that need to be accomplished and what needs to be done with the innovation projects to help him achieve those goals. Innovation at the center results in managers "pulling" rather than "pushing" innovation projects. That is, in order to meet stretching goals, which can only be satisfied through innovation projects, they devote time and energy to actively search for innovation ideas, as was the case with Honeywell. They participated in green-lighting these projects, actively adding value to them, and managing risks. They, therefore, construct and manage budgets differently.

In contrast, "push" lacks a systemic process of linking together the process with the mainstream of decision making. In a push approach the generator of an idea tries to find a sponsor to fund it and politically push it forward. If and when the idea succeeds, such a person becomes a hero for his tenacity and perseverance. In essence that's what happened with 3M's Post-it notes. Don't get us wrong. Serendipity can result in breakthroughs, but they are unpredictable and sporadic. Our key point here and in this book is that innovation can result in sustained organic growth only through a systematic process. Constructing and operationalizing their annual and long-term budgets demands that business unit managers actively incorporate in their thinking and behavior the management of the process of innovation through robust review and reprioritizing when necessary.

Whether it is a shoe store, a corporate division, or an entire company, every organization has a budget or what some call an annual operating plan. All the rhetoric of innovation, of grand strategies, and big visions, culminates in reality in the budget. It is here where ideas get the resources they need to turn them into realities. The budget is how management makes choices between short and long term, low and high risk, productivity and growth.

Budgeting is where individuals and departments are assigned specific commitments over a specific period of time, such as quarterly earnings for a company, or X percent revenue growth for a division. At P&G, each business unit has to identify all the innovation programs of a certain size in the context of the budget and the business plan. If Business A is forecasting $1 billion in sales, it has to identify seven to ten innovations that are the primary building blocks. The business is also required to track where each innovation is in the process—going to market, in development, or being qualified. This is tracked over a period of three to five years.

Successful leaders have mostly made their names by making

bottom-line numbers. No question: These numbers matter. But it also matters *how* they are made, something a number alone cannot measure. It is possible, for example, to meet a target by deferring expenses and/or maintenance, cutting growth projects, or trimming everything by the same amount. These are all common strategies; none, however, is particularly healthy for corporate performance in general, or for innovation in particular. If you want to gauge the center of gravity of a business, go through the lens of how the budget is constructed, administered, and appraised.

Budgets for a business unit are usually extensive and detailed. Typically, there are one or two lines for revenues and hundreds for costs. Most do not account for innovation. The money is there somewhere, buried in the lines, but it can't be seen. A budget that looks like this, that has no clarity on where revenues will come from, betrays an obsession with cost that focuses the mentality of people inward. That is death to creating an innovative culture.

The better approach is to aggregate costs by innovation project—linking the cost for each with forecast of revenues and gross margin improvement. This should not be difficult. Almost all innovation projects are costed; the teams know how much they have to work with, and what the expectations are. Embedding this in the budget should be simple. But the effects of doing so are profound, building an innovation-related architecture that lets managers know what they have to do. It makes innovation part of mainstream decision making, integrating it into managerial behavior that drives everyday innovation. A company-wide innovation budget cannot exist if the constituent units do not have information; so one good effect is that an *innovation-centered budget* makes managers think in these terms, and then deliver them up the chain. For another, it makes the different silos—marketing, manufacturing, operations, etc.—cooperate to share information and come up with estimates of future performance. Acknowledge that certainty of those numbers increases as time frame shortens; that's OK but means numbers must be updated as projects progress.

A bare-bones budget of money in and out in a given year is a straightforward accounting. An innovation budget is aspirational.

So what happens when stuff happens, and there is demand in the short-term to meet profit targets? In that case, leaders have three choices: spend more money earlier in the year to get higher revenues later in the year; cut spending from innovation projects and meet the profit target; or do more aggressive productivity improvements and free up funds to continue innovation projects. The first and third options assume the leader has a little give. If times are really tight, though, and cutting spending from innovation projects is necessary, don't use the salami-slicer, trimming little bits from all of them. It is better to cut out the projects with the worst ratio of costs to projected revenue on a risk-adjusted basis and to maintain funding for the rest. This is more likely to keep momentum going. The 3×3 matrix described on page 197 should be helpful in this unfortunate situation.

THE INNOVATION-CENTERED BUDGET

An innovation budget defines not only what a company expects to earn in revenues from innovation—from now to as much as five years out—but how it plans to pay for those efforts. By making innovation a visible part of a budget, available for all to see, leadership is saying, loud and clear, "This company is serious." Like any other kind of budget, one that includes innovation needs to be audited, and then reviewed. If there is a line for $100 million in revenue growth from innovations in Business Unit X, and the following year it has delivered only $50 million, the gap must be noticed and addressed. Otherwise, it is just wasted ink—and a dishonest rendering of reality.

An innovation-centered budget that is transparent for all is an energizer. It builds trust that management is making the trade-offs between the short and long terms and building the future of the business. Repeatedly communicating the existence of the innovation budget and the architecture of the mix of innovation projects inspires employees to compete for the resources that will build the future. Better people are thus attracted and retained for longer periods of time. And, though there is a time lag, investors place a higher value on the company because real innovation is a differentiator. It also gives investors confidence.

ASK YOURSELF ON MONDAY MORNING

• Do you have a robust, regular cycle for business strategy and planning? Is the innovation strategy linked to the business strategy?

• Do you have a process for determining whether you have a revenue gap, and how it can be filled through the end-to-end process of innovation?

• Do you have clear definition of your needs in detail so that the search for ideas, whether internal or external, can be focused? Have you prioritized these needs?

• What is the reliable social process for selecting and green-lighting an idea, and what criteria are used?

• What is the process for selecting a team leader and team members that will nurture the idea to reality by moving it through its several phases?

• Do you have milestones and measurement tools similar to the online tracker?

• How are ideas vetted through prototyping, experimenting, and the go-to-market process?

• How good and consistent is the linkage of innovation to the mainstream of managerial decision making, especially the budgetary process?

• Do you have an innovation budget that is explicit and transparent?

• How are innovation initiatives linked to your unit's discipline of budgeting? Are budgets altered as conditions change?

• When projects are not on time or on budget, how robust is your reprioritization and resource reallocation?

• Are you using tools like the building block end-to-end process in an organic way, emphasizing the human aspects and social dynamics of the innovation process? Do you see how this human side of innovation can have huge implications for the outcome of an innovation project?

CHAPTER EIGHT

MANAGING THE RISKS
OF INNOVATION

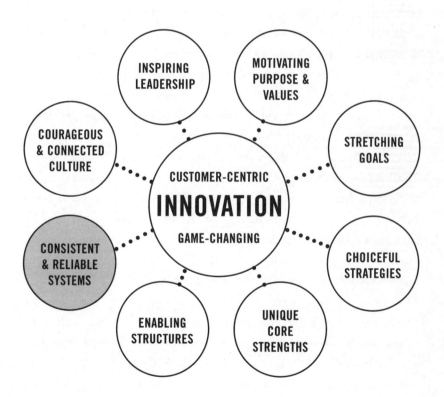

Is innovation risky?

Of course it is, but so is building a manufacturing plant or rolling out an advertising and marketing campaign for a product launch. The difference is that people have more experience managing operational, marketing, and financial risks. Financial risk is better understood than ever. Currency and commodity risk can be hedged. None of that exists for innovation, which is why so many people are afraid of it—or at least of tying their career to it.

We believe that innovation is really no different than any other business process. As P&G has demonstrated for the past several years, the yield from the process of innovation has risen from a 15–20 percent success rate to 50–60 percent; that means more revenues from innovation at lower rate of investment. The LEGO Group, as we will show later in this chapter, has a similar record.

The risks inherent in innovation are manageable, and they can be reduced as people learn from their experiences. Still, innovation is different because it is so much more dependent on unquantifiable human factors. Consumers may not tell you what they want or what they really do; it's not that they are lying, they honestly don't know. That was probably the case with Fit, an all-natural fruit and vegetable wash P&G launched several years ago. They thought it was a good concept that suited people's desires for cleanliness and natural ingredients; the product, the packaging, and the brand name were all tested. Consumers said repeatedly and with apparent enthusiasm that they wanted the product, liked it, and would use it.

When Fit went to market, it flopped. Three times. That's because P&G didn't take the time to understand how to communicate to consumers the behavior change that was required to use the product. Old habits die hard. After losing something like $50 million, it was sold to a group of venture capitalists; maybe they can make it work. P&G took a risk and failed, expensively.

A perfect success rate is not possible, or even desirable, when it comes to innovation. Not only is taking chances part of the fun of doing business, but an innovation record that lacks failure is probably pretty dull. A success rate of 50 to 60 percent is about as high as P&G wants to go; much more, and it would be a sign of playing it too safe. It is not possible to manage all the risk out of innovation; it is possible to mitigate it, and to improve over time. The loser's game is to be so fearful that you never get started. And to those who think that they can simply buy the innovation they need, think again.

Believe it or not, there is actually a museum in Ithaca, New York, named the Museum of Failed Products that is home to more than sixty-five thousand different brands and products that have failed in the marketplace—from peanut butter to deodorants to cigarettes. Robert McMath, museum curator, has kept himself busy collecting failed products for nearly four decades.

WHAT CAUSES INNOVATION RISK?

Innovation is riskier than it needs to be because of lousy social mechanisms—the gulfs between silos that separate ideas and the lack or underuse of linking mechanisms that keep people from connecting these ideas.

One gulf separates technology people, who produce and shape ideas, from the upstream marketing people who do segmentation and study consumer behavior. A second exists between those who produce final prototypes of an innovation and the commercialization people who have to take it to the first moment of truth. Eliminating these gulfs and creating *simultaneous interactions among experts* for making the right trade-offs—through a smooth functioning integrated process of innovation—reduces risk and expands the opportunity.

It is up to the business unit leader to understand the reasons for the gulf and to keep the marketing, technology, and commercialization people reading off the same page. Teams and reviewers must be psychologically inclined to confront reality when an innovation project fails to meet its milestones. In most technology-push situations, technology people, because of their narrow area of specialization, are driven to advance their cause and get funded. The reason is both simple and practical: Failure to get a project funded can have a huge adverse effect on a person's career.

These problems can be overcome if business unit leaders and team leaders develop the skills and willpower to make the right trade-offs and to have interactions and dialogue that are candid, creative, and practical. By doing so, they start moving in the right direction to overcome the traditional jealousies and loyalties among people that keep ideas alive long past the date they should have been killed.

Many believe that innovation fails either because the technological breakthroughs couldn't be made or because the product would be too expensive to produce and thus not affordable by the consumer. Our observation is that in most cases these are not the main reasons for failure. The cause more often lies in ineffective interaction between experts, team members, and team leaders. It can be fixed through well-designed social mechanisms and effective leadership. Here are some leading reasons for innovation failure.

• Disruptive and incremental innovation projects get the wrong leaders assigned to them. A leader of a disruptive innovation project led by a person who is an incremental thinker, or vice versa, will often fail.

• The consumer is boss is not an integral element from prototyping of the idea through commercialization. All too often, a concept moves from idea to functioning prototype with a technical focus; then it is "thrown over the wall" to the second process, called commercialization, where market considerations are introduced.

• Leaders are appointed on the basis of their domain expertise, rather than their ability to inspire, direct, and lead a group of high-powered, imaginative thinkers to fruitful outcomes.

• Despite competent leadership of a team working on an innovation project, team dynamics are dysfunctional or corrosive because certain personalities are unable to work together.

• Real considerations of commercialization, such as design, requirements of retailers, price points, cost factors, scarcity of materials needed for production, and operational capability are not factored into the functioning prototype.

• Upper management interferes with team functioning behind the scenes, or refuses to collaborate when expert resources are needed to make the breakthrough necessary to move forward.

• Business unit managers lack the skills to conduct reviews of innovation projects, skills that differ from those needed to conduct operational reviews. Those skills include decisiveness in killing projects early; the willingness to reprioritize as projects do not meet milestones; pressing to define the killer points of failure early in a project; not letting teams avoid dealing with problems until later project stages; not dealing with team members or a team leader who aren't working out as the project moves forward.

• There are too many ideas and too many projects in the pipeline relative to the managerial and professional skills and financial resources. For example, products are developed without the necessary go-to-market capability or availability of funding.

• Lack of clearly defined success criteria and/or arbitrarily passing through decision gates without meeting criteria.

• Not identifying/addressing the right or most important killer issues as early as possible in the innovation process.

• Poor or nonexistant connection of the innovation project with revenue goals.

While all of the above can be under the control of management, the following three problems are outside that control and also lead to failure. Management needs to recognize them early and either find a solution or cut their losses.

• Uncontrollable external factors, such as recession, currency volatility, or the rise of an unexpected competitor, make an innovation economically unviable.

• The required breakthroughs don't happen. The prototype may work and the customer likes it, but a breakthrough in the manufacturing process, such as meeting special tolerances and scaling to meet cost requirements, doesn't happen. Companies win when a new technical development and the ability to make the product in a cost-effective way happen simultaneously.

• A competitor takes your idea. Other companies can neutralize your ability to differentiate a product by copying your product's physical design, positioning, and delivery. Some companies will even steal your patents.

Remember that *minimizing* risk will almost certainly squelch innovation. With that in mind, here are eight ways for the leader of innovation to anticipate the risks of innovation and lead the team in managing them.

1. Know your customer.
2. Do prototyping.
3. Do rigorous consumer testing.
4. Manage the portfolio of innovation projects.
5. Be open to experimenting.
6. Identify the killer issues early.

7. Learn from the past.
8. Use metrics to measure innovation.

KNOW YOUR CUSTOMER

Keeping the customer at the center of things requires the members of an innovation team to have the timing and footwork of a dance troupe, lest they trip all over one another.

One frequently underestimated risk is that consumers and developers see new products differently. Developers can become too product-centric and say, in effect, here's a really cool new toy. Consumers frequently respond with a yawn. Why bother? What we have is good enough. For companies, the key is to identify where each innovation is on the scale, and invest accordingly, in both time and money.

The clearer, the more precise, and the more accurate is the definition of consumer need—and its incorporation into the entire process of innovation—the higher the ratio of success. All too often, technology or passion has pushed an idea into the market that consumers just didn't want—consider the relaunch of the Ford Thunderbird or the late, unlamented C2 (a low-calorie Coke) in the United States.

Knowing the consumer is a way to spot mistakes earlier. P&G had a great idea for a new product: Tide with a Touch of Downy. It figured out the chemistry—no easy thing—then tested the concept. It got a good reception, and P&G went ahead and designed the bottle— Downy blue, with the distinctive Tide target logo and an orange cap, combining the strongest visual elements of the two brands. Confident that it was an appealing model, shoppers were brought to the retail lab and asked to shop for household products. Sure enough, they picked up the bottle—the first moment of truth. A good start. Then, seeing the distinctive blue, they put it down again. Out of twenty shoppers, all twenty thought it was a fabric softener that Tide was endorsing— and they were looking for a laundry detergent. That was more than enough to say enough. Going to market with that design meant Tide with Downy would bomb. By taking the time to learn from the bosses, months and millions were saved while increasing the chance of success. When Tide with Downy did launch—in an orange container with a Downy blue top—it worked.

Such experimentation with consumer behavior is still a relatively new idea; it feels like common sense, but it is an uncommon practice. Skipping it creates unnecessary risks. Focus groups, of course, have been used for decades; they can be useful in getting a broad feel for what consumers do or do not want.

Gillette, for example, had a fascinating experience with a consumers group when the company was considering launching what became Mach3, a three-bladed razor. In a classic misalignment, the tech guys were thrilled—the thing shaves like crazy, they reported. The marketing folks were not at all thrilled—after the triumph of the Sensor, just adding another blade didn't seem like much. And they could prove it; at one early consumer shaving experience, the men actually laughed at the crude prototype (nicknamed "Frankenstein" because of its unsightly bolts). They ridiculed the big bold idea of three blades: "Is this all you can come up with?"

Mary Ann Pesce, who managed the project, realized that not enough was known about the customer. She then did something unusual, checking the transcripts of the tapes. And what she found shocked her. Some of the "verbatims," as they are known, were positively lyrical: "Like skating on a fresh sheet of ice," said one. "It moves like a hot knife through butter," said another. She realized that Gillette had gone the wrong way around, emphasizing the three-blade technology, which no one (other than the lab guys) gave a damn about. Once Gillette reoriented the message around performance—the closest shave ever, with less irritation—everything fell into place. "The key moment was when we stopped obsessing over the technologies and thought about what it did," says Pesce. "It was listening to the guys, with my face pressed against a one-way mirror for the better part of a year, that made the difference."

This is an example of the shrewd use of consumer immersion. Still, there is no substitute for actually walking with shoppers through a market, as P&G did for Tide with Downy, or watching and observing them use a prototype. When it comes to making a launch, consumers are the deciding factors.

DO PROTOTYPING

Prototyping is a required practice in the process of innovation. It instills the idea that the journey is going to be difficult, and that hitting dead ends is not only acceptable, but expected. The essence of prototyping is try and try again, iterate and reiterate. The key is not to seek perfection at any single step, but, through trial and error, to get a little improvement all along the way. Learn; get closer; learn more; get a little closer. And continually build on the insights of the user.

James Dyson counted 5,127 iterations of his eponymous bagless vacuum cleaner before he was satisfied, selling his first machine in 1986. Does that mean Dyson failed 5,126 times? Of course not. A project is not a failure until it is killed. Until then, any disappointment is trial and error. Every iteration produces insights. Capturing these insights cumulatively builds muscle for successful innovation. Prototyping is the process of finding mistakes, and of adding value, so don't worry about perfection; at this stage, speed is more important than polish.

The key is to get the ideas out there in tangible form; the more people are comfortable with this show-and-tell, the more ideas they will generate, which is the point. For services, the equivalent of prototyping is doing pilots. Bank of America, for example, has used specific bank branches in Atlanta to test service innovations. McDonald's has a customer experience studio—basically, a warehouse with pretensions—so that it can see firsthand how diners react to a new experience. "Anyone developing new products and new technology," Dyson once said, "needs one characteristic above all else: hope." Relentless prototyping gives form to hope.

The first step, then, is to know the questions that need to be answered: for whom, at what price and cost, and at what desired volume. With Mr. Clean MagicReach, P&G wanted a world-class cleaning tool, but was not interested in one that cost $500, but one that retails for about $12.99.

During prototyping, the team for technical or marketing reasons may discover a different target. It needs to be open to that without giving up on the original idea at the first glitch.

Second, there needs to be a very clear sense of where the perceived competitive differentiation is. *If there is no differentiation, there is no innovation.*

Third, you need to show the prototype to real people, and listen to what they say. It's human nature for the maker of a lovely something, even at a very early stage, to be proud of it and want to see it accepted. There can be a subtle pushing of the consumer by the tester to seek approval of the idea.

DO RIGOROUS CONSUMER TESTING

Learning about customer needs and habits is important, but it is not enough. Putting customers through a pre-market simulation of purchase and the usage of the product, either face-to-face or virtually, provides a source of knowledge. It helps you decide whether to commercialize, if the timing is right, whether the offering needs more tweaking, or not to proceed at all.

Let's say P&G is testing a new kind of fabric softener. The team might describe ten different kinds, and ask how likely a consumer is to purchase it in favor of all others—yes, no, or maybe. What if the price changed? Do you like this benefit? P&G always does this in relation to other products on the market. From running such tests, it can see where it is in relation to the competition. If the result is better than most of the competition, that is usually reason enough to keep going.

P&G can also isolate what is driving purchase intent—the name of the product, the price, the taste, the packaging, whatever. Consumers aren't asked whether they like the product; that doesn't give us a useful answer. Instead, they are asked whether they are definitely, probably, neutral, probably not, or definitely not likely to buy it. Having even metaphorical skin in the game makes for better answers. To test this further, transaction tests are used, running consumers through a simulated store for up to twenty-six weeks. Even packaging effectiveness can be measured, by assessing how and where shoppers' eyes look at products on the store shelf. Putting it all together, these tests help P&G refine the product offering; it won't go to market with a product that isn't meaningfully better than the competition.

Marico, an Indian consumer products company, has that country's second-largest distributor/retail network. Through its three-pronged method for knowing the consumer it has been able to create new adjacent segments for growth, and it is beating its very large multinational competitors. Its deep exploration of consumer behavior has improved its success rate:

• First, after having decided what category and segment it wants to pursue, it observes the targeted consumer.

• Second, Marico observes their chosen consumers buying various products in different segments. Observing the same consumer buying in different segments helps Marico get better insight about consumer behavior. For example, a well-off consumer buying an expensive perfume could also buy an expensive Mountblanc pen, thus reinforcing her personal image. Such information is useful to Marico in gaining further insight for such a consumer segment.

• Third, in countries like India there are third parties that influence the buying behaviors and the choices that consumers make. Marico observes these third parties in action and obtains additional information. For example, barbers have heavy influence regarding hair-care products.

By factoring in multiple ways of looking at the consumer in developing and commercializing the products, Marico better understands their habits of consumers and repeat purchase patterns. The consumer as the boss is thus an ingrained part of the way Marico operates. It is winning, because unlike many of its competitors, it is not pushing products, but rather pulling in consumers.

MANAGE THE PORTFOLIO
OF INNOVATION PROJECTS

Business unit leaders need to continually reprioritize and rebalance the portfolio of innovation projects to reallocate resources, including killing some projects when appropriate. Here are the questions to ask.

• Are there a sufficient number of projects to meet your business and financial goals or is there a gap?

• How good is the balance among the projects in the portfolio with regard to short term/long term and low risk/high risk?

• Are you doing the "peanut butter spread"? When a project doesn't come in on time and on budget, as is usually the case, there are three decisions to make: provide more funding; delay it; kill it. In most cases, small incremental funding is given, often borrowed from other projects.

Place your innovaton projects in a 3×3 matrix, as on page 197. Risk and reward are on the vertical line; time is on the horizontal.

The result is a nine-box square. The definition of *high risk* depends on the context. If losing the bet means "betting the ranch," it is a big risk; that is, if the project doesn't come to fruition, the whole business is endangered. Low-risk bets are those you can lose—and, in fact, you can expect to lose a few and be able to shrug them off.

Ask these questions about innovations in your pipeline that are placed on the matrix:

• What kind of balance do you need to achieve your goals? And does this portfolio have the potential to deliver? P&G looks at least

TIME HORIZON

	Short Term 1–2 Years	Medium Term 3–5 Years	Long Term 6+ Years
Low Risk / Low Reward			
Medium Risk / Medium Reward			
High Risk / High Reward			

RISK AND REWARDS

five years down the line. By comparing how much the projected innovations in the portfolio are expected to bring in against the goals for revenue and value creation, you can see if there is an "innovation gap," either absolute or related to specific goals such as reaching low-income consumers in developing markets. One year P&G was 1 to 2 percent short. That wasn't good news, but there were options—accelerate the timetable for projects already in the pipeline, scaling them up or adding new ones.

• Will it deliver innovation for the most important drivers of revenues and margins, such as P&G's biggest brands? If not, then they will be vulnerable to competitive attack. For example, it's not good for P&G if all the innovation in the diaper category comes from Luvs, and Pampers is stagnant.

• What is the balance between disruptive and incremental innovation? If the portfolio is heavily tilted on disruptive innovations, you could miss big if a few of them are duds.

• Does the portfolio have the right time balance? If the portfolio is heavily weighted in one or two years, you may lose momentum.

• Does the mix of high-risk and low-risk projects match the ability of the business to sustain the risk?

• Are you putting the right mix and right level of resources and people into each of these innovation initiatives? Or are you "sprinkling the desert with a teaspoon"? The people and resources necessary for high-risk/high-reward projects are qualitatively different from the ones needed for those that are low risk/low reward.

An innovation portfolio is not unlike a financial portfolio—think diversification and balance.

BE OPEN TO EXPERIMENTING

Experimenting is part and parcel of the innovation process. One example of making experimentation a routine is P&G's creation of an off-site laboratory to give intense attention to a specific idea, to allow people to test it out before taking it further. This is the Innovation Gym, which runs along lines that are similar to that of Clay Street (see chapter 9), but for much shorter periods—typically, three days or less. P&G worked with IDEO, adopting their principles to create this 10,000-square-foot gym, housed in two warehouse buildings outside Cincinnati. Among the principles: Create a dedicated space; have lots of wall space for sketches, posters, and random acts of innovation; stock the place with lots of creative tools, such as toys and colored paper; and provide teams with a skilled facilitator to guide them through the innovation process.

John Cheng, manager of the Innovation Gym, believes that P&G was too slow in the 1980s. Multiyear test markets were not uncommon, a lugubrious pace that now seems almost funny. In the 1990s, it was too diffuse, funneling too many ideas (not all of them high quality) through the product development system. "In the early 2000s, we realized we needed processes and systems for idea development," Cheng says. "How does the Gym help? If designed correctly, the process brings most stakeholders and key decision makers together in one room. Things happen *fast,* and if the results are poor, people feel confident that it is time to move on."

A business unit contacts the Gym with a problem it wants to explore intensively; the unit pays for the Gym's services, less than if contracted to an outsider, but enough to ensure that the facility covers its cost and delivers value. The problem may be in packaging, say, or refining an idea or deciding which five of twenty ideas to pursue. The home-care team, for example, wanted to think about a new floor-cleaning product; after two days of workshops and prototyping, they thought they had the answer. The only problem was that it looked like a knockoff of a competitor's product; they realized it was not going to work and went back and rethought all their assumptions—a process that ultimately resulted in a line extension for Swiffer.

Before a team even steps into the Gym, they meet with one of P&G's expert facilitators who designs a session to match the desired outcomes. Then the team seeks out sources of inspiration, often in the form of consumers, customers, or competitors. On entering the Gym, the team shares their inspiration. Then, led by the facilitator, they use whiteboards to start spraying out ideas. The ideas get grouped into themes. The team then "power dots" the themes, voting for which ones seem most pertinent to the problem at hand. Then they break into smaller groups and go to a large space used for prototyping. It's equipped with materials to develop prototypes and includes everything from fabric to hula hoops. Then consumers are brought in to look at the prototypes and concepts and the groups get instant feedback. The whole team meets again and the groups debrief each other. At this point, says Brice Westring, Gym operations manager, "the teams quickly understand that what seemed like a winning proposition on paper might be a dog." Before the Gym was created, it would take a year or more for a team to learn they had a bad proposition. Now they can learn this in a matter of days. The good news is there are almost always one or two great ideas that come out of this process and are the impetus for a great product, like a Swiffer line extension or Olay Ribbons body wash.

There are two advantages to doing this sort of experimentation outside the business units. First, the seven staffers who run the place, all longtime P&Gers, have skills unique to the process because they have seen hundreds of groups cycle through, and have a broad knowledge of the company. They have built, through experimentation, benchmarking, and experience, different modules to meet the needs of a range of innovation challenges from driving trials, to product and package innovation, to franchise innovation strategies. If there is a learning curve in building manufacturing excellence, that is also one for building innovation excellence.

And second, being even a few miles away from their day-to-day environment can help loosen people up and make them less likely to be interrupted. "If you ideate in the same space as you work in," Westring concludes, "you are going to come up with the same solutions." The Gym helps P&G identify good (and bad) ideas earlier, saving time and resources.

P&G has also significantly increased its use of computer-aided engineering (CAE), computational modeling, and simulation to test ideas. It used to use CAE to improve production and manufacturing; now it is applying CAE to everything it can think of—formulas, materials strength, raw material selection. The idea is to "explore digitally and validate physically," as one P&G engineer put it.

Shifting more R&D into the virtual world reduces development times by months and maybe years. There is a positive dimension to this, too, enhancing creativity and allowing P&G to explore more options. But one of its most important functions is essentially negative: It allows P&G to fail much, much faster.

One of the star features at the Beckett Ridge Innovation Center is the Virtual Wall. This is an eight-by-sixteen-foot wall, on which images from twenty-four projectors can be displayed. P&G adapted the idea after a visit to DreamWorks; it wanted to do something with digital imagery, but this was, of course, hardly its expertise. Working with the University of Aachen—Connect and Develop again—P&G ended up with something akin to what oil companies use for seismic imagery. What had to be done with it, though, was project packaging—from shelves to categories to a whole store.

There is video that can connect to remote tech centers around the world, so that people can call in questions. At a few touches of the button, the shelves can be realigned. The P&G team can run shoppers through many more iterations than if they had to drive them from store to store, assuming they could even find what they wanted. Fifteen minutes on the wall can replace months of dithering. Failed ideas get nuked much faster; good ones are accelerated.

Once P&G brought in executives from Iams, the pet-food division, to evaluate some packaging. The team did the usual—projecting pet-food aisles from different stores, and bringing in shoppers to make their picks. It didn't take long for the Iams folks to realize their concept was not working: Shoppers kept choosing the competition. That kind of understanding would have been very expensive if the team had launched and waited for the product to fail before realizing the need to change it.

P&G's Envision Center takes the Virtual Wall to another dimension. It's a paneled wall eight feet high and thirty feet long; the panels can be moved to create a three-walled cave. Through this, P&G can project the top ten stores of its top retailers. With goggles, gloves, and a virtual reality device, it is possible to navigate through the aisles (or above them), testing new concepts and store environments, flipping through the wrong ideas on the way to finding the right one.

IDENTIFY THE KILLER ISSUES EARLY

Ted Williams once said that hitting a baseball was the most difficult single act in sports—and in his best year, he failed six out of ten times. Like laying off a bad pitch, killing ideas is an essential part of raising the corporate batting average. The failure rate for new products starts at 40 percent, and may be as high as 90 percent, depending on who is doing the study and how. Quickly cutting off projects that will not succeed in the marketplace helps to focus time and energy, and frees up scarce expert resources and money for those that have a better chance.

People hesitate to kill projects for two reasons. First, anxiety. Am I killing something that might be big? There are always a few examples of how someone persisted for years in his quest, and finally succeeded. But persistence alone does not explain the success. In almost all cases, the project succeeded because it was reframed, or there was an external technological breakthrough that facilitated it, or the timing became propitious. Second, the leader does not want to challenge or say "no" to a person with a great track record who is passionate about a project.

Once a team has identified a possible product, the natural tendency is to want it to succeed. This creates a prejudice in favor of going forward, rather than a hardheaded reckoning of whether it should. And the team can further tilt the analysis by addressing the easy problems first, and leaving the tough ones for later. P&G has flipped this sequence. Teams must identify so-called "killer issues"—problems that must be solved for the innovation to succeed. They have to try to solve the toughest problems first, to clear the highest hurdles early. P&G calls this "doing the last experiment first." This is an important best practice, because it not only conserves and focuses scarce human and financial resources, but also forces the innovation team and team leader to come to grips with the nature of the particular innovation challenge.

In consumer household and personal-care brands and products, P&G encounters a wide range of "killer issues." A series of questions can bring these to the surface.

• Is there a market? Will (enough) consumers buy and use the innovative new brand or product?

• Is the new product or technology feasible? Can you really make it in commercial quantities?

• Will the new innovation be affordable? Is it a good consumer value, or better than the alternative? Can you get the capital cost and/or the cost of goods down?

• To be successful, will there have to be a change in consumer habits? Can you change them?

• To be successful, will you have to create new channels of distribution? Can you do this?

It takes someone with both authority and emotional distance to accept the answers and to kill a project. There is almost never enough money to fund everything; a senior manager is in a better position to evaluate the portfolio and prioritize who gets how much. Undoubtedly, some less-important, less-promising projects will end up dead.

Culling needs to be a continuous process—a minimum of four times a year, so the pipeline stays clean. Killing a project can be devastating to the morale of team members, who tend to argue that a solution is just around the corner. This is why it is critical that people know that a specific failure is not a general judgment on their capabilities. And remember, draining resources on a no-hope idea also hurts morale.

"If you want to succeed, double your failure rate," IBM's Tom Watson advised. "Fail often to succeed sooner" is the mantra of IDEO. It's tough advice to take. No company, and certainly no manager with an eye on the next rung of the ladder, wants to take ownership of a failure. But there is such a thing as a smart failure, or a failure that works. Companies will not find creative people, however, if they are bent on punishing or deterring failure. A corporate culture is a living thing; it will not breathe if employees are holding their breath in fear.

LEARN FROM THE PAST

Enthusiastic chatter in the coffee room is a good thing, but a truly innovative company has to be a little more organized than that. There can be no innovation culture if every project is a one-off event, unique unto itself and cut off from the rest of the company. Knowledge is too important to be hoarded. Companies need to make conscious efforts to build the social networks that spread knowledge and experience using tools such as an in-house intranet. Jeff Immelt of GE uses day-long webcasts to discuss what is working and not working with the company's eighty Imagination Breakthrough projects. The people actually working on these projects are an integral part of the webcast. With the webcast, Immelt reaches all employees with the learning that is taking place and the message that the leadership values both successes and failures. He is transparent and candid about the latter. Everyone gets his point of view without the filtering of intermediate layers of management.

After every innovation project—successful or not—the team leader should be required to write, and the selection group to review, a post-mortem (or, if that term is too depressing, an after-action review) of what went wrong (or right) and how. Toyota has been doing this for decades; it calls it *hansei*, or reflection, and has *hansei* meetings after every major initiative. Toyota not only explores why something succeeded, but also what could have been done better. If a team has succeeded far beyond expectations, for example, it is asked to figure out why it didn't grasp its potential in the first place. Failures, naturally, get a detailed grilling.

In these reviews, work backward from process to decisions, assumptions, resources, and quality of the team; only then should the culpability of people and their judgments be considered.

In this analysis you need to assess: Was it carelessness of the individuals, temperament, lack of inclusion or imagination, or a know-it-all pride that led to failure? These are flaws that must be addressed and sometimes punished. On the other hand, if these were not the problem, did the team and leader learn anything from the experience that will enable them to do better next time?

After-action reviews should be a narrative, with an emphasis on cause and effect. They should be short (length is often a form of obfuscation). Then they should be made accessible for consultation. The usefulness of this database for an innovation review committee, for example, should be obvious.

The risk of the after-action review is clear; it's a golden opportunity for blame and self-aggrandizement. But that is not a reason to forego it. To some extent, you have to trust your people; having other members of the team see the report, and having a business leader be required to sign it, can help to ensure intellectual honesty and decent behavior. Moreover, the tone of the report should be analytical, not personal. The discipline is important. For big successes, figure out how you did it; for failures, figure out how to avoid doing it again.

This is tricky stuff, but then if the U.S. military can do after-action reviews—as it has since World War II—it's hard to argue that it's too difficult for any company to do them. Learning from the past is crucial to improving over time—and therefore an important link in the process of continuous innovation. Typically, this after-innovation report (or AIR) should be done either when a project is killed (of which more later), or when it reaches (or fails to reach) the first milestone established for it.

What should such a report contain?

• A description of the outcome of the project, with reference to its goals.

• An analysis of the major causes responsible for the outcome. Did we do the right research? Did we have the right team? The

205

right technology? Sufficient resources? Did we choose the right goals and stick to them?

• A definition of the unexpected effects.

• A consideration of what might have been done differently to get a better result.

• An explanation of the lessons learned.

Remember: It's not personal; it's business. Discourage the mention of people by name, in other than a positive manner.

Compiling this database needs to be systematic, with a common method of recording events; it must also be comprehensive and include both successes and failures. By making this routine, a company can take a lot of the sting out of it. A successful database is not one that is chock-full of success stories, but one that is intellectually honest. The company that does not learn from its past may or may not repeat it—but why take the chance?

Organizations are more than happy to learn from success, but failure is often far-more instructive. Under Jack Welch, GE had a rule that at quarterly management meetings, everyone had to bring one idea that could be reapplied to other businesses. That seemed like an excellent idea for meetings at P&G, and there was certainly no problem getting the presidents to bring in something that succeeded. These meetings were getting a little boring. As Tolstoy said, all happy families are alike; unhappy families have their own stories. People needed to hear some of those stories. Even after they were asked to bring in one story of something that failed, people wanted to bring in one more success. It's human nature, and it has to be resisted if you are to create a social process that comes to grips with the reality that, well, stuff happens.

Failure is not so much the opposite of success as part of a successful innovation process if you learn from it. Toyota knows this. Its Toyopet

Crown, a 1950s sedan, had been a hit in Japan, so when Toyota saw an opportunity in the United States, it confidently shipped off the Crown to foreign shores. The Crown debuted in California in 1956, with the goal of becoming the second car of choice for American families. Instead, it became a joke; the Crown was too cramped for bigger American bodies, and it shivered at highway speeds. Toyota fled the U.S. market and did not return for eight years.

By any standard, the Toyopet was a failure, even a humiliation. We doubt that the managers involved in its export were proud of themselves or got any awards. But what matters more is how Toyota reacted. It reviewed what went wrong and learned from it. "That glaring failure," writes Matthew May in *The Elegant Solution*, "became a driving force behind Toyota's newfound respect for systems. Toyota leaders at all levels vowed never again to design and market another product in a vacuum."

A company, a team, a leader, or an individual who can accept and learn from failure is going to be more creative—and happier—than an equivocator who avoids risk lest something go wrong because something will always go wrong. In every P&G innovation since 2000, there has been at least one glitch. No one in the feminine care unit will forget having to haul in workers over Memorial Day weekend to hand-pack Tampax Pearl because the carton machine wasn't working, and a last-minute change in price meant needing thousands more displays.

While in the case of Tampax Pearl, P&G was able to make the right last-minute interventions to save the launch of the innovation, it has also launched a number of innovations that have eventually failed in the marketplace. However, each has taught new lessons that help develop experienced judgment that can be applied to new innovation projects.

Accepting the inevitability of failure does not mean that leaders should sit back and wait for it. Rather the opposite. For one thing, some failures cannot be tolerated—a contaminated food product, for example, or a faulty jet engine. Factories must be safe; accounting precise. It is the job of management to ensure that everyone knows where failure can and cannot be accepted.

In the realm of the acceptable, the benefits emerge only when the failure is recognized earlier rather than later, and the reasons for it are learned, absorbed, and passed on. Though it may seem counterintuitive, an innovation process that embraces failure requires more management, rather than less. One of the reasons for an end-to-end flow process (see chapter 7) is to ensure that projects get the right attention at the right time. Executing such a process sometimes means executing—in its other sense—projects that don't quite work. For those who have invested their best efforts, this can feel a lot like failure; in fact, it is the process working the way it should.

Great leaders of innovation are able to talk openly about an innovation failure. For example, Howard Schultz, founder and CEO of Starbucks, keeps a copy of the ill-fated (and unmissed) *Joe* magazine in his office. This attempt to extend the Starbucks brand into publishing failed miserably, and was, by all accounts, no great loss to literature. But Schultz keeps it out there for all to see. What kind of impression do you think that makes when someone comes into his office with a new idea to present or a mistake to 'fess up to?

Jeff Immelt even wrote an article for *BusinessWeek* in July 2006, called "My Favorite Mistake." His error, which cost around $20 million, was going ahead in 1992 with an inadequate plastic product called Nuvel. "I let the need for speed overwhelm doing enough upfront market research and testing" was his diagnosis. And his cure: "It made me learn about listening better. I'm more disciplined on the upfront stuff now than I was then."

Google all but brags that it is going to blow money on things that will never work; here is an excerpt from its April 2004 IPO prospectus.

We will not shy away from high-risk, high-reward projects because of short-term earnings pressure. Some of our past bets have gone extraordinarily well, and others have not. Because we recognize the pursuit of such projects as the key to our long-term success, we will continue to seek them out. For example, we would fund projects that have a 10 percent chance if we place smaller bets in areas that seem very speculative or even strange.

A. G. LAFLEY'S 11 BIGGEST INNOVATION "FAILURES"		
BRAND	**IN MARKET EXPERIENCE**	**KEY LEARNING**
1. Fit Fruit and Vegetable Wash	Still in market, owned by another company	Required significant consumer habit change
2. Dryel At-Home Dry-Cleaning Kit	Still in market, owned by another company (for niche audiences)	Required significant consumer habit change
3. Oxydol Laundry Detergent	Still in market, owned by another company	Bad/small idea
4. Lemon Dash Laundry Detergent	$75+ million in retail sales for P&G, discontinued	Good idea. No difference vs. other detergents
5. Bold 3 Laundry Detergent	Discontinued	Small idea
6. Solo Laundry Detergent	Discontinued	Small idea
7. Olay Cosmetics	$100 million in retail sales for P&G, discontinued	Didn't do the right consumer testing before launch
8. Physique Hair Care	$100 million in Year 1 retail sales, discontinued	Didn't sustain brand differentiation vs.competition
9. Vidal Sassoon Hair Care	$50+ million in retail sales, discontinued in U.S., business still strong in Asia	Didn't do the right consumer testing before launch
10. Torengo's Salted Snacks	Discontinued	Competitive walled city
11. Tempo Tissues	Discontinued	Small idea

As the ratio of reward to risk increases, we will accept projects further outside our normal areas, especially when the initial investment is small. . . . Most risky projects fizzle, often teaching us something. Others succeed and become attractive businesses.

Companies that really want to show their commitment to innovation, and fearlessness when it comes to failure, can promote someone whose project failed—and make the promotion totally transparent. The skill here is to demonstrate the award is based on the leadership's assessment of how well the project was done based on how well it could have been done. Good innovation leaders are hard to find; they need to be preserved, protected, and promoted. The only reason to punish someone because an innovation project failed is carelessness or laziness. Actions, such as promotions, speak louder than any webcast from the top about how committed the company is to rewarding risk taking.

The talented people in P&G's feminine care, one of P&G's stars, have a lot to celebrate. But for the past several years, Melanie Healey, as part of the FemCare Delight Awards (known, naturally, as the "Femmies") presents the President's Fail Forward Award to the "team or individual that enabled the organization to significantly learn from a failure and as a consequence enables a future project or team to move forward much faster and/or better." The recipient—under the circumstances, one hesitates to say "winner"—could hardly be more exposed. Is this really the right way to run a business?

Yes—emphatically so. It's easy (and necessary) to celebrate success. And while it may feel unnatural to do the same with failure, a company that is interested in innovation has to get used to the idea that not everything is going to work. *Fortune* magazine recently told the story of a manager at Google who realized that she made a multimillion-dollar mistake. She told CEO Eric Schmidt about it—and was sent off with a pat on her back: Better to try and fail, she was told, than not to try. (But please, let's not make a habit of it.) "Somebody has to be on the team that fails," explains Gail Fogg, marketing director for global feminine care "and they have to understand that they are not going to get their heads chopped off."

A story that has circulated around P&G for years—and may even be true—is about a big project that collapsed in a heap. The project leader felt so awful that he offered to resign. "I refuse to accept your resignation," his boss told him. "I've just spent a lot of money on your education." Something P&G has learned over time is that it is better to fail early and cheap. In a smooth-running innovation process, this is what happens—and these are the kinds of failures that are worthy of awards.

Just as the creation of new ideas is a constant process, it helps to see killing them the same way. The market can change midstream; great ideas can go stale; bad ones can be transformed into winners because conditions change. This is where self-confidence and flexibility become crucial. In innovation, death is not always final; these decisions must be continually evaluated.

USE METRICS TO MEASURE INNOVATION

Business processes, such as selling, manufacturing, and logistics, have well-established metrics. The reasons are obvious. What gets measured gets done; and what gets measured can be improved. The conventional wisdom is that innovation, unlike other processes, can't be measured. The reality, though, is that it can. You need the right tools and know-how about the various stages at which innovation progress can and should be measured. Our experience and research have shown that some companies have made breakthroughs in measuring the productivity and effectiveness of the innovation process.

The right metrics help mesh different parts of the organization, such as technology and marketing, lay the foundation for resource allocation, and form the basis for rewards and promotion. For example, a goal for innovation profit output of 5 percent more organic growth in the next fiscal year provides the motivation, context, and rigor for people to work together to achieve it. At P&G, the benefits of clear metrics have gone beyond improvement of margins and increased rate of revenue growth and include perceptible, tangible benefits such as the strengthening of some brands; stronger relationships with retailers; and the internal organizational mental muscle and confidence to change the game in the emerging landscape.

THE PRINCIPLES UNDERLYING THE CHOICE
AND USE OF INNOVATION METRICS

1. Think about measuring innovation as you would an investment portfolio, where you are concerned with the total return rather than individual stocks, bonds, or mutual funds. The key is not to measure each project individually and then declare victory or defeat, but to measure total investment over a period of time compared to total output. This pools high- and low-risk projects and encourages people to take canny chances.

2. The payoff from innovation has a time lag similar to other investments you might make, such as building and then fully utilizing the capacity of a manufacturing plant.

3. Simply because something can be counted doesn't mean it is worth counting. Count what counts despite the difficulty and imprecision. Imprecise measurement of the right thing will tend to become precise measurement tomorrow.

4. Some aspects of innovation can be precisely quantified, such as the percentage of new products over a specific time period. Other measures are qualitative and can be measured only on a relative scale. For example, you have several innovation teams and determine that on a scale of 1 to 10, Innovation Team A rates a 9 on discovering consumer insights and incorporating them into effective decision making, while Team B rates just a 3. Qualitative measures often zero in on the most mission-critical issues that determine success or failure

5. Other aspects are physical measures that form the foundation for the eventual financial results—such as speed in developing a prototype and the number of iterations that are tested with "the boss," the consumer.

6. Each phase of the innovation process should have rigorous output measures and milestones. For example, one hundred ideas are green-lighted. How many then make it through for nurturing? Then how many make it to market? (It is at the go-to-market stage that major investment decisions are made and the yield is finally determined for the outcome.) Finally, how many then become successful in the eyes of the consumer and meet financial criteria?

7. The output of innovation results from a sequence of decisions at every stage and every phase, each building on the previous one. Thus, the better the metrics and the better the decisions at each stage, the better the effectiveness of the whole process. The discipline of reviewing each stage has a very important effect on the outcome of innovation.

8. The number of people developed for future promotion, especially to the general management level, by building their experience curve in the process of innovation.

HOW LEGO MANAGES RISK

Understanding consumers and customers lowers risk. It is important to create social processes that bring those insights to bear on critical decisions, including which ideas to bet on, especially when it is time to make major investments. In industries such as fashion, toys, or patio furniture, where buying is concentrated and onetime decisions are crucial, a single missed season can be devastating. That's what happened to LEGO Group in the early 2000s. Its products missed the mark and the company nearly went bankrupt. When Jørgen Vig Knudstorp became CEO in 2004, his first mission was to survive another day. He divested noncore assets to create some cash flow and decentralized decision making. Then, he built a management team to revitalize the brand, improve relationships with suppliers, and improve LEGO's supply chain.

As he did this, he set his sights on increasing the percentage of revenue that would come from new products, but with careful attention to improving the chances that those new products would sell. About half of toy purchases are made in the six weeks before Christmas. If you have the wrong products on the retail shelves, there's no time to recover. You're stuck with inventory that you have to discount heavily, and you know you're going to have a bad year. Knudstorp took a major step toward lowering risk by bringing users and retailers into key decision points.

LEGO has a process for mapping the general direction product development should take based on trends in play habits, patterns in society, what's happening at the toy fairs and in the media landscape, and what appears to be exciting children. First, product concepts start to take shape. Then, in the initial phase, the first big reduction in the portfolio is made. Of the fifty or so ideas that get presented, about one-third are eliminated. The best ideas get fine-tuned and subjected to user testing.

Decisions about which ideas to pursue are made by a team that not only includes designers and product managers, but also people who are closer to the market: those who service LEGO's key retail accounts and work on the consumer and trade marketing side in various countries. People with marketplace experience have what Knudstorp calls a "practical intelligence," a good feel for which products will appeal to real customers and users. The CEO makes sure those people are not just present, but also listened to. He knows that if he himself voices an opinion, people will weight it heavily because of his position. That's a problem, because he doesn't see himself as the best source of insight about what will sell. "I don't have the information, and frankly, I don't have the experience," he says.

So Knudstorp sits in the back and observes the people and how they listen, imagine, connect, and build on one another, watching for comments that shut down ideas too early. Such comments often start with "Yes, but," as in: "Yes, but we tried that in Germany and it didn't work. It will never work in the U.S." He watches to be sure that people's opinions have facts behind them, that everybody is involved, and that the external view is represented. "While people with deep experience are a great source of insight, younger people who lack it are often a source of fresh ideas," Knudstorp explains."It's like gardening. You have to protect the young seeds."

As he participates in these sessions, Knudstorp develops an expertise in evaluating and improving the social system of experts making decisions relevant to the process of innovation. While he does not make decisions about when to green-light, he does make the leadership decisions of how to change the social system by changing one or more key people.

The most critical juncture is when decisions are made about which products to put into production, triggering major investments to acquire the tools and molding equipment and thereby raising the company's financial risk. Those decisions are made some eighteen months before the product goes onto the shelf (though the cycle time is shrinking); so, for instance, LEGO decides in February 2008 what will be on the shelves for Christmas 2009.

At this point, LEGO taps another perspective that improves its chances of making the right choices: that of its customers. These are the big retail chains and distributors like Wal-Mart, Toys "R" Us, and Top Toy, Scandinavia's dominant force in toy retailing. Over a two-week period, LEGO brings senior merchandisers and buyers from key accounts to its headquarters in Billund, Denmark. Staff members give tours of the facility, explain the company's philosophy of doing business, and spend a full day going through the entire portfolio. When LEGO started this process in 2005, it was a first even for longtime customers. Top Toy, for instance, has traded with LEGO since the day it opened forty-two years ago, but had never been invited inside the company before.

The idea behind the Billund visits is to leverage retailers' collective wisdom while there's still time to make adjustments, whether that means adding a product line or canceling one retailers think will bomb. Small comments give important clues: "Why do you have a robot in that series when there are robots in another series as well?"

"Why is this model in the BIONICLE series rather than EXO-FORCE?" "These models look a lot alike; do you need both?" Knudstorp says those reviews are among the most insightful product reviews he's ever had. The visits are a rich source of insight. They also make selling easier. Because the buyers are familiar with the product lines and may have helped shape them, it's almost as if they've tacitly agreed to purchase them.

Merchandisers, like all human beings, have their biases. Expanding the range of people you listen to helps. When LEGO presented its idea to create a Viking series, buyers at Top Toy were skeptical that it would have global appeal. They thought it was "too Scandinavian." But some U.S. retailers had expressed interest, which convinced LEGO that Vikings was a global play theme, and they went ahead. The series was a big success, especially in the United States.

No one at LEGO expects to eliminate risk, but finding ways to reduce it makes business more predictable. In 2004, it was not unusual for the annual sales forecast to be off by as much as 20 or 30 percent. For the past three years, the company has hit its top line within a 5 to 10 percent window.

Yes, innovation can be risky, but not innovating is much riskier. It is, in fact, a guarantee of failure. As the great economist Joseph Schumpeter put it, companies that resist change are "standing on ground that is crumbling beneath their feet." That has always been true; what is different is that the ground is shifting faster than ever.

ASK YOURSELF ON MONDAY MORNING

• How are you using the measures of innovation to influence behavior?

• Are you measuring the total innovation portfolio of innovation, not just individual projects?

• How good is the granularity in grouping projects in your portfolio for measurement: disruptive high risk/high reward (long term); low risk/low reward (short term). Such groupings demonstrate that managing disruptive projects is different from managing those that are short term.

• How good are you in pinpointing the break point at the phase when a decision is made to launch or go to market? Until then, while the intellectual investment is high, the financial investment is low.

• How well are you building your experience curve by learning about previous innovation projects and improving decision making at each milestone?

• How good are you in ensuring there is intellectual honesty? A common problem is that a team may want a project to succeed so much that it brings in poorly designed research or plays down the negative information.

• How persistent are you in your resolve in making judgments about when to pursue a project or kill it?

PART THREE

THE CULTURE OF INNOVATION

Does an organization exist that doesn't make the effort to develop a culture of teamwork and collaboration? After all, it's how work gets done. But why, if teamwork exists, does it often fail to result in organic revenue growth and profits on a consistent basis? The reason is that, in actual practice, collaboration and teamwork are limited to the silo or function where people spend their workdays. Innovation requires something different—collaboration and teamwork *across* silos and inclusion of people from outside the organization. That means leaders have to think and act differently for innovation to happen. Leaders set the pace by establishing and modeling the values, beliefs, attitudes, and behaviors conducive to innovation.

In addition to traditional qualities, leaders of innovation have unique characteristics, traits, and skills. It is an imperative to identify these kinds of leaders early in their careers. Leaders of innovation nurture other leaders by creating new, often very different, pathways in the organization.

In this section we share with you our firsthand observations and experiences for how to build cross-functional teams that make innovation happen, and how to identify, coach, and develop leaders of innovation.

CHAPTER NINE

INNOVATION IS A TEAM SPORT

Courageous and Connected Culture

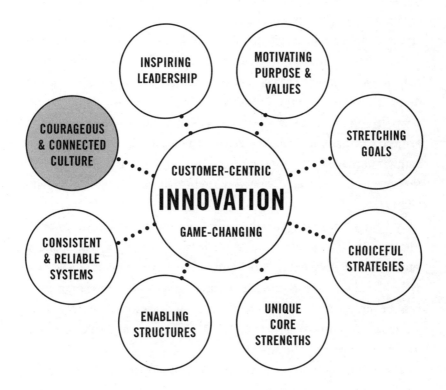

When I joined P&G in the 1970s, everyone wanted to work on big, established businesses; that seemed like the best way to move up. The job you didn't want was on the least well-defined projects. That is what I got. I spent two years working on a secret new product innovation called H-85. It never made it to the marketplace. I was concerned: Would I get another assignment after toiling on a failure? I did, and I have had a long career. Still, the story illustrates the culture that existed—conservative and a little too cautious. People feared, rationally, being associated with risky innovation—with anything that was not a clear well-established success.

Since becoming CEO, I have tried to promote a more-courageous, more connected and collaborative culture—one in which people want to take risks to identify game-changing, life-enhancing innovations. It takes a certain kind of nerve to deal with the unknown, to work on the frontier. Being ahead of the market can be lonely. Dick Byerly, a maverick researcher, kept Project X alive long after everyone else had given up on it, even to the point of not disclosing his work on his weekly reports. In retrospect, he was not only ahead of the game, he created it. Project X turned into Tide, the first synthetic laundry detergent. Innovating can mean sticking your neck out; a courageous, connected culture means it won't get chopped off, and that you are not alone with taking risks.

What I am seeing now is that more and more P&Gers are embracing the idea of exploring the frontier. It's becoming a way of life, a value they embrace without being told. We have an open job-posting system, and we have no trouble staffing most of our innovation projects. People are excited about being in the innovation game, which not only provides intrinsic satisfaction, but is also seen as a path to recognition and career advancement.

Obviously, we want to have a lot of winners; but we also want to encourage a set of what I call "connecting behaviors": If we get the behavior, the winners will follow. An innovation culture fosters openness, curiosity, networking with suppliers and customers, and the ability to say, "I have a problem I can't solve. Can someone help?" That is the attitude that both describes an innovation culture and helps to create one. It is one in which people want to go above and beyond the norm because they have a sense of mission. To do that, you need the social mechanisms and tools to mold diverse experts into highly functioning teams.

While there are many ways to build innovation teams, the two we present are Clay Street and co-location. Clay Street is a methodology for bringing together people who haven't worked together before to become a highly functioning team. All have great expertise. Some have very human egos. They learn how to submerge their egos, listen to each other, and build on each other's ideas—quickly and without being critical of others and without the selfishness that the owner of an idea often exhibits.

Co-location, simply having the opportunity to spontaneously interact with people, helps a business unit to be culturally innovative. To convert an idea into a reality, the unfiltered free flow of information has to exist. Getting people together on the spur of the moment so that everyone hears the same thing and builds on each other's ideas increases the chances of reaching the click point.

THEATER OF INNOVATION

For an example in miniature of a place where innovation teams are built from scratch, connecting behaviors are the norm, and the culture is courageous, come to an edgy and bohemian neighborhood in downtown Cincinnati known as Over-the-Rhine. Step inside the converted brewery on Clay Street, and the place looks like a combination of think tank and playground. There are desks and whiteboards, computers and conference areas. But there are also crayons, toys, and chalkboard walls; it's not unusual to see people sitting in a circle telling stories. There are even what look like pinups of children's art around the walls.

For those who like to think of P&G as full of stereotypical Proctoids (i.e., men with short hair, white collars, and serious issues about the Cincinnati Reds), don't go to Clay Street. All illusions will be shattered. It is headed by Dave Kuehler, a designer/theatrical director/ engineer who may not even own a white collar. On any given day, you might see people playing improv games. Or talking about Arthurian mythology. Or listening to a lecture on the latest breakthrough in bioscience.

If you think it's all play and no work, don't fool yourself. Teams at Clay Street do work hard. They just work differently. Clay Street, as it is known, is a systematic approach to create groups who wrestle with the unknowns and solve critical business problems. "People are creative by nature. It's part of being human. We organize around that," says Kuehler. "We try to reframe everything." According to Kuehler, Clay Street is not a process. It's an approach. Every team is unique, and their processes will reflect that. If you create the right initial conditions—people, purpose, and environment—a group will create their own culture, tools, and processes to accomplish their task. "Multifunctional barriers, common to many work teams, aren't an issue here. We serve the consumer, the idea, and each other," says Kuehler.

Innovation is a group activity. An effective group is both practical and willing to explore out-of-the-box ideas. One way that P&G does it is Clay Street.

The way it works is that a P&G executive—typically a president or a general manager—identifies a problem related to growth, such as relaunching a brand or devising a new product to fit a market segment. The manager needs to select an idea that links with business strategy; otherwise, it is not worth doing. The sponsor puts together a team of eight to twelve people and pays Clay Street a fee; the idea is not to make a profit, but to ensure that the business is serious. Moreover, the internal market for Clay Street is a stern test of its value: If no one is willing to pay, that would be a sign that its services are not considered worth it. In that sense, Clay Street has clearly proved itself. Two projects run at a time in the old brewery, but there are many more requests, so the Clay Street folks pick and choose the most important projects with the biggest payoff. Small problems need not apply.

"The project has to have a goal," says Claudia Kotchka, P&G's head of design, who was responsible for opening the door for Kuehler and the Clay Street concept to come to Cincinnati from Mattel. Of Clay Street, she says, "We are not interested in some wacko idea. It has to make sense; there needs to be an answer we can do something with."

The members of the team are released from their usual duties for several weeks to work exclusively at Clay Street; they are even discouraged from e-mailing their erstwhile colleagues. It is *total immersion;* everyone is deeply concentrated on the same task and constantly accessible to each other. That is the recipe for breakthroughs.

The team is crafted carefully to ensure a variety of disciplines are represented; there are also a couple of outsiders included on the grounds that they are more likely to make "the emperor has no clothes" kind of comments. Even if it is a marketing project, for example, there will likely be participants from finance, human resources, and manufacturing; there will also be a range of ages, both sexes, and people from a variety of cities or countries. "If you cast it right," says Kuehler, drawing on his theater background, "the rest is crowd control." The full-time staffers at Clay Street—there are only four—put together hand-crafted starter kits, including brand strategy, description of the product and category, introductions to the various speakers, and so on.

DIVERSE TEAMS MAKE BREAKTHROUGHS

For the first two weeks, led by a facilitator, the team does no nitty-gritty business. Their jobs are to become sponges. To see things with fresh eyes, build deeper capacity as a team, and build collective knowledge. In this early phase, exercises and experiences are designed with one thing in mind—to develop trust. Team members eat lunch together every day (without the facilitator for the first few weeks)—another element of team building. Then the team might start free-associating about ideas connected with their project: What does a mother want from diapers? What does "organic" mean? They literally draw their thoughts and fears on big sheets of paper that are pinned up around the room—an act that itself requires trust. Some people are clearly more gifted than others when it comes to expressing their ideas artistically, and they have to believe that even the most awkward stick figures will not be subject to ridicule. Speakers are invited who can shed insight on something related to the business problem—for example, an anthropologist who studies how busy American families spend their time discusses her work with a diaper group. A feminine care group heard from an academic whose expertise is social taboos.

Over time, the process becomes more structured and focused on the business problem. But every day starts with a "good-morning circle," in which each person says, "Good morning," to every other person, followed by conversation, which can last anywhere from a few minutes to a few hours. The idea is to begin each day as people, first, then address real problems early, in an environment that allows difficult things to be said.

Around week six, there is a period of chaos. There is no directive that says "chaos week," but it inevitably happens around this time. The team, typically, isn't quite sure where it is going, or how it is going to get there; it is fretful and sometimes fractious. They can't believe they are going to be able to complete their task and can be irritated with both the process and the people running it. Kuehler calls this period "adolescence." Like the real thing, it is blessedly brief.

At this point, the facilitator begins to step back, and the team gets on with the job; by week seven or eight, it should be autonomous. "We know we are on track," says Kuehler, "when they tell us, 'You don't know what you are talking about.'"

THE "EUREKA!" MOMENT

Although innovation cannot depend on hoping for "Eureka!" moments, Clay Street is all about building an atmosphere in which each team has one (and so far, they all have). "The room is a disaster, a mess; people are frustrated; and someone comes in and says this-and-that—it all comes together out of chaos, a novel and higher order always emerges," is Kuehler's scientific description of what happens. "There are always little ideas all along the way, and then comes a moment when they figure it out. It's magical. You can't exactly plan for it. You have to be awake, aware, and ready when it does."

Think of it as a productivity versus time graph in the shape of a hockey stick. For the first half of a Clay Street session, the line is horizontal, with perhaps a slight upward arc; sometime during adolescence comes the click—and after that the line angles up steeply the rest of the way. The point of the good-morning circles, the games, the relationship building, and all that is to get to that angle of ascent.

LOOKING AT CONSUMERS IN NEW WAYS

The members of the Herbal Essences team remember the Clay Street click well. Their task was to revive a brand, bought in the Clairol acquisition in 2001, that was so stale that major retailers were threatening not to stock it. At Target, Herbal Essences had slumped from a 10 percent market share in 2001 to half that in 2004. Snippy P&G internal memos used the term "death spiral." The stakes were high. Susan Arnold, then the vice chair of global beauty and health (and now president of the global business units), turned to Clay Street in January 2005, then a new and unproven outpost, and chose the team from across P&G who would be participants. Many of the chosen were ungrateful for the privilege. "Most of us came kicking and screaming," recalls Tiffany Stevens, a team member who went on to become a Clay Street staffer. And they were disconcerted by how un-P&G the place was—no e-mail, no hierarchy, no talk sheets or charts, no milestones or briefing papers. Just ten people in a circle saying, "Good morning," every damn day. Over time, they began to relax and work the process—and to believe in it and each other.

One eureka moment came, as such moments tend to do, at a time of extreme frustration. The team was trying to redesign Herbal Essences to attract young women in their late teens and early twenties. However, they were really struggling to find ideas that would resonate with this group. In particular, they were struggling with how to reposition that brand's "natural ingredients" into something that would "wow" young women. The breakthrough came when they went shopping.

The team sent two groups shopping for "natural/organic" products. One group was made up of women in their thirties and forties; another who were in their teens and twenties. The older group came back with things like lentils, nuts, and granola; the younger group with smoothies, flowers, and fructose-sweetened dry fruit. There was not a single item that was the same in the respective shopping baskets. At that moment, the team realized their fundamental mistake. The young women they were designing for were from a new generation (Gen-Y) and had fundamentally different beliefs and attitudes to just about everything. This insight drove the team to abandon their own Boomer/Gen-X preconceptions and start to immerse themselves in everything Gen-Y and create a re-launch proposition that Gen-Y young women would love.

"The common starting point is always the consumer," says Sean Sauber, another Clay Street staffer. A team needs to find a way to let go of their own biases and know their target consumer inside and out. To encourage this, Clay Street creates innovative ways for teams to interact with consumers. "We look at the consumer in ways you never have before." By encouraging teams to think and act like the consumer, not just talk about her, and defining a total consumer experience, Clay Street can figure out how to meet the consumer's needs. For the Herbal Essences folks, their first critical breakthrough came only when they designed a human experiment whose entirely unexpected results got them on the right road.

Eureka moment number two came as the team was trying to find a way to update the brand's packaging. The team was inspired by mythology, as the original Herbal Essences packaging had a goddess figure rising from a shell. There was a nub of an idea here, so they brought in an artist to sculpt bottle shapes, informed by the idea of feminine sensuality. However, the team struggled to find shapes that worked for their consumers. The team went back to consumers and immersed themselves in how Gen-Y women wanted feminine sensuality to be portrayed. This immersion made them realize that packaging needed to be very subtle versus the overt sexuality of Gen-X. In other words, just a suggestion of sex and youth. Out of that came the idea of "nesting" the bottles—to shape the shampoo and conditioner so that they fit into each other. Stevens recalls the word associations that got the team to the idea: "goddess, human form, tango, flirting, Gaultier." If Henry Moore had ever designed shampoo packaging, it might have looked something like this.

At the end of the twelve weeks, the Herbal Essences team had recommended that P&G change every single thing about the old shampoo, from the formula to the packaging to the language to the brand equity. The new proposition was completely grounded in a deep understanding of Gen-Y women. Then they had to sell the revamp—first of all, to the decision-makers at P&G. The Clay Street team made its pitch to about hundred people, including Gil Cloyd, the chief technology officer; Jim Stengel, the chief marketing officer; and Susan Arnold. The team did a presentation not typically seen at P&G. They eschewed charts and started with the finished product, then talked about the process that got them there, including mistakes. They told a story, using props such as a mock-up of the tested models. Most importantly, the "story" was based on their deep immersion in the consumer. And the narrative proved compelling with many of the P&G old guard blown away by the teams' depth of understanding of their consumer.

Except, that is, for one important thing. At a purely intellectual level, the story worked. However, executing the transformation is a complex project, one that typically takes several years. Susan Arnold knew that Herbal Essences, with its plummeting market share and growing customer discontent, did not have that long to survive in the cutthroat hair-care category. She charged the team to have the revived product in the market in twelve months, which was two to three years less than typical and had never been done before at P&G. Needless to say, the project team was nervous. However, Susan backed the team to deliver. The most important thing she did was to take personal ownership of the risk. The project leader vividly recalls Susan sitting her down early in the project and saying "I know that what I am asking you to do is unreasonable and has a high chance of failure. However, my commitment to you is that I will bear the risk. If the project fails, I will take ownership for the failure. All I ask is that you tell me what the team needs to succeed, what risk I am taking, and to try your hardest."

The project team tested Susan's commitment many times during the year, including asking her to commit over $1 million in capital to retool the manufacturing line. Susan made this decision in less than five minutes and without qualified packaging. However, she made the decision in a way that was consistent with her promise; she asked the team to lay out the risks, explain the alternatives, and then personally called the head of hair-care manufacturing to ensure he understood that she had made the decision and that she owned the risk if it failed.

About eighteen months later, the new Herbal Essences was on the shelves and put the brand back on track to eventually become another P&G billion-dollar brand.

Molding diverse experts into a functioning team, through total immersion in an innovation project, is a unique experience, substantially different from the way people participate in other types of teams. Total immersion involves every member of the team listening, often simultaneously, to different viewpoints about topics outside the expertise of any one individual, then going further and connecting and integrating those viewpoints to push forward imagination and thinking to create new insights until the whole team has a breakthrough.

ELEMENTS OF TEAM BUILDING

Clay Street, by nature and design, is a special place. People who have participated in such experiences—other companies have similar setups—report a huge expansion in their ability to connect unrelated ideas and design creative experiments and make breakthroughs they could not have done alone. This is so tremendously enriching that there is something of a recovery period after Clay Street—people don't want to leave, because they are so strongly bonded with their team and the total immersion process. When they do go back to their day jobs, they bring their experience with them—as well as their intellectual flexibility, self-confidence, and a certain unclassifiable sixth sense of what is possible. An added cultural benefit is the building of wide and deep social networks that can last a lifetime.

In real life, you can't always shove a dozen people out the door to work together for months at a time. That said, the lessons of Clay Street are widely applicable because they are about two things. One is knowing the consumer: The Herbal Essences breakthrough did not come in the chemistry lab, but in the store aisle, with the team experiencing shopping as a consumer would. Nothing else would have worked without those insights.

Second, Clay Street is about building a team totally driven by the idea of creating breakthrough innovations. When it comes to making innovation a nucleus of corporate life, creating a culture of teamwork inside the organization is crucial. You might argue that game-changing innovation is simply the by-product of highly connected, collaborative, and purpose-driven cultures. The fairly extreme example of Clay Street is a useful template for thinking about teamwork more broadly. It is a proven human phenomenon, from Edison's New Jersey lab to SAMSUNG's innovation center, that when you have a clear goal and you put together a team (ideally six to ten people) with the right blend of intellectual diversity and real expertise for an extended period, you create conditions that can lead to breakthrough ideas. Given the right social processes, such as trust, time, deep concentration, and total immersion in a well-defined problem, finding the right insights becomes likelier. This is something that can be done, improved, done again, and improved again. It is replicable.

THE POWER OF CO-LOCATION

It is important to design accessible consumer immersion experiences as a focal point for where and how innovation teams work together so that it is part of their daily work. The Pampers Baby Discovery Center, located a few miles from downtown Cincinnati, is the epicenter of Pamper's business operations. Beginning in 2001, P&G put all of its previously scattered baby-care functions—research, management, marketing, and so on—here. Having all the relevant people and disciplines together means that everyone can hear the same thing at the same time, without distorting filters. Spontaneity matters. And it also allows people to bounce ideas off each other in odd moments, around the coffee machine or walking in from the parking lot. Given the growing power of the virtual world, co-location might not appear all that important. Just the opposite: Co-location helps create a more-rounded, better-integrated team, in a word, *holistic*.

Quite simply, co-location is about building relationships; sitting next to team members from different functions makes it easier to integrate all stages of a new product right from the start and to deal with tough challenges quickly. An idea can be taken from a concept to test at a single site, even as data is pulled from around the globe. Then, as technology is developed to meet the need, product researchers and marketing work in parallel and collaboratively to develop the product, make the right trade-offs, and figure out how to communicate it so that it succeeds in the marketplace.

Having everyone in the same place also makes it more likely that research serves both commercial and technical needs. (Diapers, believe it or not, are drenched in technology. In the lobby of the P&G headquarters, there is a copy of the patent application for the first Pampers. If you didn't know you were at P&G, you might think it's a part for the space shuttle. And that diaper was primitive compared to modern ones.) Innovations don't just get handed over to the marketing people; everyone gets things off the ground together.

The Baby Discovery Center is not a place for people who like quiet and order. Babies run the joint. There are three large rooms where, drawing from the database of fifteen thousand families, product research is done with the experts—babies, moms, and the occasional dad. One recent day, a new color for the Kandoo wash—a soapy foam in a frog-shaped plastic container that is designed for toddlers—was being tested. A sweet-faced three-year-old named Josiah was the day's star. He sat with his mom, two sisters, and a P&Ger at a low table. After a little chitchat, Josiah scrambled up a step in a nearby bathroom to wash with Kandoo. "Oh, it's green," he said happily, and scrubbed it in. Sitting back down, the P&G researcher tried to engage the youngster about the soap. Josiah wasn't having it: "I want to play." His mother attempted to get him back on track. "Won't it be fun to talk about soap?" Josiah was dubious, but managed to offer a little something: "I like the green. I like the smell."

Back Josiah went to test another version. He looked around, then asked where the bathtub is. (There isn't one.) He scoffed, "We have a bathtub at home." Back to the table for more soap talk. The researcher gamely tried to get Josiah going again.

> Did you like this soap?
> I like it.
> Why?
> Because we are best friends.
> Did you like the light or dark color better?
> I like both of them better.
> The first one or the second one?
> I like three.
> Was there anything you didn't like?
> I like to jump up and down.

No one said any of this was easy.

But something was learned from this session. Judging by his behavior, Josiah seemed more interested in the first, darker version, using a bunch of it. His mother wondered aloud whether he will use too much of it because he likes it so well. She also worried if the dark color will stain. Food for thought.

Next door, the room was crawling with youngsters from nine to eighteen months old. They were there all morning, and had four diaper changes. Each time a mom came up to the changing table, she was asked about fit, look, leakage, stretch, and fastening, on a scale of 1 to 5. How the diapers move, marking the diaper when it was put on, and then where it was when it was taken off were also measured. Here was where, for example, a version of the "bikini diaper" that is popular in Latin America was tested. It's a lower-slung version that is cooler and uses less material. Babies didn't seem to mind it, and it works just fine. But mothers said no thanks. American moms are used to high-waisted diapers and were skeptical that the bikini versions were good enough. We didn't force the issue. The Discovery Center will do almost four hundred such studies this year—just for diapers.

"The challenge is to find what is meaningful for parent and child, and to communicate that to them," says Jane Wildman, vice president of the global baby care and Pampers franchise. "That's why the Discovery Center and our other similar facilities across P&G are so important. When you are able to quickly assess a portfolio of technologies and get firsthand experience with the consumers, it can really help to make the smart choices." It all has to do with treating the consumer as boss—even when the consumer is an infant.

Which is all very sweet, but does it work? Absolutely. Redefining Pampers as a brand that supports child development and creating a team to deliver that promise was key to our introduction of our Pampers Stages line. P&G regained its competitive edge. "When we hit that sweet spot of knowing the consumer and delivering what she wants," says Wildman, "our business—and parents—respond." As of fiscal 2007, Pampers has a 10-point share lead over the next branded competitor. Pampers is now a $7 billion brand—P&G's largest brand.

Another example of co-location is SAMSUNG. In recent years, it has been a game-changer against bigger, more established companies such as Sony and Philips Electronics. It redefined where to play and became better focused, positioning itself as a leader in digital convergence. It upgraded, by an order of magnitude, its technologies and supply chain process. It made design part of its fabric with the creation of the Innovative Design Lab and appointment of a chief design officer. It also found a way to accelerate its fast consumer-based product development and launch.

SAMSUNG created a Value Innovation Program (VIP), housed in

the VIP Center in Suwon, Samsung's main manufacturing site just south of Seoul. There product planners, designers, programmers, and engineers immerse themselves in data and brainstorm ideas. Their aim is to arrive at the basic outline of a product. The details get worked out later by designers and engineers.

With thirty-eight bedrooms, a kitchen, and even a gym, the VIP Center is designed to facilitate the kind of discovery that often happens when people are deeply immersed in a topic for an extended time. Most people live there for the length of the assignment, which can be several weeks or months, and test their ideas on their teammates whenever they strike. They can meet to brainstorm almost at will. The intensity and immediacy allow for creative solutions and the esprit de corps that helps them hash out the enormously conflicting trade-offs between price and cost requirements, technological capability, and consumer preferences. The team that worked on the flat-screen TV, for instance, realized that although SAMSUNG had the technical capability to make a sophisticated TV with lots of whizbang features, customers were more concerned about how the TV looked. What might have been an overdesigned and too-expensive technology flop became the number one LCD TV brand in the United States.

VIP teams are small but productive, completing nearly a hundred projects. They include a notebook computer that doubles as a mobile TV, yet is thin and light enough to be carried in a handbag, and the CLP-500, a color laser printer that was built at the same cost as a black-and-white model.

BUILDING AN INNOVATION TEAM

Innovation comes not just from thinking up new ideas, but from combining and recombining them—and then putting together the people who can turn concept into reality. That is what we mean when we say innovation is a social process. It is a team sport. Just as a sports team has certain defined positions—quarterback, kicker, tackle—so must an innovation team.

The idea generator   You have to have conceptual people who are able to push beyond the plausible to create provocative ideas. This person is a nonlinear thinker, someone who sees connections and patterns that are not obvious. Idea generators are impatient with constraints and unafraid to say what they think. They do not need to come from obviously creative functions, such as research or design, but you should ensure every team has a couple of people who fit the profile.

The project manager   In a nutshell, think type A, with a sense of humor. Project managers are accountable for making sure that all the pieces come together. They need to be disciplined, attentive to detail, and able to organize complexity. They also need to be able to get the team to the finish line on time, and together; that is where the sense of humor is essential. A project manager who lacks social skills will be seen as a nag, not a leader, and provoke guerrilla resistance.

The executor   These team members are the watchdogs of executional excellence who make things happen. They make sure that the milestones are met, and that the right factors are in place to commercialize the product in a cost-effective and scalable way. If you don't execute, the consumer doesn't care what the strategy was. Execution is the only strategy that consumers see.

The team leader   In any project, the selection of the team leader is crucial. "Recruiting the right genius for the job," writes Warren Bennis in *Organizing Genius*, "is the first step in building many great collaborations." How does Bennis characterize such a leader? As a "pragmatic dreamer," which sounds exactly right. The leader's most important job is to create a culture in which people feel free to express ideas—in short, to take the fear out. (See "Rules of Brainstorming," pages 246–250.) That is one of the strengths of Clay Street. In a typical group of ten people, there is usually one person who talks a lot; two more who speak regularly; a couple who try to get in a word edgewise; and a few who are silent before a group, but always say something pertinent in private. The Clay Street groups are different: Everyone chips in; everyone listens; no one dominates; no one is looking to the senior person for approval or brownie points. Such indifference to the organizational chart is one mark of a team with good leadership.

In the case of Herbal Essences, the facilitator played the part of team leader early on. But Clay Street does not operate in a corporate vacuum. Remember, it was Susan Arnold who not only released a dozen people to attend—an unmistakable sign of commitment—but also backed her people's concept on the production line, to the tune of $1 million. And she let them get on with the job. Arnold knew what she wanted—a strategy to save the brand—but did not tell the team how to get there. This is the kind of structured flexibility (or perhaps flexible structure) that makes success more likely. The leader's job, says Bennis, is to "inspire, communicate, and choose"; the ideal is not to micromanage the project as it goes along, meddling as people try to work out problems, but to settle issues when the team has gone as far as it can (e.g., giving the go-ahead to the nesting bottles).

Team leaders need expertise in the field, both to win respect from other members and to know what is going on; they do not need to be the leading expert. An ambitious software project, for example, need not be led by the best programmer; it needs someone who understands both the product and the market. The leader's most important tasks are to listen, to know the talents and preferences of the members, to manage personality conflicts, to recognize when outsiders need to be brought in, and to keep the team focused and optimistic. The art of team leadership is to ask the right questions to keep the project moving forward.

The composition of the team itself is another task that falls to the leader. The principle here is diversity—not in the sense of affirmative action, though a range of ethnic and social backgrounds can certainly be useful. The more important kind of diversity is intellectual, to draw in people with different ways of thinking. This needs to be done strategically. Throwing a bunch of people from different backgrounds into a room and calling it diversity misses the point, which is to bring varying kinds of expertise to bear that are related to the problem at hand. The team that reinvented Febreze started with just five people; in a video explaining their experience, they described themselves this way: an artist, an archaeologist, a scientist, a philosopher, and the head honcho. All were acknowledged experts in their fields; they brought a self-confidence and mutual respect to the endeavor that allowed the creative juices to flow.

There also needs to be risk diversity. Some people tend to see barriers and assume this can't work. They are blocked; their brain architecture is linear and intensely practical. High rollers do not worry so much about whether something can be done; they conceive impossible things and work backward. They may not know how to do it, and sometimes it can't be done—but the journey toward finding that out can be valuable in itself. An innovation project needs both types of people. In the early stages, the wild things are particularly valuable; later, the practical folks come into their own.

Diversity is not, however, a virtue in itself. Heterogeneous teams, by definition, are less tight knit and can be more difficult to motivate because the bonds that tie them are looser. Trust, mutual respect, and open debate have to be encouraged right from the start—an essential element of the social process of innovation. Done right, the advantage of diversity is that there are many different kinds of minds crackling all around a subject. A team of people who think alike may, in fact, be more cohesive and report less friction—but it is also less apt to come up with answers that move the needle.

Teams need deadlines, both because we're in business here, not a social experiment, and because constraints spur creativity. A team with time on its hands is probably not being productive. Bennis describes the development of Disney's *Snow White* as a "dream with a deadline"; that is the right spirit. Teams also need to be contained—a dozen people at the very most (some social science research suggests five or six as the ideal). Amazon has the two-pizza rule—no team so big it cannot dine on two pies. Google typically has three-person teams that work for three to four months on a project. A permanent team of many people is just another way of saying *bureaucracy*.

Leaders need to do three more things—make sure the team is

communicating, say no to bad ideas, and keep the team connected to reality. The whole point of a team is to take advantage of the potential of having diverse minds pointed to the same goal; if ideas are not shared, it's no longer a team. And it is the nature of group dynamics that sometimes people can get very excited and go 180 degrees in the wrong direction. A confident leader pulls them back. Even more important, though, is to keep your eyes on the prize. Business history is, unfortunately, not short of great teams in great companies who discovered great things— and let someone else profit from them. The classic example is of Xerox, whose Palo Alto Research Center developed the first personal computer. But it was the folks at Apple who toured PARC, saw the potential of the PC (complete with mouse), and took the idea to market. PARC was well led in terms of generating ideas; but it was poorly served by its failure to conceive of these ideas in business terms and convert them into profit. It is the job of the leader to get product out the door.

GETTING TEAMS TO GEL

One of the most common reasons teams fall short is that they fail to design the business model at the same time they are creating the actual product or service. The classic example of this comes from one of the world's greatest innovators, Apple, which created the Lisa in 1983—a PC that could do everything but the dishes. But the Apple team failed to realize that few businesses wanted to pay ten thousand dollars for a computer. The Lisa was inventive but not, in our definition of the term, innovative—because it failed in the marketplace.

Businesspeople tend to think about the business first, then look at the technology or product and ask what to do with it. Designers and engineers do the opposite; they fall in love with the new new thing without figuring out how it works as a business. That is why teams need to be multidisciplinary, so that they can balance out their predispositions and ask all of the right questions. Tim Brown of IDEO says that the ideal team is actually *interdisciplinary*—full of people who themselves have diverse strengths and are flexible enough not to simply protect their own institutional interests. The term IDEO uses is "T-shaped"; it looks for people with depth in one subject (like, the downstroke of the *T*), but also a breadth of curiosity and willingness to consider other people's skills. "T-shaped people collaborate better," says Brown. "They know what they are doing; everyone tries to solve the challenge." Because the world is not brimming with such empathetic polymaths, the next best thing is to create teams of widely varying expertise and to build in expectations that they work and play well together.

The most important way to make that happen is to define a goal to reach, a problem to solve. A clear, precise, common goal helps a team to gel, to see the outcome of their work as more important than their individual interests. In the case of Herbal Essences, for example, the goal was to innovate to take back lost market share. It also helps to have team members live together—not necessarily in space, though that helps, but in time. They each need to give focused attention to the task—and trust others to do so. Clay Street offers another lesson here—time spent building trust is not time wasted. Tiffany Stevens recalls a moment when the team was just not working; they had hit a point they called a Hot Spot. The team was blocked, relations fraught. And yet time was running out on the project; there was no time for psychological mumbo jumbo. So they kept plugging away. And getting nowhere. It was only when the team stepped back and cooled the Hot Spot by reestablishing relationships of trust that they got back on track.

For an example of excellent teamwork done more conventionally, take the creation of one of our most successful new products in years—Crest Whitestrips. Research showed that while half of the population wanted whiter teeth, only a tenth of that number did anything about it. That was understandable; whitening required going to a dentist and paying hundreds of dollars. OK, but now what? Here is where P&G's ability to connect internally came to the fore.

Analogy can be a rich source of insight; and there can be no innovation without insight. But this is often not a linear matter. It requires synthesis. So P&G put together a team of film and adhesive experts from the corporate organization, dental experts from oral care, and bleach experts from laundry. They defined the problem: They needed a way to deliver peroxide gel to the teeth in an easily applied and removable system; they needed a process that could be completed in about thirty minutes without interfering with other activities; they needed a product that could be manufactured at high speed, and affordably; and they needed a product that could be packaged for long shelf life. Then they looked for analogies. They found it in a food wrap P&G was researching, which provided a tight seal, but was still easily unrolled. And then P&G did the kind of technical research it is known for. The breakthrough result was Crest Whitestrips. These are clear adhesive strips that are applied to the top and bottom teeth for thirty minutes; unlike trays, users can talk while wearing them or walk around without looking like a hockey goalie. Crest Whitestrips are affordable, convenient, and widely imitated, but still better than anything else on the market.

The team thought it had a winner on its hands; but since many people at P&G regarded the Crest brand with something like awe, feared taking it into new territory. "The prevailing mind-set at the time," chemical engineer Paul Sagel told *Strategy & Innovation* in 2004, "was that an oral-care product had to come in a tube. There weren't a lot of other people in the company who thought Whitestrips were going to be a blockbuster product." Thanks to strong leadership, the team was able to quell these doubts and press ahead.

Early sales—it went into test markets in 2000 and rolled out nationally in mid-2001—were strong. But many people were not repurchasing the product. To understand what was going on, the team went back to the bosses: consumers. In an innovation lab, people came in and went through their morning ablutions. The team watched them from behind a one-way mirror. What they saw were people frustrated and often not using the product correctly. Why? Because the instructions were in the box and not easy to find. So directions were put on the box instead. Problem solved. Oh, and Crest Whitestrips has a 50 percent share and is a very strong profit contributor. That is the power of teamwork in action.

None of this happens by serendipity. All projects, right from the beginning, are expected to have multiple connections from multiple functions and partners, such as market research, design, marketing, agency partners, retailers, and suppliers. Marketing people are part of P&G upstream R&D programs to ensure that innovation will advance the brand equity and can be commercialized. P&G has tried to create a seamless connection between R&D and product supply to ensure scalability and cost efficiency.

One way the Clairol retail hair color business team ensured they had the right mix of people on their innovation team was to create what they call the "Consumer Community." Simply put, the Consumer Community is a multifunctional, consumer-focused community of marketing, R&D, market research, and design experts. This community is charged to work collaboratively to develop and deliver holistic consumer innovations. *All* functions in the community are held accountable for the success of an innovation based on deep consumer understanding—not just R&D or marketing. Before this cultural intervention, R&D might not be invited to participate in consumer interactions organized by marketing. It wasn't because marketing didn't want R&D involvement, but didn't see it as useful. Now, marketing folks complain there aren't enough R&D people to support the various brand efforts.

Second, there are almost two dozen "communities of practice" (COPs) built around areas of expertise—biology, packaging, sustainability, chemistry, analytics, and so on. Some of these are relatively formal, with annual meetings to share best practices; others are mostly virtual, communicating via P&G's intranet. All, however, are run from the grassroots, led by someone in the field who steps up to keep it going.

Finally, the end-to-end product launch (see chapter 7) is intended to push connections. Each phase forces the different elements to engage with each other—within the company, with consumers, and with retail partners and other stakeholders, such as regulators.

PULLING IT ALL TOGETHER

Simply put, culture is about everyday behavior. Changing the culture, therefore, requires changing behavior. That means clearly defining both business and personal development expectations. (An example of the former: that 50 percent of innovations will come from the outside; the latter, that you develop actionable insights about the consumers your business serves.) It also means changing the consequences that follow, both positive and negative; for example, recognition, rewards, and performance feedback. Peter Drucker believed that for an existing business to be capable of innovation "it has to make sure its incentives, compensation, personnel decisions, and policies all reward the right entrepreneurial behavior and do not penalize it."

Creating an innovation culture takes time, especially if you want to have it permeate an entire business unit or company. However, by starting small and by focusing on four important elements—*c*ourageous, *c*onnected and *c*ollaborative, *c*urious, and *o*pen—an innovation culture can be created and nurtured.

Think "4 Cs and an O." For each element, the table below outlines specific how-to ideas for interventions that can jump-start the transformation into an innovation culture.

INNOVATION CULTURE ELEMENTS AND INTERVENTIONS

INNOVATION CULTURE ELEMENT	WHAT IT LOOKS LIKE	EXPECTATION INTERVENTIONS	CONSEQUENCE INTERVENTIONS
Courageous	- No fear - Learns from failure - Knows how to manage risk, relying on most meaningful indicators/measures	- Use innovation portfolio as way to manage risk (see chapter 8) - Qualify few, meaningful measures for innovation that should be broadly applied - Establish "there's no bad idea" operating principle - Test, prototype, and iterate to reduce risks	- Limited human and financial resources are sufficient to support most promising game-changing innovation projects in a well-managed portfolio - Capture learning from failed innovations and share with other teams for reapplication - Broadly reward and recognize teams who fail

INNOVATION CULTURE ELEMENT	WHAT IT LOOKS LIKE	EXPECTATION INTERVENTIONS	CONSEQUENCE INTERVENTIONS
			- Assign talent from a failed innovation to a new high-profile innovation project
Connected and Collaborative	- Works effectively and productively with others—inside and outside of the company - Works seamlessly across functions, business, and geographies to develop, commercialize, and execute - Uses personal and professional networks to seek out innovation ideas	- Create in-house infrastructures, communities of practice to foster knowledge exchange - Select team leaders who facilitate connections and expect collaboration - Establish ways to encourage employees to leverage and extend their external networks (e.g., industry conferences, trade associations, supplier/retailer relationships)	- Include in performance evaluations - Be prepared to change the leader and/or team members - Continuity of team members builds trust
Curious	- Remains childlike, naive to enable best learning - Looks for unobvious patterns - Explores and likes to discover new possibilities - Looks for analogies and metaphors - Asks "Why and why not?" "What's possible?" "How does that work?" - Use the "Columbo" approach to solve the "mystery" (aka, the innovation problem)—he	- Set an expectation of ongoing learning - Brainstorming - Consumer, shopper, and customer immersion - External connections and diverse experiences	- Challenge the team's thinking beyond the superficial - Keep asking, "why" and "why" again

INNOVATION CULTURE ELEMENT	WHAT IT LOOKS LIKE	EXPECTATION INTERVENTIONS	CONSEQUENCE INTERVENTIONS
	focuses on the problem to be solved and exercises curiosity by asking "just one more thing"		
Open	- Open-minded to new ideas—from anyone, anywhere, anytime - Open to learn with assumption that others' idea will ultimately make a product or service better - Open to empathy to the consumer/customer to best understand their needs and wants - Open to suspend judgment	- Institute an "open architecture"—even on a small scale—to enable ideas and innovations to flow in from outside (the project team, the business or function, and the company) - Establish and communicate clear goals for what's expected from sourcing innovation from outside (e.g., P&G's 50% of innovation will have an external partner; see chapter 6) - Eliminate "not invented here"—instead encourage "apply and reapply with pride"	- Reward and recognize those who seek out/commercialize innovation opportunities from outside (essential especially early on to create momentum) - Reward and recognize those who reapply others' success to their business - Include open-mindedness in performance evaluations

An example that brings these elements to life comes from P&G Asia, where the leadership team has made creating an innovation culture a fundamental organizational strategy. They use the concept of "IDEAS" to emphasize the need for out-of-the-box ideas as a source of game-changing innovation, as well as a reminder of the behaviors required to create a more innovative culture.

Inclusive: Reaping benefits of diverse thinking and ideas needed to foster game-changing innovation

Decisive: Eliminating organizational swirl, debate, and overanalysis to enable faster innovation development, qualification, and commercialization

External: Externally focused to get and stay in touch with consumers, customers, suppliers, and the need for honest and objective benchmarking versus external competition

Agile: Quickly reacting to changing consumer and marketplace conditions, being forward-thinking, becoming more comfortable with taking (calculated) risks

Simple: Ongoing streamlining and simplification of work structures/processes to free up more time for innovation

RULES OF BRAINSTORMING

In a bland conference room near the entrance to IDEO's office in Palo Alto, there is the usual long table, chairs, sockets for PowerPoint presentations, and a whiteboard. Yawn. There is, however, one interesting note. Above the whiteboard, right where schoolteachers might put the alphabet, are a series of commandments written in large letters.

Defer judgment
Encourage wild ideas
Build on the ideas of others
Stay focused on topic
One conversation at a time
Be visual
Go for quantity

These are IDEO's rules for brainstorming, and while the room itself could not, frankly, be more boring, the work that gets done there is not. IDEO is the MVP of design consultancies, regularly winning more awards than anyone else. Its rules make sense, and we agree with IDEO's general manager Tom Kelley that companies that "build a culture of brainstorming . . . [have made] a great start toward nurturing a culture of innovation." But because brainstorming is so much a part of what IDEO does—the people there are schooled to be good at it, the way writers absorb the rules of grammar—we think the IDEO rules may assume knowledge some people might not have. So here are our ten rules for effective brainstorming.

1. Get a facilitator. This is the traffic cop of the session, and should be an outsider. An insider brings baggage that can inhibit the free flow of ideas. HR consulting organizations are one possible resource; if you are working with a design firm like IDEO or Continuum, they may be able to help. If bringing in an outsider is difficult for some reason, the second-best option is to bring in someone from a different group inside the company. Facilitators need to be skilled at group dynamics, able to read when the team is flagging or when it is hitting on all cylinders. They have to be patient, yet willing to exercise discipline if one person can't stop talking or is becoming aggressive. It is more a matter of personality than formal training, but it can't hurt to bring in people to watch a well-run brainstorming session to see how it works.

2. Be prepared. The Boy Scouts have it right. Preparation is a key to success. In terms of brainstorming, this means two things. First, the topic needs to be well understood. Balance is required here. The subject needs to be specific enough for good answers to be possible (a session on the theme of "new ideas for cleaning" is going to be deadly) and general enough to provide room for creativity ("industrial abrasives for stainless steel sinks" is not going to get anyone excited). What could work: Well, IDEO did a useful session with P&G on "how to reinvent bathroom cleaning." The topic needs to be defined in terms of either the market or of consumer needs and habits; all the participants need to know what it is, and also have a little time to think about it. You want them to bring something to the party; this can be the glimmering of an idea, a competitor's product, a color pattern, a series of useful words or images, or an interesting question. Something—anything—to get to the launch pad.

3. Relax. Fear blocks both the generation and expression of ideas. Not every company or team will be comfortable with this, but consider doing some kind of word game or ice-breaking exercise to loosen people up (e.g., the improv circles at Clay Street). Discourage negative comments; as the session goes on, it is going to become apparent which ideas have any kind of future—bad ones do not have to be shot down on sight. At Clay Street, the buzzwords are "Yes, and . . ." Not "Yes, but . . ." Trust is the word here; people need to believe that they can say what they think without the risk of being ridiculed.

4. Leaders should follow. The whole idea of a brainstorming session is that it be open and freewheeling. But everyone at the table is going to be aware of who else is there, and where each person sits in the corporate hierarchy. There is going to be the usual human desire to please one's superiors. Consciously or not, some people some of the time will try to do so by agreeing up the ladder. So leaders should be careful about when and how they talk. General Peter Pace, former chairman of the Joint Chiefs of Staff, says when he wants to get an honest opinion, he asks a question neutrally and then gives his opinion last. If he gives his thoughts first, that colors the entire discussion. The whole point of brainstorming is that everyone participates, so we are not suggesting that leaders simply shut up; but they should think carefully about how they join in. Don't close down discussion; don't be the first to weigh in on everything; do tap into other people's ideas; ask questions.

5. Get everyone to contribute. This should be obvious, but group dynamics are such that it does not always happen. And it won't if people are intimidated or the tone is brutal (see rules 2 and 3). The wrong way to get everyone involved is to go around the table or to single people out—that can be scary. The right way is for the facilitator to know why each person has been selected to be in the room and try to play to each individual's expertise. Discourage interruptions; not only can this be rude, but it can silence those who lack the personal style to persevere through them.

6. Keep track of ideas. Obvious, but essential. Use a whiteboard or a big sheet of paper so that everyone can see what has been said and make connections between ideas. Allow people to write down their own ideas; it lets them refine them as they go along and also gets them out of their chairs, which can be rejuvenating. Discourage taking notes. If necessary, tape and transcribe meetings; or bring in someone to do so. If people have their head down writing what has just happened, their mind is not in the moment. Number new ideas as they occur for easy reference; this also builds a sense of accomplishment as the number accumulates, or as incentive for action, if it doesn't. Quantity matters in brainstorming.

7. Think ahead. Done right, brainstorming can be fun, sort of like a college bull session, but with full pay. Of course, that is not the point. Brainstorming is supposed to be a start of something, not an end in itself. At the end of the meeting, the participants should figure out what to do next to refine the insights generated. Brainstorming is itself a kind of Connect and Develop; generate ideas, then connect them, and repeat. This is not the time for considering practicalities, but for simply exploring ideas on a conceptual basis.

8. Use props. One of the reasons for rule 6 is that some people think visually; putting stuff up for them to see is a way to engage their mind. Others think best with their hands. So bring in prototypes of related things, versions of current (or competitive) products, even just bits and pieces that seem relevant—a color wheel, say, or advertisements, or a deconstruction of what you are talking about. Anything to get people thinking in practical terms about what you want to achieve. And again, this helps to keep them awake and interested. IDEO brings things like foam, duct tape, glue, straws, and markers to make models or just get the physical juices stirring.

9. Go outside the lines. Consider the metaphor contained within the word *brainstorm*. A storm is wild, volatile, and often random; it is weather with a passion. But it also has a beginning and an end. A good brainstorm should be something like that; without a degree of impulsiveness, of something very like whimsy, it will end up as a puddle, not a storm. And that is a waste of time. So let people stray into odd territory and let others follow; this just may lead in the direction most likely to get you to the ultimate destination. The facilitator needs to have the judgment, though, to reel people in if they are too far gone or go on for too long.

10. Follow the rules. From the outside, a brainstorming session may look chaotic; in fact, it has its own discipline. If this is not adhered to, people might have fun, but they will not produce ideas worthy of their time.

ASK YOURSELF ON MONDAY MORNING

• What are you doing to encourage courage and eliminate fear of failure that is an inherent part of the innovation process? Are you explicitly recognizing and learning from successes and failures?

• How are you fostering a culture of curiosity and openness that enables individuals and teams to suspend judgment and open themselves up for collaboration and connections?

• How are you eliminating unnecessary bureaucracy to encourage connections, collaboration, and experimentation?

• How are the team leader and team members chosen? Are you betting on the right people to get the innovation revolution you want? Have you ensured there is diversity of thought, experience, and skill on the team? Have you included "T-shaped" people on the team? Are team member changes made as the project progresses and different skills are required? How do you know when it's time to change the team leader or other team members who may be affecting overall effective team collaboration and performance?

• What are you doing to encourage open communications within an innovation team; across business units and with external parties to ensure maximum connections and learning, and maximum application and reapplication of effective innovation approaches, products, and services happen?

• How well do you manage the development of an individual's innovation skills?
  * How are individuals trained to become better innovators—both on the job and through other experiences?
  * Are innovation skills included as part of each individual's performance assessment?
  * How well does your team build an experience curve by working on other innovation assignments?

• How do you enable individuals to reenter more traditional assignments in the most productive way—that don't frustrate the individual, and enable him to effectively infiltrate what he's learned about innovation culture into his new work teams? Are you fully leveraging innovation hot zones and tools?

• Do you use special approaches/environments/experiences (e.g., Clay Street) to enable teams to immerse themselves in the customer to accelerate their ability to identify innovation opportunities and solutions?

• Do you use co-location to help business units build innovation into their everyday work approach? How can the consumer/customer co-locate to cocreate and coinnovate?

CHAPTER TEN

THE NEW JOB OF THE LEADER

Innovation and Growth

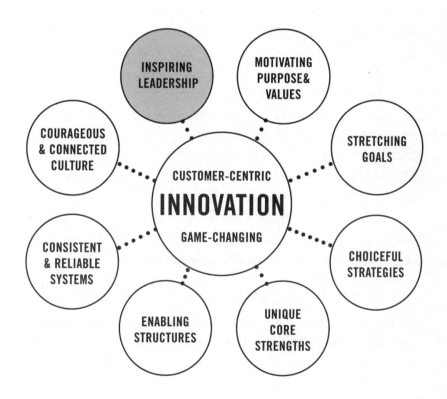

Achieving sustained organic revenue and profit growth will, as we hope has been made clear, require innovation at the center of your business. When all is said and done, it's your job as a leader to make it happen.

In our research and practice, we have found that leaders of innovation take their game to another level through a unique set of skills. Don't get us wrong. You still have to earn your stripes through a track record of delivering consistent results and effectively leading teams and organizations. But there's more, and the purpose of this chapter is to show how you can evolve your leadership approach to ensure that you develop the tools for becoming a leader who delivers organic growth through innovation.

It is our belief that *leaders of innovation are made, not born*. That was certainly true at DuPont. The transformation of its innovation strategy and leadership culture enabled it to break out of an innovation slump and increase its rate of organic revenue growth. The story that follows brings to life the significant impact an innovation leader can make. The members of the DuPont team responsible for this achievement had earned their reputations as great operators, or functional leaders. But when they chose, or were chosen, to lead a major innovation project, or program, they discovered that success required a "whole new leadership ball game." Because of their experience, they knew how things worked in the real world of business. This gave them the foundation to build on as they assumed responsibility for more complex and more uncertain innovation programs.

Following DuPont we will provide the tools to help identify the steps you can personally take to become an innovation leader. We will also take a careful look at the qualities of innovation leaders, and show how leaders of innovation are developed through performance evaluation, early identification, job experiences, and reward and recognition. Further, we will also show how to develop and nurture a strong management team and a pipeline of innovation leaders.

HOW DUPONT GOT ITS GROOVE BACK

DuPont, the two-hundred-year-old chemical company, has an out-standing record of technology-based innovation, including such breakthroughs as Kevlar, Teflon, nylon, and Lycra. These innovations created huge markets and, with the company's scale and manufacturing prowess, enabled DuPont to expand globally. But breakthroughs such as Kevlar hadn't happened for many years, and organic growth through innovation had sputtered. Complicating matters, DuPont, as was the case with almost all chemical companies, got caught in a web of declining prices and increasing costs over several decades. When commodity prices spiked and the value of the U.S. dollar declined, even DuPont's steady expansion in emerging markets couldn't offset an earnings slump.

When Chad Holliday became CEO in 1998, he laid the foundation for DuPont to return to its roots as a science-based company that converts technology into profitable customer offerings. Using "miracles of science" as the centerpiece for building DuPont's future, he had the leadership tenacity required to shape the path and stay on it, while confronting the day-to-day realities of productivity improvement and pressure from Wall Street.

Holliday believed that DuPont's deep and broad scientific expertise and ability to scale production capabilities could translate into growth and profits, provided they were channeled toward the right market opportunities. He raised the bar, saying the company would deliver 6 percent growth in revenues, a third of which would come from the sale of new products by 2006, and 10 percent growth in the bottom line. He and his senior team identified "growth platforms"—safety and protection; electronic and communication technologies; coatings and color technologies; performance materials, agriculture, and nutrition; and, since then, applied biosciences. Together they define the market space where DuPont would put its science to work. These platforms also became the basis around which the business units are organized. In doing so, Holliday was demonstrating something every innovation leader must provide: focus.

Holliday chose Tom Connelly to lead DuPont's process of innovation, seeing in him the ability to *integrate* what were two separate worlds at DuPont: technology and marketing. In addition to impeccable credentials as a chemical engineer and researcher, Connelly is also one of DuPont's top three executives under Holliday, responsible for research and development and several line functions. He has also been a successful growth leader and P&L general manager of several DuPont businesses, including Kevlar and Fluoroproducts.

THE MISSING LINK

The ongoing effective *intersection* of marketing and commercial people in a business unit with the separate technology units was the missing link in DuPont's culture. Its innovation projects were neither clearly defined nor properly prioritized. Also missing was "ownership" by leaders who would be responsible for delivering the projects to realize targeted revenues. Connelly immediately began to deal with the nonexistent intersections between the two silos. He put in place the mechanisms, social processes, and people to make innovation happen routinely and with rigor and discipline to translate scientific exploration and ideas into successful products and business results. Since 2001, when Connelly was named senior vice president and chief science and technology officer, DuPont has more than doubled new product introductions and revenue from new products (defined as products introduced within the previous five years), all achieved by prioritizing and reallocating existing resources.

DuPont has tremendous scientific expertise. But as its senior leaders considered why they weren't achieving the growth they needed, they had to admit that researchers too often pursued projects that were technologically exciting but not right for the market; while at the same time some projects with big commercial potential were stalled for lack of attention or resources. In 2000, most of the company's resources—some 60 percent—were focused on maintaining existing businesses, improving plant yield, and productivity. They are important, of course, but they would not help build DuPont's future top line growth. With growth and earnings goals before them and the growth platforms as the frame of reference, the need for serious leadership was obvious. It was obvious there was room for improvement. Connelly concluded that he had to lead the effort to achieve intersection between marketing and commercial people, on the one hand, and technologists, on the other.

One of Connelly's first steps was to get the company's technology leaders together to try to make better sense of what DuPont was working on. He created a process called Technical Effectiveness Planning, or TEP, to address the issues of focus, resource allocation, and the competitive positioning of technology, market by market. He and Uma Chowdhry (now senior vice president and chief science and technology officer after Connelly's promotion to senior vice president and chief innovation officer) led a discussion with a group of business unit and technology leaders, including director of technology planning Dick Bingham and the general managers of all the business units. The general managers enjoy a high degree of autonomy and generally are free to run each business as they see fit, within the approved framework of financial and other corporate goals. Working collaboratively was a new experience. Together they assessed their strengths in various areas of technology, what technology bases were emerging, what was happening in new and familiar market spaces. They debated where DuPont was or could be positioned in those markets. It led to a discussion of where they stood in key technical areas and what they needed to improve.

INNOVATION REVIEWS

Connelly and Chowdhry have made the TEP review an annual process which culminates in a half-day meeting for each growth platform. The meeting involves business and technical leaders reviewing technical resource allocation within their platform. The purpose is to ensure that each platform has its resources deployed where they will have the biggest impact. They sometimes make decisions on the spot.

The TEP review is directly linked to the annual strategy sessions and the reviews the corporation does for each platform in every business. This linkage is transparent because the people in TEP also participate in the annual discussion of strategy. The linkage provides the continuity that keeps the tech strategy and business strategy in sync. It's the job of the leader to create the linkage.

HOW LEADERS MANAGE INNOVATION

Technology research projects three to five years from commercialization were the feeder system for DuPont's future revenues and margins. There were lots of them, all consuming precious resources, particularly the expertise of key people whose efforts were diluted over too many projects. In Connelly's view, so many projects could neither be properly managed nor given the proper amount of resources. He and Bingham looked at the hundreds of projects that were within three to five years of launch and picked seventy-five (limited to no more than a handful per business unit) that they judged had the highest probability of success. The top seventy-five projects had to meet three criteria: address a well-defined unmet market need; the business must have or be reasonably expected to develop a unique solution to the need; and the business must have an effective route by which the solution could be delivered to the market. For a company whose development efforts had been driven by R&D for most of its two-hundred-year history, that shift represented a major turning point. Suddenly, commercial considerations were part of decision making. As a result, the focus was sharpened and expert resources were used more appropriately.

By 2006, the key initiatives for developing technology had been defined and were in place, and Connelly was ready to take innovation to the next level. He turned his attention to projects that were almost ready to launch or had been commercialized recently. Some products would get introduced to the market but take many years to become widely adopted. Those were precious years, because they delayed the company's ability to recoup development costs and increased the risk that competitors would catch up. Connelly and the technical and business unit leaders began to think beyond the point at which a product was introduced to the market, to the time it hit its peak market share. Obviously, achieving profitable peak market share sooner would mean not just higher sales, but also better pricing and higher margins and lower risk—an enticing combination. They set their sights on reducing the time to peak market share from the typical four to five years to something closer to two to three years.

THE CRITICAL 50

To make this happen routinely, another notch of leadership was needed. This time Connelly and Bingham looked at the total portfolio of projects across the businesses to identify fifty that were within six months of launch or had been launched within the past two years and had the greatest potential to boost revenues and margins within the next eighteen to twenty-four months. These "Critical 50" were, in Connelly's words, "the sweet spot." At least 80 percent of them should be focused on revenue growth, they decided, and the rest could focus on cost reduction or productivity improvement. They didn't all have to be technology based; a business model innovation was equally important. Of course, choosing fifty projects to focus on is harder when you realize how important it is to get the focus right. Connelly knew that projects failed for one of three basic reasons: the technology got out in front of the market, the market got out in front of the technology, or the company didn't have the appropriate route to market. He and Bingham integrated all three of those perspectives—in selecting the projects.

A few of the Critical 50 were for business model innovations, but most of the projects centered on new technology based on identified market needs. Some were broader, involving new technology, new equipment, and even a new supply chain. Successfully launching them required bringing a whole system together and was therefore complex, but those were the projects with the greatest potential to change the game. A new dry process for printing graphics was one of them. It was clear that switching from a liquid printing process to a new dry printing technology brought consumer benefits, such as faster printing speed and less environmental harm. But adopting the technology meant that DuPont would supply the technology, the equipment, and the consumables. All of those things had to come together from several parts of the organization. This was enabled, at least in part, by its designation as a Critical 50 project. The dry film technology was given priority access to engineering and marketing resources needed to drive the program forward at a faster rate.

Next was the question of how to manage those Critical 50 projects. DuPont promised the resources to accelerate time to peak market share and help came from a core team of technical and marketing leaders led by Bingham. The catch was that there were expectations around how those projects would be run. Each Critical 50 project was assigned a leader (usually from marketing) and team members with a mix of expertise. Because the projects had to be managed in a way that integrated diverse and equally important viewpoints, the team leaders had to be good at drawing people out, synthesizing ideas, and facilitating debate, yet getting the group to be decisive and action oriented. They had to be innovation leaders in the making. For many, leading the teams was a new experience, but they quickly got used to the fact that delivering on the project was their sole purpose. Team members moved on or off the teams as projects progressed; they needed more technology expertise early on and more emphasis on developing first a value proposition and then market positioning. Also, team members were more accustomed to taking direction from functional leaders than having a single project leader, so that, too, took some adjustment.

REWARDING INNOVATION

Reinforcing the change in how people worked was a financial reward tied to quickly making the project a commercial success. Each team could earn a cash bonus not for hitting milestones in the development process, but for meeting and exceeding annual revenue and earnings targets. A typical award is from $50,000 to $100,000, depending on the results. The bonus increases as they exceed their goals. For instance, if they get to 150 percent of their goal, the bonus doubles. The team leader gets a set amount of the bonus, then decides how to distribute the rest based on people's contributions.

Assigning teams and leaders, giving them a clear sense of purpose, incenting them, even inspiring them—none of that is sufficient to compensate for a shortfall in capability. As the Critical 50 teams got to work, Connelly discovered company-wide shortfalls in capability. For example, DuPont lacked strong skills for developing and executing comprehensive launch plans. In fact, DuPont had relatively few people with those skills. So Connelly and Bingham began to work with the HR organization to find the right people to fill the gap. They also developed a product launch diagnostic to help the teams assess whether they were fully prepared.

THE ROUTINE OF INNOVATION

Using existing reviews, new mechanisms like the TEP sessions, and plain old-fashioned hallway conversations, Connelly and Bingham stay fully engaged to ensure that the Critical 50 project teams are running right. Periodically they reassess the overall direction and mix of the company's innovation efforts. They now routinely adjust the priorities as new information comes to light or to shift resources accordingly. They've created a number of other formats to keep people and their innovation projects focused and aligned. Team leaders are expected to meet with their teams at least once a week to discuss progress made, issues encountered, and key action items for the following week. And every Monday Bingham meets with his own core team. These people stay in constant touch with each of the fifty teams to keep abreast of what is going on and where they need help. Touching base with each other once a week maintains project rhythm and discipline toward meeting milestones and provides early identification of any emerging issues such as resource availability. Relationships are developed, and this in turn helps information flow.

Once a month the Critical 50 team leaders meet by teleconference to share their stories about what's working (or not working), so they can learn from each other. Also quarterly, they meet as a collective group to talk about where they stand with their quarterly goals, multiplying their capacity by sharing knowledge of fifty projects.

The linkage goes all the way to the CEO. Holliday holds a monthly Critical Growth Review in which he selects typically three programs and spends an hour on each. Holliday gets the discussion going with comments or questions such as "Tell me what are the most critical hurdles your team is facing" or "What makes you the right person to lead this team?" It's usually a positive experience that gives people a chance to have their work recognized or gets them additional support or inspires them. He helps people see that what they might think of as a huge risk might not be one in the context of the corporation as a whole. It's another way of building confidence that innovation is on track to produce revenue and margin gains.

Connelly, as an executive vice president, also participates in the company's annual strategy sessions and in quarterly operating reviews the business units conduct, so he sees where the revenue from innovation is going to come from and how the most important projects are progressing. He carries in his pocket a list of the Critical 50 projects, so whenever he runs into anyone associated with one of the projects, he can pull out the card and say, "I see you're down for this many units this quarter. How are you doing? Where do you stand versus the objective?" Sometimes those casual conversations unearth a problem Connelly needs to know about or can help with. There is never any ambiguity about the fact that people have a commitment to deliver the numbers.

Connelly realized the importance of selecting the right people, so part of his effort to make DuPont more innovative included choosing the right leaders. There isn't anyone in a leadership position, including lower-level supervisors, who he and Bingham didn't help to choose. Over the last five years, they have built a core of leaders who understand what they are trying to execute. Leaders of the Critical 50, in particular, are getting just the practice they need to be innovation leaders in the future.

Connelly's leadership of the process of innovation has led to a measurable shift in resources. The impact is easy to see. It used to be that 40 percent of resources were devoted to growth. The problem was lack of focus. Today, 65 percent of resources are focused on targeted growth. Around 2000, roughly 20 percent of revenue was coming from products introduced within the previous five years. In 2006, it increased to 34 percent. Now the goal is to get 35 percent of revenue from products introduced within the last *four* years by 2010, representing even more revenue from new products and achieving it faster. Margins are significantly better, too. When Performance Materials compared the variable margin of every new product it had commercialized in 2006 with the margin for related products in a given market segment, they found the average difference was in the double digits. In one market segment, margins were between nine and twenty points higher. Even in parts of the business that were most commoditized, variable margins markedly improved.

The change in mind-set is not measurable, but it is real. In fact, it's the leadership that drives the numbers. Projects are no longer driven by technology alone. Instead, they are selected based on the integration of two important perspectives, technology and marketing, and with an aim toward not just bringing products to the market, but to achieving peak market share. The innovation and growth focus, and the goals, strategies systems, and culture, enabled by Holliday, Chowdhry, Connelly, Bingham, the Critical 50 team leaders, and others are consistent with the innovation drivers model we have presented. Through their leadership, the DuPont leaders created the conditions to make innovation happen at a new, game-changing level that, in turn, drove significant business results.

TAKE YOUR LEADERSHIP GAME UP WITH INNOVATION

As we said earlier, innovation leaders are made, not born. DuPont's Chad Holliday, Tom Connelly, and the Critical 50 project team leaders first developed a track record of consistently delivering business results.

Their experience gave them the foundation for implanting the process of innovation. Warren Bennis said it well in *The Character of Leadership* when he referred to leaders as "pragmatic dreamers."

Leaders of innovation dream differently, not just looking at the world as it is but what it can be. They try to conceive how they can change the game. They view the external landscape in a new way, imagining possibilities that elude others. They are thus able to generate new strategic alternatives, select more ambitious goals, choose the right ones, and then convert them into reality.

Leaders of innovation are, however, more than just dreamers; they effectively balance the possibilities with the practical realities of the business. First, by being the *role model of the unique behaviors* required for creating and sustaining an innovation culture. Second, by *performing the unique value-added work* that only an innovation leader can do. And, third, *by honing personal skills* in the most critical areas to take their innovation leadership to the next level.

Responsibilities of an Innovation Leader

Hone
Critical Skills

Provide Unique
Value-Added Roles

Role Model Behavior of
Innovation Culture

ROLE-MODELING THE BEHAVIORS
OF AN INNOVATION CULTURE

DuPont's leaders were the role model of five behaviors—collaborative, connected, curious, open, and courageous (the 4 Cs and an O; see pages 243–245) that laid the foundation for successfully integrating innovation into the fabric of their business.

Collaboration ensures that the right people are at the table for key meetings, reviewing and making the difficult decisions that people often avoid. Tom Connelly's personal behavior and daily interactions enabled a group of autonomous general managers from individual businesses to work together. They created a thorough assessment of the marketplace based on their combined knowledge and factored important innovation priorities into their work. This collective effort resulted in a stronger innovation program for the total DuPont company. The leaders of DuPont's Critical 50 projects were selected in part because of their proven collaboration and facilitation skills of drawing people out in productive and actionable ways—especially those with differing points of view.

At many companies a virtual firewall exists between people in technology and those in commercial areas, such as marketing and sales. While practically everyone understands this problem, solving it eludes most. Connelly was a great connector by effectively bridging the gap between technical and commercial functions. He role-modeled this connection through monthly conference calls in which they not only shared best practices but also dealt with the knotty questions facing one or more members.

Connelly was also *curious*. Getting DuPont's innovation portfolio prioritized and focused simply wasn't enough. He wanted to learn how to accelerate the time it took for innovations to achieve profitable peak market share. His curiosity led to action as he and Bingham identified the Critical 50 innovation projects to apply his findings. He also had the courage to extract resources from other projects, which is never an easy task, especially in collegial organizations.

Continually exhibiting such behaviors is the foundation for how innovation leaders create, nurture, and develop a culture of innovation that leads to successful commercialization.

THE UNIQUE, VALUE-ADDED WORK
OF AN INNOVATION LEADER

Game-changing innovation leaders, in their day-to-day work, have four value-added tasks that differentiate them from other leaders: setting the vision that cannot be accomplished without innovation, and inspiring, integrating, and making the right things happen by dealing with the real issues.

SET THE VISION THAT CANNOT BE ACCOMPLISHED
WITHOUT INNOVATION

Leaders of innovation *convert their vision into long-term priorities.* While excelling at delivering short-term results, they set the right balance by building a long-term foundation via innovation projects. They do it through continuous linkage with open networks to discern and connect external changes.

Steve Jobs's success with the innovation of iPod and iTunes turbocharged Apple into a high-growth trajectory. This, in turn, has accelerated the growth of its original core business, the personal computer, and enabled the Apple brand to achieve new heights in the mind of the consumer.

By virtue of his being a leader of innovation, the fundamental definition of Jobs's vision expanded from personal computers to consumer entertainment. He saw a new opportunity in telecommunications by successfully initiating the first major change in the industry's business model since the breakup of the old AT&T in 1984. Makers of cellphone handsets, for example Motorola and Nokia, sold them through carriers such as Verizon and retailers such as Costco and Radio Shack at deep discount, committing end-users to lengthy contracts for access to the network. Jobs changed the game with the iPhone by controlling the distribution of the handset in two ways: through building his own retail network and with an exclusive relationship with one of the carriers, AT&T. Such a game-changing innovation gives Jobs control of the positioning of the Apple brand. Apple, then, won't be commoditized, as has been the case with the rest of the telecom industry. Thus, Apple has better control not only of the brand but of its pricing and margins as well.

Another earth-shaking innovation is building a revenue stream not just from the sale of the handset, but from a portion of the revenues that telecom carriers get from each consumer using a handset. Thus, Jobs not only has the sale of a product, but an annuity from service revenue. This has resulted in a new trajectory of profitable growth, taking Apple to new heights of revenues and profits.

Jobs was cautioned by many not to build his own retail network, being told that "your head will be handed to you." Jobs charged ahead and innovated a radical concept for retail outlets based on a new vision of what the customer experience needs to be in the store. While his first prototype failed, he was courageous and persisted until he executed a revolutionary new design for ambience and the distinctive experience customers have from the time they enter until they leave. It's a design no one has yet been able to replicate and has resulted in Apple stores having among the highest—if not the highest—dollar per square foot of space in the recent history of retailing.

INSPIRE

Since the process of innovation has inherently uncertain outcomes and is riddled with risk, leaders of innovation *inspire and redirect emotional energy of knowledge workers,* both individually and on teams. They are patient if things don't go as planned, not getting frustrated if a team takes longer to work through qualifying a prototype with a customer. In fact, they know when to encourage a team to go off for further exploration to ensure they have considered all possibilities. And, they know when to converge and move on to the next stage of development.

Through their participation in innovation project reviews, they inspire individuals and teams to help them see new possibilities by asking questions unique to innovation: What haven't you noticed? What can be connected that hasn't been connected? How can you harness the diverse thinking of both internal and external people? Overall they inspire people that they can do it, that they can make the breakthrough. For example, improving the lives of consumers was a significant inspiration for people at all levels of P&G, as was the personal interaction many experienced through the *Living It* and *Working It* programs (see pages 48–49).

INTEGRATE

One of the most critical aspects of the day-to-day work of the leader of innovation is *seamlessly integrating the tasks of different members of the organization*. (Horizontal integration across silos is very uncommon, especially with innovation projects.) They integrate innovation into the daily operations of the business, not allowing people to think of it as discrete and "special." They make sure individuals go through experiences together as one team, not as separate businesses or functions. For example, innovation reviews are held with the entire team and not just with one function such as R&D. Often these teams include customers and suppliers when that is appropriate.

MAKING THE RIGHT THINGS HAPPEN BY DEALING WITH THE REAL ISSUES

Innovation can be messy at times, but innovation leaders have the *discipline, judgment, and courage* to ensure that a team works only on innovation projects with a chance to be successful in the marketplace, being decisive and killing those destined for failure. They don't let projects linger without a clear next step or action plan. They know, as the adage goes, "the buck stops with me." As a routine, they ensure that real killer issues are identified as early as possible and then dealt with. Given the uncertainty inherent in innovation projects, they continually reprioritize the assignment of resources and have the discipline at each milestone to do so. They help the team clearly define the real success criteria and find ways to get them the resources needed, resorting when necessary to the "art of scrounging." They are action oriented, as they know the competition is not letting up and the only innovations customers see are those that ultimately reach the market.

In the end, how the innovation leader performs these unique tasks can make or break the potential of a business to become an innovation powerhouse. It's up to the innovation leader to bring the vision, inspiration, integration, and action orientation to bear on innovation strategy, portfolio, and individual project decisions.

HONING CRITICAL PERSONAL SKILLS

The leadership bar is higher when it comes to the more complex, uncertain, and long-term game of innovation. It means operating at a higher level with relentless courage, integrative thinking, and balancing IQ and EQ.

RELENTLESS COURAGE

Innovation leaders are not afraid of risk. They know how to pinpoint, define, and manage it. They have a willingness to try and try again. They're not afraid to fail since failure can be an important source of learning. They experiment and iterate. They are not afraid to kill an innovation, even if it is someone's pet project. In fact, the best innovation leaders can pinpoint at an early stage potential reasons for an innovation to fail. They are not afraid to ask the tough questions to ensure the most important killer issues are addressed.

On the flipside, they have the *courage* to stick with an innovation for a while, even though the team hasn't yet figured it out. That's because they believe in the people working on the project, the innovation's potential to make a difference for the customer, and in the technology underlying the innovation. They have the courage to instigate change in anticipation of what's needed to win versus waiting for the market to dictate the need for change. They have the conviction to constantly challenge the status quo and look for opportunities where innovation can make the difference, such as things that can be done better, cheaper, simpler, and faster. They are not afraid to set the bar higher. They resist accepting trade-offs for the customer, the retailer, and the company.

People who seek solutions for customer problems must have incredible courage and remain steady in their resolve to reach the final outcome, because the journey from idea to final product is fraught with ups and downs, budget cuts and increases, and changes of bosses, strategies, resources, and team members. Innovation leaders who focus on achieving a higher purpose to delight customers, versus pursuing personal gain, affect the culture and inspire others.

Take Andy Wong, who led the team that was trying to find a market for 3M's optical film technology. He tirelessly networked with potential customers over several years, across many unrelated industries, attempting to match various combinations of 3M technologies against the needs of customers. Wong's sense of purpose, courage, and confidence never wavered.

Wong demonstrated his personal commitment at several critical junctures. At one point, when senior management wanted to shut down Optical Systems, Wong went to the team and explained what he was being asked to do. He said, "I don't think it's in the best interests of the company, and I'm willing to put my career on the line and fight for this business. But if you think it's time to call it quits, we will." The team wanted to keep going, and Wong was able to persuade headquarters to give them more time. That was two years before they struck their most successful product innovation and cracked the PC market just as the industry was taking off (see pages 46–47). Optical Systems is now a major contributor to 3M's profits.

Wong's personal commitment, even risking his own career, created an environment in which others were willing to do the same. Many team members passed up chances for more money or prestige to stick with it. "Why have so many of us stuck with Andy Wong all this time?" asks Jeff Melby, the optical systems business director and former technical director. "Because," he said, "the job's not finished. The team has more to do, and that's more important than looking out for your own career. That's the kind of commitment Andy's built."

Courage and a higher sense of purpose sustain the energy of people as they withstand the ups and downs and uncertainties inherent in the innovation process.

INTEGRATIVE THINKING

There are many different ways of thinking, including linear, conceptual, inductive, deductive, and integrative.

For innovation, *integrative thinking is more central for success*. As Roger Martin, the dean of the Rotman School of Management at the University of Toronto, puts it, an integrative thinker finds unobvious connections and patterns from a diverse set of factors. They see *more* things as relevant and important, such as contradictions in what customers say and what they actually do. They then bring it all together by synthesizing and translating salient information into simple insights that lead to action. Integrative thinkers are creative problem solvers because they find solutions to break the tensions of opposing ideas.

Hartwig Langer, president of P&G's Global Prestige Products, is an integrative thinker. When determining the best way to innovate the business model for P&G's fine-fragrance business (see pages 101–103), Langer opened his mind and found more aspects of the category salient than were previously considered. He and his team looked at the category from a consumer-centric vantage point, including identifying different consumer segments to whom specific innovations and brands would appeal most. They carefully looked at total system costs—an aspect most people in the fine-fragrance business paid little, if any, attention to. They focused on building long-term brand equities of fragrances like Hugo Boss and Lacoste instead of using more typical holiday promotions as the primary way to sell product. Langer, in sum, understood that for P&G's fine-fragrance business to win, he and his team needed to consider more data and connect the dots in different ways than other industry competitors. His way of thinking was unique for this industry and provided him with the intellectual ability to turn the traditional business model on its head.

IQ AND EQ BALANCE

Innovation leaders have different thinking patterns and broader influencing capabilities and skills. They have *well-balanced intellectual and emotional skills*. They have mastered the social process that comes with innovation. They are aware of their impact on others and, therefore, exercise self-awareness and self-control. They are intrinsically motivated. They have a well-developed intuition to understand and appreciate people's intentions, feelings, and motivations. They trust and rely on their gut. They think with their head and their heart. They have strong social skills that enable them to have productive relationships. For example, innovation leaders have personal passion for the customers they serve. They won't settle for superficial understanding of their customer. They dig deeper to understand and empathize with their WHO by uncovering unarticulated needs, which lead to game-changing innovations.

BUILDING THE PIPELINE OF LEADERS OF INNOVATION

We have been describing what differentiates leaders of innovation, but at this point we need to reiterate a key point made at the beginning of this chapter: *that leaders of innovation are made, not born*. For the process of innovation to be sustainable it is imperative to have a systematic methodology for developing these unique people as a continuous process. The four key building blocks of this process are performance evaluation, early identification, developmental experiences, and reward and recognition.

PERFORMANCE EVALUATION

Performance evaluation is a proven way to grow and develop individual innovation leaders and is, thus, an essential element in building a pipeline of leaders and ultimately an innovation culture. Selecting and developing the right people and giving the most promising managers assignments that enable them to learn how to manage innovation is an investment that will result in more experienced, and therefore, more successful innovation leaders in the future. If a company hires, develops, trains, and promotes people who do not have the skills or passion to do what it takes to develop and lead innovations that delight the customer, nothing else they do is going to matter.

For example, as part of the performance-evaluation process, P&G systematically increased its emphasis on the qualities that foster innovation. In 2001, in a major study, two thousand people, mostly current and former P&Gers, were interviewed to isolate leadership behaviors that result in success. In 2003, a new performance evaluation was introduced to all employees. It consisted of three dimensions: power of minds, power of people, and power of agility. Innovation is integrated across all dimensions. Within each dimension, specific attributes are evaluated.

1. **Power of Minds** P&G, as does every business, wants people who think and act decisively and have mastery of a function and/or business. These attributes are taken to another level to achieve game-changing innovation by harnessing diverse thinking and linking it with real consumer insights—thus generating innovation—and reapplying thinking and insight again and again.

2. **Power of People** The performance attributes evaluated—demonstrates leadership, builds collaborative relationships, and grows the capabilities of others—are taken to another level for game-changing innovation when the leader actively searches for the right diversity of people and leads, inspires, and works with them.

3. **Power of Agility** P&G evaluates how an employee understands and appreciates customer needs and wants, embraces change, and operates with discipline. A leader of innovation takes these attributes to another level as she naturally becomes comfortable in identifying the ever-changing needs of customers in a very dynamic and competitive

marketplace and demonstrates agility to convert those needs into reality of revenue growth.

Working on an innovation project enables an employee's performance to be assessed across all three dimensions. For example, an innovation project team leader can demonstrate his ability to think and act decisively by the quality of actions taken (for example, asking for more resources or identifying and having the team work against the most important killer issues). They can show their effectiveness at inspiring, leading, and collaborating with a diverse team consisting of people who are "creatives" as well as those who are more logical thinkers. The leader can also encourage and enable the team to deeply understand and involve the customer in each step of the innovation development and qualification process to improve the odds of commercial success.

For general managers and presidents of businesses (the top 150 P&G leaders), there is an additional level of scrutiny. A scorecard is used to measure their performance against these three dimensions, but with more detail and with higher expectations. For example, factors like whether innovations are meeting customer needs and winning at the first and second moments of truth, and whether the leader is creating a sustainable innovation pipeline that drives business results to help assess the innovation leader's strength and opportunity areas. These annual scorecards are evaluated over a multiyear period. They are also checked the year after a manager leaves a job. If business results deteriorate, it may be a signal that the way the person got results was unsustainable—something that will be looked at further. For example, a P&G business may experience strong growth under a specific general manager's leadership. However, if the business results start to suffer in the year following the general manager's move to a new assignment, this would indicate that he had not developed a strong enough innovation pipeline for the future, and in fact may have just been reaping the benefits of the innovation pipeline developed by his predecessor.

Scorecards play an important role in promotion. "The ability to lead innovation is really important. We need to know that a strong general manager can run a good innovation program," says Dick

Antoine, then P&G's head of human resources. "It's something we look at very, very carefully." In general, those who aspire to lead a global business unit have to show a consistent record of business-building innovation. There is no way to win in P&G's consumer businesses unless consumer-winning, profitable innovations are delivered to the market on a regular basis.

Finally, these performance evaluations and scorecards send a message. They say to managers that you may not become a line group president if you have not demonstrated an ability to manage innovation, even if you are well qualified in other ways. As GE's Jeff Immelt tells his managers, "You're not going to stick around this place and not take bets." That's a different outlook than one solely focused on making the numbers—although it is expected that people deliver the numbers, too.

LOOK FOR FUTURE INNOVATION LEADERS FROM DAY ONE

From day one, new hires at P&G are intentionally thrown into innovation projects to see how they do right from the start. More P&Gers in more functions are tested this way. If they do well, they get a bigger project. To move up into the senior ranks at P&G, an employee has to be able to consistently demonstrate his ability to run a business operation; to define clear, game-changing strategies; and to effectively run an innovation program. It's that simple.

Dimitri Panayotopolous is a great example. He was raised in Tanzania and educated in the U.K. He joined P&G as part of the sales organization in Europe. He also worked in the Middle East. During the initial years of his career, he worked on and led numerous innovation projects for the brands he was responsible for. Dimitri then led P&G's rapid growth in China by identifying the winning strategies and by introducing a strong pipeline of innovations that met the needs of consumers in this developing market. He was then responsible for leading the business and innovation program in Central and Eastern Europe, the Middle East, and Africa. His ability as an effective business and innovation leader helped deliver record-setting growth in the global fabric care business. Today, he's vice chairman of the company and heads P&G's global Household Care business including overall responsibility for the household innovation program.

DEVELOPING INNOVATION LEADERS

A good operational leader becomes an innovation leader through the right combination of coaching, experiences, and learning opportunities that develop innovation judgment and skills. If a company wants to place innovation at the center of its business, developing innovation leaders is not optional. Support mechanisms can help strengthen the skills of current innovation leaders and are also necessary to ensure the development of a strong pipeline of future innovation leaders (such as DuPont's approach to selecting the Critical 50 project team leaders).

While there are many different support mechanisms to consider, here are three key ways to help provide current and future innovation leaders with the informal and formal opportunities they need.

• **Personal Coaching by Other Innovation Leaders** Great innovation leaders develop other innovation leaders. They have a serious commitment and give priority to coaching and teaching others in everything they do. They make the time, either one on one, on the job, or in more formal training to help other innovation leaders learn how to think, make judgments, take action, mobilize resources, and inspire organizations. They have, as Noel Tichy of the University of Michigan says, "a teachable point of view." They think about their own experiences, draw lessons from what they know, and share those lessons at teachable moments. For example, when P&G was looking to expand Febreze into Japan, the team received discouraging data that the idea and product were not appealing to the targeted segments of the Japanese population. The Febreze innovation team was asked by Bob McDonald, then leading northeast Asia and now the COO, to dig deeper into the data and look at the responses from passionate consumers. What did they like about the new product? Why was the promise appealing to them? Based on the team's findings, McDonald encouraged them to change what the "passionates" did not like about Febreze. Modifications to the product fragrance and packaging enabled Febreze to better satisfy the needs of the Japanese consumer. Those "teachable moments" between the coach and the team resulted in a successful launch of Febreze in this market. The business is still going strong with a continuous pipeline of new innovations that appeal to passionate Japanese consumers.

• **Support Systems and Training Opportunities** This includes more formal mechanisms, such as encouraging innovation leaders to attend specific training courses (for example, P&G offers courses in design thinking and improving innovation success rates); providing leaders with short immersion experiences (such as participating in the *Living It, Working It* consumer immersion program); spending time at a design firm to learn about the role of design and innovation; and creating specific places and forums for innovation leaders to share and discuss learning (for example, P&G's Clay Street and its Innovation Centers).

• **Intentional Assignment/ Experience Planning** When working on innovation, you can't rely on numbers alone as most innovations have never been done before. Innovation leadership requires relying more on personal instinct and developing experienced judgment. The more diverse the experiences, the better the instincts and judgment of the innovation leader. It is important to include an element that ensures an individual continues to build experience across a variety of innovation situations with increased complexity, increased uncertainty, and increased risk. It is also important to give them experiences across a variety of businesses, geographies, and multiple functions. An example of a P&Ger's assignment plan might look like this: Lead an innovation project of a new line of flavored Crest toothpaste in a manufacturing role; then move to marketing and lead a project that is more important and complex as it will revolutionize the category, like introducing Crest Whitestrips; then move to China to run the Crest low-income consumer innovation program for all developing markets; and finally lead the entire oral-care category innovation program for P&G (including such brands as Crest, Oral-B, Scope, Fixodent). Assignment plans like this ensure the innovation leader gets the right kinds of experiences and is well equipped to be able to take her game and the innovation programs she is responsible for to the next level.

REWARD AND RECOGNITION

By publicly recognizing people for winning innovations and rewarding them, companies build pride in achievement and create a positive psychology. It's not only a positive recognition of an individual's accomplishments but an inspiration for hundreds, if not thousands, of others to follow the path to become a leader of innovation. It influences the behavior of people the day they enter the company and alters their aspirations. It muscle-builds the culture for innovation.

For example, in P&G's R&D division, the Vic Mills society (founded more than twenty years ago) is named after the man who invented Pampers. There are only sixteen active Vic Mills members at the moment (plus twenty retired members), including the scientist who figured out the odor-eating technology behind Febreze and the biochemist who created much of the skin-care technology underpinning the reinvention of the Olay brand. The vice presidents of R&D call for nominations; a team of senior managers, including the chief technology officer, evaluates nominees; and the CEO makes the final decision. The winner gets a medal—some have been known to wear it around the office for weeks—and is recognized by the CEO with his colleagues and family in a large company gathering. Other functions at P&G have similar recognition programs for outstanding contributions to innovation and the growth of the company's business.

There is also an annual Cost Innovation Award given to teams that bring innovation to the market in a way that provides consumers a better value at a lower capital and/or cost structure than competition. P&G started this program to recognize people who are crucial to commercializing innovation in a way that gives consumers great value. It is given during an annual award dinner, and again, senior management is on hand to recognize and salute the winners.

These examples work for P&G; different companies will have their own recognition programs, depending on what they want to achieve and how. Regardless of program specifics, recognition should reinforce the behaviors of an innovation culture the innovation leader wants to create.

WHO SHOULD BE THE CHIEF INNOVATION OFFICER?

The characteristics we have discussed are common to innovation leaders at almost all levels. However, the broader the scope of the innovation leader, the broader the responsibility. At the CEO level, the job is to take the mid- to long-range views with an eye for balancing short- and long-term goals, high- and low-risk projects, and disruptive and incremental innovations. They have to be able to see the company from 30,000 feet up (setting goals) while also keeping a close eye on the infantry on the ground (tactics and execution). For example, one of the first things DuPont's Chad Holliday did was reestablish higher growth goals and commit that one-third of sales would ultimately come from new products and innovation. A. G. Lafley set the goal that at least 50 percent of P&G's innovations would need to come from the outside to enable P&G to deliver target growth goals.

As innovation is becoming a more recognized business growth driver, many companies have carved out room in the C-suite for a new position—the chief innovation officer. There has been a notable increase in such positions, including at such companies as Citigroup, Coke, Wrigley, Humana, and Kellogg. Most CIOs have direct access to the CEO, always a sign that a company is taking the job seriously. P&G, however, has decided not to create a separate CIO position. They think accountability belongs with the business unit leaders and, ultimately, the CEO.

In effect, A. G. Lafley is the CIO of the company as a whole, but he partners very closely with the chief technology officer and with the group presidents who are the CIOs of their respective businesses. P&G's goal is to create a structure that can deliver innovation on a regular basis; for that to happen, line business leaders have to buy into the idea. P&G doesn't see the need to create a separate, high-level executive to do what current business leaders should be doing—namely, being the innovation and growth leaders for their businesses. In fact, they believe that creating this position goes in the wrong direction by creating another silo, when the ideal is to integrate innovation into the businesses and with the participating functions.

ASK YOURSELF MONDAY MORNING
PERSONAL ASSESSMENT

• From a scale of 1 to 10, how would you rate yourself on the following leadership of innovation characteristics:

1. Do you set organic growth goals that cannot be accomplished without innovation?
2. How do you ensure that the consumer/customer is really the boss in the process of innovation?
3. How good are you at integrating the end-to-end process of innovation, within your area of responsibility?
4. How well do you review and assess innovation projects?
5. Do you experiment? Do you iterate to learn?
6. Do you know the tough questions to ask? Do you have the courage to kill projects?

7. How good are you in molding a group of diverse individuals into an innovation team that can deliver game-changing innovation?

8. How good are you at performing the primary responsibilities of the innovation leader?

 * Do you consistently role-model the behaviors of the innovation culture you are trying to create?

 * Do you set the vision, inspire, integrate, and provide the action orientation needed for innovation to become a growth driver for your business?

 * Are you continuing to immerse yourself in experiences that enable you to hone your innovation leadership skills?

9. Do you actively search for new ideas? Are you open to new ideas?

10. Do you take advantage of all the possible connections— inside and outside your company—for innovative ideas?

DEVELOPING OTHER INNOVATION LEADERS ASSESSMENT

• Have you clearly articulated the qualities, traits, and experiences required of innovation leaders at different levels of the organization (e.g., project leader, business unit leader, functional leader, senior executive, and CEO)?

 *Do your high-potential leaders balance operational leadership *and* innovation leadership to deliver sustainable business growth? Are they able to balance possibilities with practicalities?

 *Do your innovation leaders have strong social skills? That is, the skills of self-awareness, self-control, internal motivation, empathy, and social relationship skills.

 *Can your innovation leaders recognize important consumer/customer insights that lead to potential innovation opportunities?

• How do you identify, develop, and nurture innovation leaders?

　*Do you have assignment planning for your top-development leaders to ensure they get the diversity of experiences required for them to become strong, innovation leaders?

　*Do you provide your current leadership team with formal and informal opportunities to learn and fine-tune their innovation leadership skills?

　*Do you take time to personally coach and teach others how to become more effectively leaders of innovation?

• Is innovation leadership an important element of the performance-assessment process?

　*Are leaders being measured on innovation performance?

　*How does innovation leadership success or failure influence their career progression and compensation?

• What processes do you use to reward and recognize innovation leaders—for both innovation success and failure?

CONCLUSION

HOW JEFF IMMELT MADE INNOVATION A WAY OF LIFE AT GE

Now you know that innovation must be built into how you ordinarily run your department, business unit, or company. How do you get from here to there? Not by changing everything at once. P&G, despite an earnings shortfall back in 2000, carefully *paced and sequenced* the innovation strategy and culture changes it made. So did GE, when CEO Jeff Immelt determined a higher organic growth goal and put innovation at the center of the business seven years ago.

Immelt did an extensive scan of the external environment and the industries GE competed in and concluded that GE could grow faster than it had been. He confidently set the organic revenue growth at two to three times GDP, which meant GE was aiming for 8 percent organic revenue growth versus its typical 4 percent. How would GE actually achieve it? Not just from doing more of the same. Productivity improvements alone would not deliver it, and GE was getting too big to sustain growth through acquisitions (remember that European regulators blocked the proposed acquisition of Honeywell). Reaching the new organic growth goal meant reaching new and existing customers with new offerings. It made innovation an imperative.

In the past seven years, GE has been building the *capacity, capability and culture* to make innovation a reality. The capacity to fund innovation has increased in part by reducing overhead and G&A expenses and in part from the reallocation of resources. New capabilities in marketing and technology have been built through targeted recruiting and new executive development programs and training programs at GE's state-of-the-art John F. Welch Learning Center, located in Crotonville, New York. The culture has evolved as a result of changes in the selection and promotion of leaders, the content of reviews, and the creation of new operating mechanisms, all of that reinforced with metrics and accountabilities designed to drive innovation. Without explicitly setting out to do so, GE worked its way through the "innovation drivers" model (goals, strategies, core strengths, enabling structures, work systems, leadership, culture, and values). Driven by Immelt's high energy and personal commitment, and boosted by breakthroughs GE made in understanding how to use its training sessions at Crotonville to shift the *social process*, innovation is becoming integrated into everyday thinking and decision making throughout the GE businesses.

Exactly how, and in what sequence, you make a change in one or more of your innovation drivers is very much up to you as a leader. Some companies will start by trying to change the culture. Many others (P&G and GE among them) have found that changing some of the "hard stuff"—goals, organizational structures, work systems, and metrics—actually helps drive the culture change. What matters most is that you integrate innovation into your business strategy and operations, and then work innovation as an end-to-end process. Bear in mind that innovation is social and not just mechanical, and exercise leadership to inspire others to keep working at it until it becomes a common thread in your ordinary business activities. What you'll most certainly find is that one change leads to and builds on another.

You'll find that even seemingly simple actions can have a big impact. Consider the following set of actions Immelt took to put customer-centric innovation at the center of day-to-day work at GE. The lessons apply to leaders at any organizational level.

Put innovation and productivity—both—on your personal leadership agenda. Immelt took the helm at GE just four days before the World Trade Center tragedy. In those first few months, the economy weakened and GE took a large write-off for its insurance business. GE's Aviation and Energy business hit tough times as well. Investors had been hoping for a continuation of GE's steady, predictable earnings, and perhaps some portfolio adjustments, but in the post-9/11 world, it wasn't clear that earnings would be sustained. The stock price took a beating.

In the face of all that, Immelt set his own agenda, and seeing untapped potential in GE, he set his sights high. He determined he could make GE a faster growth company, despite its size and the increasing complexity and uncertainty of the external environment. Early on he imagined that GE could be great at both productivity and organic growth at the same time, and that the two *core strengths* would work together. GE in the Jack Welch era was a productivity engine. Immelt wanted to continue to sharpen that productivity edge to drive the bottom line, but he wanted to apply the same kind of rigor and discipline to growing the top line. He believed in his heart and mind that GE could do it. He made his *goals* specific—and public. He even tied his own compensation to them.

It has taken time for GE's people and investors to be convinced, but his *motivating purpose*, or vision, to become a growth company has been constant. Immelt's unwavering commitment to customer-centric innovation as the key to growth—even in the face of questions like "Can GE really do innovation?" and "If it can, will it lose its execution edge?"—has inspired people and provided the focus for specific actions that would follow.

LESSON: Consider how innovation could breathe new life into your existing business, segment, or product area and achieve higher goals. Become the source of inspiration for others who don't see it yet. Make it part of your personal leadership agenda. Communicate it clearly and repeatedly, but don't stop at inspirational words and positive thoughts. Be prepared to make innovation happen.

Give innovation a seat at the table. GE is a "doing" company. Among the first things Immelt did to jump-start innovation was create what he called a Commercial Council. This was a *structure* that brought together some sixteen sales and marketing people he picked from throughout the company not because of their job title or position but because of how well they could influence others in their businesses and their excellent marketing skills. The idea was to get them to help develop and share their best practices around marketing and innovation and to take those practices back to their businesses. This would put the *customer at the center*.

At the time GE had already started to hire some marketing leaders, and while some businesses had a strong marketing function, in others marketing did little more than support sales. Pulling together a small group of salespeople and marketers to conference with the CEO, who worked shoulder-to-shoulder with the chief marketing officer, was a powerful signal that marketing was important and had a real job to do and that Immelt was making a shift in GE's operations-driven *culture*. Having Dave Nissen of GE Money cochair the Commercial Council with chief marketing officer Beth Comstock helped ensure buy-in from the businesses.

The Commercial Council has since grown and evolved and is now run by Dan Henson, chief marketing officer, though Immelt drives the agenda, focus, and discussion. It includes about twenty sales and marketing people from across GE's businesses, only two of whom report directly to the CEO. The Council continues to be a forum to share best practices to drive the growth and innovation agenda, now through one-hour monthly phone calls and four-hour quarterly meetings at the Learning Center at Crotonville. Those meetings sometimes include customers. The meetings bring people from disparate businesses together to exchange ideas and send them back with tools or ideas they can translate for their individual businesses. The Commercial Council creates social connections across the businesses and infuses the company with a marketing and customer orientation. It drives *culture* change on a tactical level.

The Commercial Council is also a sounding board for identifying and testing ideas for growth and innovation, particularly those that have implications across the P&Ls. In that sense, it is a mechanism to do a kind of *internal connect-and-develop*. Through discussions in the

Commercial Council, GE recognized, for instance, that the Olympics was an opportunity not just for NBC to broadcast but also for GE to provide security systems, mobile health-care units, lighting, and financing to the tune of around $600 million in potential revenue from the Beijing Games alone and about a billion dollars for all of the Games under GE sponsorship. Immelt put representatives from each of the relevant businesses on a team to pursue the combined opportunities and gave the team leader clear accountability.

LESSON: Don't expect to innovate without getting closer to your customers. Send a signal by finding the people who know customers best and elevating their position or at least their input. Take simple, repetitive actions to drive a culture of innovation at the tactical level. In the beginning, you can't delegate this.

Find and follow up on the best ideas. Before the October 2003 business review session, Immelt sent a note to all of the business unit leaders asking them to bring a list of innovation project ideas. The ideas had to show promise to generate between $50 million and $100 million in incremental revenue. The best ones would get pulled out of the pile so Immelt could personally track them and ensure they got properly funded and commercialized. He would help evaluate them from his CEO-level-view of the risk and time horizon, so good ideas wouldn't get passed up because of short-term profit pressures on a business. He gave those project ideas the name "Imagination Breakthroughs."

Imagination Breakthroughs (IBs) have been a companywide edict ever since. Each business unit leader has to not only bring new ideas forward but also "own" three to five IB projects. That means he or she must fund them (even if it means taking funding from something else) and is accountable for making them happen. Each project has to meet specific milestones along the way, and is measured against a specific set of metrics. Generating IB ideas and tracking them is a *consistent, reliable work system.*

Immelt personally devotes time each month to review about ten IB projects with their leaders (a handful of people from the same or other businesses are also present so people can learn from each other). In the early days, people tended to tell Immelt what they thought he wanted to hear in those reviews—that everything was going fine, even when it wasn't. To break that mind-set, Immelt would intentionally praise people for taking a project off the list because it couldn't meet the metrics. Over time, with repetition and deft leadership, reviews of the IB projects have become direct and deep. "The leader looks me in the eye," Immelt says. He or she describes the project succinctly, and Immelt asks incisive questions to understand the barriers they might be facing, whether they have to do with technology, funding, magnitude of risk, or commercialization, and how to overcome them. Review of a portable ultrasound project, for instance, led to discussion of a new kind of distribution and what they had to do to reach the customer base and in what time frame. Another IB session generated the idea of using imaging technology from the health-care business to test the structural integrity of infrastructure parts. "Nondestructive testing" didn't even exist until 2004. It is now a $700 million business and a global leader, growing 25 percent a year.

GE even makes reporting on Imagination Breakthroughs part of its Corporate Executive Council, or CEC, its twice-a-year meeting of senior executives at GE. Frequent periodic reviews of new ideas and their progress creates an operating rhythm in how people work and what they spend their time on. Initially, business leaders brought ideas forward because they had to. As they've practiced spotting and evaluating opportunities, they've become better at finding them, and they bring them forward because they're excited about them. Generating imagination breakthroughs has become part of the innovation and growth process. Shahira Raineri, Imagination Breakthrough leader at headquarters, is charged with overseeing the portfolio of Imagination Breakthrough projects to address which ones belong where and what intervention might be needed. The business leaders handle the projects that represent growth by adjacencies and bring the more radical ideas to senior management's attention. Immelt focuses on the ones that could truly be game-changers.

LESSON: Chances are your people have lots of good ideas for growth and innovation. Create a disciplined process to sort through them. Select the good ones and create mechanisms to track them. Be sure they get funded. Keep them on the radar screen by asking about them often and formally reviewing them on a regular basis. You know innovation is taking root when there's rhythm to the review of projects and rigor in the milestones they must meet.

Shift the focus to customers and the longer term. For many years, GE's annual strategic planning session was a time for each business to take stock of the industry and lay out a roadmap for where it was going next and what it would deliver, and for the CEO to drill into the business to make sure the thinking behind the plan was bulletproof. Immelt now refers to these sessions as the growth playbook to reflect the different orientation he brings to the process. Now when people convene, they have to cover several prescribed "chapters," starting with the external environment, technology, the competition, and market trends. This requirement puts the realities of the *customer's world at the center*. Then they move on to discuss how they will build on the growth plays where GE has strategic advantage, such as environmental technology, to drive toward the *goal* of long-term organic growth. And then things are tied into the operating and financial plans.

The sessions are no longer than before, but the front end of the discussion generates a lot of ideas and gets people thinking more strategically. In other words, Immelt redesigned the social architecture of the existing strategy review *structure* so it is linked to the *customer, financial goals*, and GE's *motivating purpose*.

The follow-on to those sessions six months later is a business review of the operating plan for the upcoming year. These reviews have been famously rigorous at GE, with a hard-nosed focus on business results. Immelt has maintained the rigor, but he starts each one with questions about how GE's product lines are differentiated and how the markets, customer industries, technology, and competition are shaping. The reviews still cover things like productivity, and earning money is always key, but there is a difference in emphasis. Rather than drilling solely on the operating details and assuming growth will take care of itself, he gives the *customer* center stage and digs into the details of the leader's growth and innovation efforts as well. Now the reviews are more balanced between the science of productivity and the science of growth. They discuss customer value propositions, market segmentation, pricing strategies, and product launches with as much rigor and edge as they do spending and efficiency improvements. At the same time, Immelt tries to show that while the current quarter is important, it isn't everything. Leaders have accountability beyond it. Repeated questions and discussion about where future growth will come from has gradually shifted business leaders' orientation to think long-term as well as short-term.

LESSON: Put growth and innovation high on your agenda. Shift the topics you focus on and ask about. Change the emphasis in your discussions. Treat growth and innovation as a science, not an art form. Dig into it and follow up on it with the same kind of edge you have in operations.

Rethink leadership. A different agenda for GE put different demands on its leaders. Immelt redefined the criteria for leaders and circulated them so everyone knew the expectation. Leaders had to think long-term as well as short-term and pursue growth as well as cost efficiencies. As he used those criteria in reviews of people, he began to make changes in a number of high-level *leadership* positions. About two-thirds of the 190 officers are people he named to their positions. He now has a leadership team that is adept at doing short-term and long-term, productivity and growth.

He made a few changes at the top that were especially significant. For instance, because he knew technology had a key role to play in innovation, Immelt wanted to energize the leadership of GE Global Research. He put bright, accomplished, relatively young Scott Donnelly in charge of the GRC (Global Research Center) and updated and globalized it. He also elevated the role of the chief marketing officer by giving the person a visible role in important meetings, including the reviews of Imagination Breakthroughs, and required that each business hire a CMO of its own. As Immelt notes, "Growth companies respect technology and marketing."

LESSON: Innovation leaders are different. People who have been successful in the past might not have the mind-set or talent for it. Be specific and explicit about the characteristics you're looking for, and make the people who "get it" more visible. Don't back off from tough decisions about people.

Build the capabilities you're lacking. GE's search for Imagination Breakthroughs uncovered lots of good product ideas, and even some for how products are commercialized. People were used to seeing new products come from a research lab, but the energy business found a $200 million opportunity over three to five years by simply doing a better job of matching GE products to market segments. As one of the business unit leaders said, "It was a basic market segmentation exercise." With Crotonville as the melting pot, the idea of innovating in how you approach commercialization spread quickly throughout the company—and brought to the surface the need for more upstream marketing capability.

GE went about building marketing skills as a *core strength* in part by recruiting undergraduates and MBAs expressly for the purpose of doing marketing. It also created new training programs at its John F. Welch Learning Center to teach marketing and innovation. As part of that training, GE brought in five different innovation firms, each with its own approach, to get people to see things with new eyes. One of the firms took people from GE's energy and water businesses, who were working on a project to treat water in nuclear plants, to NASCAR to glean insights from how the pit crew services the car. A group from GE's Scandinavian health-care business that was reengineering some anesthesiology equipment visited with airplane pilots to better understand what goes through the minds of those who oversee other people's lives in a stressful situation; the outcome was a totally integrated suite of technology that improves the quality of anesthesiology care in operating rooms. People also learned specific marketing tools, such as segmentation. Career moves also began to change to ensure leaders were getting experience with Imagination Breakthrough projects.

Meanwhile, Immelt continued to build GE's technical capability. He invested $100 million to modernize GE's R&D facility in Niskayuna, New York; expanded the one in Bangalore; and opened new facilities in Shanghai and Munich. In 2005, he created the Ecomagination initiative and pledged to raise GE's investment in core research from $700 million to $1.5 billion over five years to develop environmental-friendly technologies.

LESSON: You might not have all the capabilities you need to be great at innovation, but there are many ways to get them. Break the cookie-cutter mold you use to hire and promote people, bring in outside experts, see things through different eyes, and learn as much as you can from others. Emphasize an external focus and learning. Provide training in-house or at outside institutions. Capabilities improve with practice.

Architect the social process of innovation. When individuals returned to their businesses following their sessions at GE's Crotonville learning center, they found that their bosses and colleagues didn't always appreciate their newly acquired marketing skills. Immelt tackled the problem after seeing in the spring 2006 session that the business leaders weren't taking hold of the marketing tools and approaches. As he wrestled with the problem, Immelt came upon a significant insight: Unlike productivity improvements, which were often driven by individuals, growth was a team sport. While people needed to continue to cultivate their individual leadership skills, they also needed to improve the *social process of innovation.* Business leadership teams had to learn to pursue it together, like a basketball team on the court. That idea led to a groundbreaking approach, or innovation if you will, for the Crotonville learning facility: to have entire leadership teams from GE's businesses attend the learning session together. It was a first at GE, which had always brought individuals into Crotonville from a mix of businesses and functions. Immelt wanted the teams to attend Crotonville to work together on leadership, innovation, and growth, or LIG, as GE now calls it.

Immelt and his learning experts—including Susan Peters, VP executive of development and chief learning officer; Raghu Krishnamoorthy, HR manager, corporate commercial and communications; and Dan Henson, marketing chief—created a course designed to focus on leadership, innovation, and growth that included marketing skills, but a chief benefit was on the *social* side. Putting intact teams through the session together and asking them to participate in areas they hadn't taken ownership of before made the *culture* shift faster.

Six teams of fifteen to twenty people attended each time. For one full week, they were exposed to teachings from external experts and to best practices from inside GE, and then were given exercises to do in ten- to twelve-hour breakout sessions. Early on, team members were asked to rate themselves on innovation and imagination using a questionnaire. The exercise was designed to be fun, but it also had a serious purpose: It got people to realize that while individuals may feel they fall short on imagination, they still can be part of a team that generates and develops ideas. As people got comfortable with that notion, they grew more confident in suggesting ideas.

In the breakout groups, the marketing person was sitting next to the finance person, who was sitting next to the technology person, who was next to the operations person—all from the same business. Together they wrestled with how to apply the learning to their business and hashed out important shifts in resource allocation. They jointly made commitments to take actions and change their orientation and behavior, whether it was deciding how to segment the market, which new ideas to pursue, or how the innovation development process should work in their unit. As a result of discussions in the breakout sessions, the transportation team resolved to hire more people from emerging markets, for instance, and the team who runs GE's water business resolved to put a global sales leader not in Philadelphia but in Dubai, where the market was growing.

At the end of the session, the teams pulled their ideas together and presented them to the group and to Immelt. Each business leader was also required to write a letter to the CEO summarizing what the team learned and would do differently. The content of the letter became part of the growth play book for that business, which gets revisited and reviewed twice a year.

After their first LIG session, many business leaders redid their calendars to free themselves from their more routine work and cleared time to pursue growth opportunities. They communicated what they had learned when they got back to their businesses, *inspiring* others to pursue growth and innovation.

LESSON: Get people together across silos to share ideas and solve problems. Figure out who needs to coordinate their work or make trade-offs and create situations that demand joint effort. Give entire leadership teams problems they must solve together. Working on challenges together reshapes relationships and clears the path for innovation to happen faster.

Create the resources you need to fund growth. Attention is more certain to shift when resources do. In 2003, Immelt invested $4 billion in technology, not just in the United States but also in new research centers in Bangalore, Shanghai, and Munich. He increased R&D spending from 2 percent to more than 4 percent of revenue. The funding wasn't a gift from headquarters to the businesses. It came from aggressively streamlining and simplifying the internal infrastructure of the company to cut overhead.

Immelt set specific targets for general overhead costs as a percentage of revenue. He told investors that of the $6 billion GE expected in savings, $4 billion would be redeployed in the company, and $2 billion would go through to the bottom line.

The target, or *goal*, caused leaders to dramatically improve and simplify the "back end" functions of their businesses, in areas like accounting, finance, sales, and general administration. GE went from SG&A expenses of around 12 percent of revenue to about 7 percent. The benefit comes at the front end in the form of innovations that fuel growth. "I could have said to the business leaders, here's a billion dollars, go spend it wherever you want," Immelt explains, "but people value things more when they work for them."

Immelt has a keen eye for resource allocation in business reviews, because he believes so strongly that resources must be directed toward growth, and he doesn't accept excuses for not funding it. "It never ceases to amaze me that somebody running a $15 billion business with a $2 billion cost base can say he doesn't have $15 million to invest in the sales force in an emerging market. It's a matter of deciding what's important."

Choosing which Imagination Breakthrough projects to pursue is also a resource issue. When GE wanted to put more intense pressure on innovation for emerging markets, they didn't just increase the overall resources. They took more than a dozen projects off the list and added fifteen that had promise in those markets. For instance, they added projects for an MR scanner that could be sold in China for $500,000, a desalination plant in India, and a fuel flexibility program in Qatar. Those projects were a way to get incremental growth and also to build capability to move into emerging markets. It was an act of *inspiring leadership* to make the shifts in resources to expand the capacity to fund growth.

LESSON: Business leaders always have budget constraints, but if innovation is an imperative, so is funding it. Find places where you can operate more efficiently and channel some of that money toward growth and innovation projects. Don't overlook people, whose time is an important resource; free up a portion of their time for innovation projects. Don't rely on the higher-ups to give you the resources you need. Generate your own and spend them carefully. Remember that productivity and innovation go hand in hand.

Open up to learn from others. GE's global research centers have followed P&G's lead in opening up to let outsiders help solve their problems. It has been a change in the *culture*. Beginning around 2006, GE started doing "technical networking," a process, or *work system*, in which the research team plots all the nodes of discovery around an innovation project in a particular technology area. It's a way to capture all the technical capabilities that have to come together for the project to succeed. A coal gasification project, for example, required close to twenty-two core capabilities. GE can then step back and say, "OK, we own twelve of these, we can partner on six, and we can source four." Opening up means success can happen sooner.

LESSON: You don't have to do everything, and small companies simply can't. Make use of the many ways you can connect with other companies that can help you overcome technical obstacles and do what needs to be done to create and commercialize your innovation.

Reorganize or restructure to get close to customers. Immelt knew that GE would be a better innovator if it got close to *customers,* and that it would have more funds available for growth if the back-room operations were run as efficiently as possible. He reorganized the business with both those important considerations in mind, creating an organizational *structure* that allowed GE to be both customer-facing and efficient. He identified six growth platforms—commercial finance, consumer finance, health care, infrastructure (geared toward meeting needs of developing countries for things like energy and water), NBC, and transportation—which became the basis for grouping similar businesses to serve those particular customer segments. Leaders of those growth platforms could tap whatever GE resources they would need to drive growth, from financing and service to information.

LESSON: In many businesses, cost drives every major decision, including how to organize the business. But innovation rests on being close to customers, so businesses should be sure they are organized in a way that allows them to get to know customers well and serve them better. Make your business "customer facing" as well as efficient.

Reinforce the culture you want. To reinforce customers, growth and a longer-term view of the business, Immelt changed the compensation plan for senior leaders. There are four drivers of compensation: paid salary, equity, variable incentive compensation, and a long-term incentive plan. The long-term incentive plan now has a metric for organic growth in addition to cash flow, EPS, and return on total capital. It's one of the metrics that allows senior leaders to make a lot of money.

Because he saw that the opportunity to grow cash and profits in appliances was at the high end of the market, he changed the metrics for that business. GE now tracks market share for the high end only rather than for the appliance market as a whole. Appliances has a 60 percent return on capital and an 11 percent operating profit rate, and generates more than a billion dollars in cash annually. As Immelt remarked, "Private equity firms couldn't run it any better." It has a well-defined distribution strategy and an organic growth rate of 5 percent, which is above the industry average.

At the same time Immelt found ways to reward organic growth, he removed the penalties for missing on innovation. Hitting performance targets has always been a basic requirement to progress at GE, and leaders take it hard when they miss. They saw innovation much the same way—as something they absolutely had to deliver. The problem was, sometimes they couldn't deliver an Imagination Breakthrough because the idea just didn't pan out. Immelt does several things to try to change that thinking and ease the anxiety that comes with it. He makes a point of praising people for heeding the warning signs and being tough-minded enough to allow things to fail sooner. The emphasis is on quick decisions and lessons learned. He tries to get people to ask the right tough questions early on so they can make an early kill. Speed and learning are the two most important things, he tells them. His questions, comments, and reactions are demonstrations of his *inspiring leadership* and help shape the *culture*.

LESSON: Use metrics to encourage growth and innovation, and beware of contradictory signals sent in other ways. Make it possible for people to feel good when they innovate, and not too bad when an innovation fails early. What you emphasize and how you react have a tremendous effect on the culture of your immediate group, regardless of the broader corporate culture.

Let innovation spread. When a leader pursues innovation passionately and takes actions that reinforce it, it filters down to lower organizational levels. As senior leaders at GE picked up the cues from Immelt, they started to apply the same kind of focus, processes, tools, and attitudes to their own businesses. The great melting pot of ideas at Cro-tonville, of course, sped that adoption. The health-care business, for ex-ample, now has some sixty mini–Imagination Breakthrough projects under way.

What Immelt emphasizes in his reviews, other leaders have begun to emphasize with the leaders who report to them. They ask different kinds of questions, and they're starting to recognize and value people who have an external focus and can generate ideas about customer needs. They're using different criteria for evaluating people and differ-ent metrics for measuring their contribution. As a result, the spirit and *culture* of innovation has been spreading. "In the end, a lot of these things intersect and are reinforcing," Immelt says, "and that's some-thing you want to have happen."

LESSON: You'll need passion and tenacity to keep driving innovation into your organization. Your behaviors, attitudes, values, and beliefs set the tone. Your actions set the pace. The more consistent your efforts, the faster the acceleration.

Immelt didn't follow a textbook sequence of events for making GE an innovation company. He went about it in his own way, based on GE's unique context. Decisions he made and actions he took naturally led to the next thing that needed to change. He tackled more as he gauged the organization's ability to handle it, and in fact is still finding ways to make GE better at customer-centric innovation. Over the course of seven years, he has maintained his own sharp focus on the vi-sion he has for GE as a productivity, innovation, and growth company, and has wrestled with the specific works systems, core strengths, and strategies that would make it happen. He has been building a cadre of leaders who have the same sense of purpose and can help reshape GE's culture. Innovation is now integrated into the fabric of the business. IB projects have generated $3 billion in incremental revenues, and GE has hit its organic growth targets for fourteen straight quarters.

You don't have to be the CEO of a multibillion-dollar corporation to be an innovation leader. At any organizational level, you can find ways to put customer-centric innovation at the center of your work.

Even when you don't have much leeway at the macro level—when, for instance, goals and strategies are handed to you—you can exert influence at the micro level, by reinventing a work system, creating a new enabling structure, or changing the culture. You can provide a motivating purpose and inspire your team and the leaders around you to search for growth opportunities and reallocate resources to them. Your starting point will be different from someone else's, but if you keep working at it, you will see innovation permeate more and more aspects of your daily work. Eventually innovation will be integrated and self-reinforcing. What's important is that you recognize that innovation is necessary to sustainable growth, that you pursue innovation with discipline, and that you start your journey sooner rather than later. It is the only way for you and your organization to become a game-changer.

AFTERWORD

As the manuscript for The Game-Changer *was completed in the closing days of 2007, Ram Charan and A. G. Lafley sat down to think about their New Year's resolutions for 2008 (and beyond).*

Learning is a lifelong journey. Working with A. G. Lafley accelerated my research work and my determination to make it as useful as possible for practitioners. Being allowed to observe the workings of P&G, GE, LEGO Group, Marico, Honeywell, DuPont, Cisco, Nokia, 3M, and DuPont opened my eyes about how little we know and how much research remains to be done.

My mission in life is to do research on significant topics in ways that produce insights and ideas for practitioners. Innovation is what maintains and improves our standard of living. There has been to date very little sustained research in innovation, contrary to what has been done in areas such as financial instruments used by Wall Street, marketing to consumers, and the supply chain. My resolution for 2008 and beyond is to continue to be immersed in researching the ways in which innovation can continue to be a game-changer, with particular emphasis on how social interaction impacts the functioning and output of the end-to-end process of innovation.

I welcome any opportunities to be permitted to do research that will further our knowledge.

—Ram Charan

Job one for P&G and for me is to "deliver the decade"—double-digit earnings-per-share growth through 2010. We have three years to go; 2008 is next.

Innovation is P&G's lifeblood—the engine of growth for P&G—sustainable, organic, long-term growth—and the only way to deliver the decade.

Innovation is P&G's strategic game-changer. Most of the company's *leading* brands and businesses are the result of category or industry changing innovation:

1. Tide: The first synthetic laundry detergent for automatic washing machines.
2. Pampers: The first disposable baby diaper.
3. Crest: The first cavity-preventing toothpaste with fluoride.
4. Swiffer: The first convenient, disposable, quick-cleaning system for homes.
5. P&G's Prestige Fine Fragrance business: The first consumer-centric, innovation-led fragrance business in the world.

Innovation creates and builds brands; sustains meaningful brand, product, and service differentiation; supports premium pricing and superior margins; and delivers superior returns to shareholders. Innovation is the game-changer that will enable P&G to deliver the decade.

What Have I Learned in 2007 About Innovation?

At P&G, *purpose-driven innovation*—whose goal is more than sales and market share and profits—whose goal is meaningfully improving the everyday lives of the billions of consumers we serve—gets every P&Ger "in the innovation game" and inspires heroic efforts on a regular basis to come up with new ideas and then to transform these ideas into brands and products that enhance and improve daily life.

At P&G, innovation is *purpose driven and people led*. P&Gers'

shared purpose and common values unite them in their crusade to make daily life a little better.

At P&G, innovation is *at the heart of our business model* and business strategy, and P&G leaders and managers have the responsibility and the authority to coordinate and integrate the proven innovation drivers—purpose, goals and strategies, structure and systems, culture and leadership.

At P&G, *the consumer is truly our boss.* When we delight her or him with relevant, important, and valued innovation, she or he rewards us with purchase and trial and loyal usage. Loyal brand and product users are the most important stakeholders at P&G. Loyal users drive P&G's financial model.

At P&G, we are trying to *involve the consumer early and often* in our innovation process. Ideally, she or he will cocreate and codesign new brands and new products. At a minimum, we will check in with her at every step along the way of development and qualification. In the end, we don't have a successful innovation until she/he tries/buys and repurchases on a regular basis

At P&G, *the innovation process is integrated* with all the other business strategy, business operations, and business management processes. And, the innovation process is end-to-end—from ideation to commercialization—with critical social linkages every step along the way. At P&G, innovation is a team sport and the team has to play together seamlessly if we are to win.

At P&G, we're *building a leadership and a management* that understands the power of "and." We need to be great operators *and* to execute with excellence in the intensely competitive, fast-moving consumer products industry. *And,* we also need to be great innovation leaders—open to change, connecting to find the best ideas, and collaborating to develop those ideas into winning products. Culture matters at P&G—connected, collaborative, creative, courageous, and committed to touching consumers' lives and improving more of everyone's life.

For now more than thirty years at P&G, I've been on a journey—a journey of learning about innovation and how innovation can make a big difference for consumers, a big difference for my business, a big difference for my organization, and a big difference for my shareowners. I still have much to learn.

1. We have a lot of good ideas at P&G—but there are still so many unmet consumer needs and unfulfilled consumer wants that we are not yet addressing. And, competitors too often come to market with innovation ahead of us.

2. We have more than our fair share of innovation success—but still nearly half of P&G's new product innovations fail to deliver their business objectives or financial goals.

3. We have a disciplined innovation process—but too often P&Gers drive through caution lights, and occasionally even stop signs. No process, no matter how robust, can overcome human lack of self-discipline. Many presume innovation stems from extraordinary creativity. Creativity is necessary—especially at the ideation front end—and creative problem-solving is necessary throughout development and qualification—but innovation requires exceptional discipline. And, the innovation process, and in-process measures, are critical to maintaining discipline.

4. We have more broadly defined innovation at P&G—but most innovation is product innovation. We have created and introduced new brands in the last decade—Actonel, Align, Intrinsa, Prilosec, Febreze, Kandoo, Swiffer, Torengo's, and Thermacare—but only a few new business models—reflect.com, Prestige Fine Fragrances, Bella and Birch, Mr. Clean Car Wash, and Juvian laundry services. And, disruptive innovations that dramatically change the consumer value equation have been challenging. The new ultra-thin, low-cost Pampers diaper we're selling in China may be one.

5. Participation in, and responsibility for, innovation are now broadly distributed and shared across businesses and functional disciplines—but, while all these functions bring passion and talent,

and considerable time and effort to the innovation task, they are still not as coordinated and integrated as they need to be to produce consistently excellent innovation results.

6. Identifying, developing, and growing innovation leaders is not easy. Innovation leadership is an acquired skill. It takes time and patience. It takes study. It takes learning from experience—a lot of experience.

I've learned so much from innovation successes I've been fortunate to be a part of. But, I've learned so much more from innovation failures—and I've been a big part of a lot of failures. Failure is such a good teacher—if you have the humility and the persistence to assess and examine what happened and, more importantly, how and why.

So, as we identify talent, we need to develop these women and men in businesses that require innovation to grow—in businesses where they can learn—from their own successes and failures.

I am committed to learn a little more about innovation in 2008 (and to try not to forget what I've learned in 2007 and before!).

—A. G. Lafley

ACKNOWLEDGMENTS

I consider *The Game-Changer*, like all my books, to be a by-product of a lifetime of learning from accomplished business leaders, who have generously shared with me their time and thoughts over the years. I am particularly grateful to the following people for their help as I researched this book: Jeffrey Immelt, Beth Comstock, Susan Peters, Pam Daley, Dan Henson, Raghu Krishnamoorthy, Chad Holliday, Tom Connelly, Dick Bingham, Michael Blaustein, Dave Cote, Tom Buckmaster, Dan Sheflin, Darryl Fogal, Byron Hill, Jørgen Vig Knudstorp, Olli-Pekka Kallasvuo, Tero Ojanperä, Hallstein Moerk, Shiv Shivakumar, Todd Bradley, Phil McKinney, Steven Sanchez, Mike Kelly, Andy Wong, Jeff Melby, Marc Miller, Donna Fleming, Angel Mendez, Tim Brown, David Kelley, David Webster, Dennis Boyle, Sam Truslow, Diego Rodriguez, Ilya Prokopoff, Brendan Boyle, Brad Anderson, Sue Busch, Harsh Mariwala, Ameya Naniwadekar, Rajiv Narang, and Shu Ebe.

Cait Murphy did an outstanding job of bringing P&G to life on the printed page. She spent time with many people in many different parts of P&G, from the research labs in Cincinnati to the streets of Mexico, immersing herself in their world and absorbing not just what they do but also how they go about doing it. P&G is very large and complex, yet Cait was able to get her arms around it and capture its spirit. Using her great gift of narrative, she gives readers that same view from inside

P&G. Cait is also a great collaborator who used her focus, drive, and keen editorial skills to advance the project through its many stages, always with a desire to produce a great final product. I am very grateful for her contribution.

My appreciation, too, to Geri Willigan, who has helped me research this and other topics for many years. She made intellectual contributions before a first draft even existed and significant editorial contributions as the book was taking shape. Thanks to my longtime friend John Joyce, for his helpful input along the way.

Cynthia Burr is the magician in my office who kept me and this project on track despite her dizzying array of responsibilities; she seemed to be able to manufacture time whenever it was running short. I am deeply grateful to her and to Karen Baker and Carol Davis for their dedicated support.

John Mahaney, our editor at Crown Business, is the editor of all editors. He is an incredible coach. He worked tirelessly, going far beyond the call of duty, to get to the bottom of the subject matter and help us shape the book so that readers could easily access the ideas. He has added to my personal capability immensely. In addition, his family has been tremendously supportive and hospitable during completion of this project.

Only once or twice in the life of a researcher does an opportunity come to learn from an outstanding CEO. Working with A. G. Lafley was one of those rare opportunities. His willingness to share ideas, his gentle coaching, and his ability to open the mind through questioning are unmatched. He is a true authentic leader who inspires people and stretches their capability, including my own. I am deeply grateful.

—Ram Charan

First and foremost, I want to thank my P&G colleagues—virtually everything I've experienced, everything I've learned about innovation over the past 30+ years has been from and with fellow P&Gers past and present.

I want to particularly thank the nearly one hundred P&Gers from across the businesses and functions, and from around the world, who interviewed with the researchers and writers of this book. Their stories, their experiences, their successes, and their failures helped us understand how innovation really works and were important sources of practical learning about innovation.

Second, I want to thank three Xavier University students—Daniel J. Saylor, Karlie A. Winnett, and Scott A. Sivinski—who helped me research a wide variety of innovation subjects and study a long list of other Company real-world examples. I hope they enjoyed our Saturday and Sunday afternoon sessions as much as I did.

Third, I want to thank Kathy King, Maria Carver, and Sheila Knollman—my P&G support team. Nothing happens without them.

Fourth, I want to thank Craig Wynett—one of the most provocative, out-of-the-box thinkers about innovation I have ever met—and Greg Icenhower, my communication partner at P&G who helps bring my ideas and my experiences to life.

Fifth, I want to thank Diana Shaheen for her conceptual and strategic leadership. She helped us organize the book around a few critical ideas. Diana pushed us hard to stay focused on themes of interest and utility to the operating manager. She pushed us hard for clarity and context as we worked to translate experiences and practice into concepts and learning that might be helpful to others engaged in the leadership of innovation.

Sixth, I want to thank John Mahaney for his mastery, his patience, and his tireless support. John coached this "rookie" through the process of collaborating on his first book. He "walked me through" each step along the way. He encouraged me when I became frustrated. He helped me translate real-world experiences into examples readers can learn from and build on.

Finally, I cannot thank Ram Charan enough for his vision and partnership. Ram understood not only the strategic importance of innovation but also the opportunity to address the practical everyday needs of practicing managers trying to get innovation done. He knew the key would be to help these managers understand how to integrate innovation into everyday business strategies and processes. As we worked closely together, Ram helped me better understand not only what I was doing and how I was doing it, but also why. He is a consummate teacher—committed to lifelong learning and to the growth and development of his students, of whom I am honored to be one.

Net proceeds I receive from the sale of this book will be donated to scholarship funds to encourage future study and learning about innovation.

—A. G. Lafley

INDEX

ABOUT THE AUTHORS

ALAN GEORGE (A.G.) LAFLEY is chairman of the board and chief executive of Procter & Gamble.

A.G. is not your typical CEO. In fact, he never intended to pursue a career in business. He grew up in a small town—Keene, New Hampshire. He went to Hamilton College, a small liberal arts school in upstate New York. His plan was to become a teacher and a basketball coach.

He took a break in the late '60s to go to Paris. He studied history, politics, art, cinema, and drama. And he hitchhiked his way around France on weekends. He came back to the United States in 1969 and entered the Ph.D. program at the University of Virginia to study medieval and renaissance European history. Then, his plans changed.

He joined the U.S. Navy where, instead of serving on a battleship, he oversaw retail and services businesses at a U.S. air base in Japan. He operated grocery, department, and specialty stores—all the retail and service operations for a "small town" of about ten thousand Navy and Marine Corps members and their families. It was his first general manager job, and he was hooked.

Instead of returning to the life of a professor when he came home from the Navy, he headed to Harvard Business School. After graduating, he joined P&G in 1977. Over the next fifteen years, he moved up through the Company's laundry and cleaning businesses. He and his teams were responsible for some of P&G's biggest innovations, including Liquid Tide and Tide with Bleach—innovations that continue to fuel P&G's growth yet today.

He went back to Japan in 1994, but the business he ran there was a far cry from the small retail businesses he ran on that American air base two decades earlier. He was responsible for all of P&G's operations in Asia. He laid the foundation for a return to growth in Japan. He helped P&G's business in China grow from less than $90 million to nearly $1 billion in sales by the time he left Asia in 1998. And he led the Company through major currency and economic crises, including the earthquake that struck Kobe, Japan, P&G's Asia headquarters, in 1995.

His experience in Asia helped prepare him for his next assignment, in 1999, running P&G's fast-growing Beauty business, along with the Company's business in North America—its largest single market.

In 2000, A.G. was elected president and chief executive of P&G. Under his leadership, P&G has nearly doubled sales—from $39 billion to $76 billion. The number of "billion-dollar brands"—those earning a billion dollars or more in sales each year—has more than doubled, from ten to twenty-three, and the number of brands with sales between $500 million and $1 billion has more than quadrupled, from four to eighteen. P&G now does more than a billion dollars in sales in a dozen countries and with seven retailers. With Lafley at the helm, P&G has generated more than $43 billion in net earnings, $50 billion in free cash flow, and the Company's market capitalization has more than doubled to more than $200 billion, making P&G one of the ten most valuable companies in the United States and among the fifteen most valuable in the world. P&G is consistently recognized as one of the most admired companies in the world and a great developer of business leaders.

Despite these many achievements, A.G. remains a somewhat unlikely CEO. In fact, *Fortune* magazine called him the "un-CEO" in an article that described him as a leader who "doesn't overpromise, doesn't believe in the vision thing," and who would be hard to spot as the boss in meetings where he spends more time listening than talking. Those who know him best will say, "that's quintessential A.G." During his tenure, A.G. received such distinctions as CEO of the Year in 2006 by *Chief Executive* magazine and was identified as one of America's Best Leaders by *U.S. News & World Report,* also in 2006.

RAM CHARAN is a highly sought after business adviser and speaker famous among senior executives for his uncanny ability to solve their toughest business problems. For more than thirty-five years, Dr. Charan has worked behind the scenes with top executives at some of the world's most successful companies, including GE, Verizon, Novartis, DuPont, Thomson, Honeywell, KLM, and MeadWestvaco. He has shared his insights with many others through teaching and writing.

Dr. Charan's introduction to business came early while working in the family shoe shop in the small Indian town where he was raised. He earned an engineering degree in India and soon after took a job in Australia and then in Hawaii. When his talent for business was discovered, Dr. Charan was encouraged to pursue it. He earned MBA and doctorate degrees from Harvard Business School, where he graduated with high distinction and was a Baker Scholar. After receiving his doctorate degree in corporate governance, he served on the Harvard Business School faculty.

Dr. Charan is well known for providing advice that is down-to-earth and relevant and that takes into account the real-world complexities of business. He views every interaction with business leaders as an opportunity to stretch their thinking and his own. Using his business acumen, insights into people, and common sense, he translates his observations and insights into recommendations leaders can apply on Monday morning. He has expertise in leadership and succession, growth and innovation, execution, and social systems. Identified by *Fortune* as the leading expert in corporate governance and by *The Economist* as a veteran of CEO succession, Dr. Charan provides practical ways for boards to improve their functioning. Directors, CEOs, and senior-most human resource executives often seek his advice on talent planning and key hires, including CEO selection.

Many people have come to know Dr. Charan through in-house executive education programs. His energetic, interactive teaching style has won him several awards. He won the Bell Ringer Award at GE's famous learning center in Crotonville, New York, and best teacher awards at Northwestern and Wharton's Insurance Institute. He was among *BusinessWeek*'s top ten resources for in-house executive development programs.

Over the past decade, Dr. Charan has captured his business insights in numerous books and articles. In the past five years, Dr. Charan's books have sold more than 2 million copies. These include the bestseller *Execution: The Discipline of Getting Things Done,* coauthored with Larry Bossidy, and *Know-How.* Dr. Charan has written several cover stories for *Fortune* magazine and lead articles for *Harvard Business Review.* His articles have also appeared in *Financial Times, Wall Street Journal,* and *Director's Monthly.*

Dr. Charan was elected a Distinguished Fellow of the National Academy of Human Resources. He is on the boards of Tyco Electronics, Austin Industries, and Emaar MGF India. He is based in Dallas, Texas.